CW00376957

Extra Naughty

Frisky Foreplaying

Hot Sex Dice Games
Get Lucky Tonight

Straight, Gay, Lesbian, Bi-Sexual & Threesome
Foreplay Activity Lists Included

Michael and Barbara Kortekaas

Succulent Enterprises Inc.

Copyright © 2021 Michael & Barbara Kortekaas

All rights reserved, including the right to reproduce this book or portions thereof in any form whatsoever except in the case of brief quotations embodied in critical articles or reviews.

The author and publisher specifically disclaim all responsibility for any liability, loss, or risk, personal or otherwise, which is incurred as a consequence, directly or indirectly, of the use and application of any of the contents of this book.

Many of the designations used by manufacturers and sellers to distinguish their products are claimed as trademarks. Where those designations appear in this book and Succulent Enterprises Inc. was aware of a trademark claim, the designations have been printed with initial capital letters.

Individuals pictured on the cover are models used for illustrative purposes only.

Cover Design: Michael Kortekaas

This book is dedicated to all couples striving to create a loving, long lasting relationship that is filled with joy and happiness. We hope this book inspires you to creatively enhance your relationship with even more fun and pleasure. Stay frisky and playful as you grow even closer together.

Play Safe

Succulent Enterprises Inc. and the authors assume no responsibility for any injury or damage incurred while playing or performing any activities inspired or identified in this book. The questions and ideas are intended for consenting adults who are knowledgeable of sex while still exploring and discovering their full sexual potential. If you have any health concerns, please consult your doctor to ensure you're healthy and fit enough to engage in sex.

Sex is a very sensitive subject. People have radically different views on what is morally right and wrong when it comes to sex between consenting adults. Although attitudes have become more accepting of a broader range of sexual practices, many laws still exist that prohibit specific types of sexual activities. Certain sections of this book may deal with activities that could be in violation of various federal, state and local laws if actually carried out in your location. We do not advocate breaking any law. The authors and publisher do not accept liability for any injury, loss, legal consequence, or incidental or consequential damage incurred by reliance on information, advice or suggestions provided in this book. The information in this book is for entertainment purposes only.

Always use safer sex practices and common sense when performing or engaging in any sexual activity. Sample activities provided are designed for couples in a mutually consensual sexual relationship. All the foreplay and sex play ideas are intended to inspire your own sexual creativity so you can enhance your relationship with more pleasure and intimacy. They are only sexy suggestions for you to adapt and perform at your own discretion.

Special Note: always clean before inter-mixing anal then vaginal activities to avoid bacterial infections. Use a dental dam for oral-anal activities. Also, avoid getting anything with sugar in the vagina. This can lead to a nasty yeast infection.

Versions

The original version of Frisky Foreplay was developed as a set of PDF files only available online from our website www.friskyforeplay.com as a digital product. A slightly modified version was included in the book **Sex Games & Foreplay Ideas For Couples** available from Amazon in both print and Kindle formats. The game was then developed into an iPhone app with the same name. Although some minor updates and corrections were made to the content along the way, it was still primarily oriented to heterosexual couples.

However, in 2020, the app was redesigned and re-implemented to support the iPad. For this major upgrade, the scope was expanded to include up to four players of mixed gender and sexual orientation. New foreplay activities were written for gay, lesbian, bi-sexual, and various other combinations of three bodies. All the new material has been repackaged into this book format.

Foreplay Idea Sets

Introduction

"Couples that play together stay together" is not just a trite cliché but rather valuable words of advice. Over time, the passion and excitement in a relationship can fade. However, couples can help maintain the quality and quantity of their intimate interactions by playing together more. While growing up, play was a fun and natural way to learn and develop essential skills. It may sound strange but, as adults, we still need to play and have fun as we continue to learn and grow together. For couples, sensual love play encourages more intimacy while also stimulating more profound levels of communication and bonding.

Even in mature relationships, many people find it challenging to bring up new erotic desires or talk about sensitive subjects involving their sexual needs. We've developed Frisky Foreplay as a fun way to introduce a broad range of sensual activities in various, random combinations. It's designed to encourage intimate exploration of mind and body with progressively more intense levels of pleasuring.

Although many relationship games focus on getting you to play together nicely, our naughty game is designed to embrace the thrill and challenge of competitive play. By agreeing to play a game and adhere to the rules, even timid lovers may be tempted to venture outside their sexual comfort zone and overcome some of their inhibitions. With an appropriate sexual forfeit or reward, your passionate desire to win can be very stimulating.

And, of course, the sensual-sexual tension experienced during your foreplay fun will lead to amazing sex play. Prolonged foreplay and extended pleasuring are the best ways to dramatically intensify your orgasms. Foreplay games not only pace your pleasuring, the random sensual activities during the gameplay will help boost arousal and build excitement. Not all erotic games will suit your interests, but there's a large variety to choose from. With the Frisky Foreplay activities in this book, you can even transform regular games you love into new erotic favorites.

There is always something new to discover about yourself, your lover and your relationship, so love play is essential regardless of your age. Whether in a new or mature relationship, we believe couples should make intimate play a priority. Take the time to have fun with each other. You'll find it improves your life in a variety of different ways too. We hope our Frisky Foreplay ideas help you spice up your love life with a creative sense of curiosity and adventure.

Sex is Fun - Why Play Games?

It's well known that great sex can actually help keep you healthy. It turns out exciting sex can help to improve your brain as well. As you'll discover, creative sex games can provide a fun way for you to improve both your brain and your relationship at the same time.

In the book Keep Your Brain Alive – 83 Neurobic Exercises to Help Prevent Memory Loss and Increase Mental Fitness by Lawrence C. Katz, Ph.D. & Manning Rubin, sex is claimed to be the ultimate neurobic workout. When you engage all your senses (vision, smell, taste, touch and hearing) and emotions in unexpected, unusual or novel combinations, you create new neural connections. You also stimulate the production of brain nutrients that keep your mind agile and healthy.

According to the research, for a neurobic exercise to be effective, you must:

1. Involve one or more of your senses in a novel context

2. Become more aware by fully engaging your attention and emotion

3. Change your routine activity or habit in a significant way

With these guidelines in mind, here are a few ideas to enhance your relationship and improve your brain. So unleash your creativity and see how much naughty fun you can enjoy together.

- Read erotic stories or fantasies aloud to each other. Activate different areas of your brain than those used when reading silently. Stimulate your erotic imaginations together and get closer by discussing mutual desires.

- Use body paints or washable markers to draw pictures or erotic designs on your lover's naked canvas. Try different types of artist brushes, a variety of stroking techniques and multiple colors. Also, try switching hands, write words for your lover to identify or use flavored oils and lick the design after you create it.

- Set up a romantic or sexy atmosphere using different types and colors of lighting. Use a new fragrance or scent dispenser. Play music you would not usually listen to. Include new touch sensations using lingerie or bedding with fabrics that have unique textures. Sample succulent fruits, decadent chocolates or exotic drinks. Mix and match different combinations of each sensory element for something new every time.

- Fully engage in role-playing scenarios with imaginary characters or situations. Use a fake accent, dress up in costumes, swap passive and assertive roles, explore different locations and even experiment with fetish or taboo activities.

- Introduce new accessories or sex toys and try new foreplay techniques. Go shopping together to a variety of stores with the intent to find novel items for sensual pleasure. Use your imagination to think about how regular items can be used to arouse your senses and enhance your lovemaking.
- Embrace new ways to play together. Try out a variety of foreplay games or turn regular games into erotic competitions. Add a sexy reward or forfeit to any game and experience new levels of exciting fun.

You may have experimented with some of these activities when you first met. But now you have a great reason to try them again and again. And if you haven't tried these ideas yet, the very first time can be thrilling. It's never too late to spice up your relationship with creative new sex ideas. By enjoying great sex in novel new ways, you keep your body and brain healthy while ensuring that your relationship thrives too.

We've designed our games with novel foreplay ideas to stimulate your mind and engage all your senses in pleasure. Your brain is your biggest sex organ, and it craves these types of experiences. We hope you enjoy keeping each other fit and healthy with creative sex. Try out these fun and simple neurobic exercise techniques any time you can. You'll transform your lovemaking and your life together.

Here are a few more reasons to get frisky playing naughty games with each other:

1. Playing a couples game is an excellent opportunity to turn off the TV and phone so you can become directly involved with your partner. Engaging in activities together will reward you in more ways than you can imagine. Keeping your relationship intact has been calculated to have a value of over $100,000 worth of happiness per year.

2. Romantic games are designed with intimate questions and activities to strengthen your emotional bond. These loving exercises help create a deeper connection and increase your level of trust, so you both feel safe with each other. A high level of trust is essential when you face challenges or want to step outside your sexual comfort zone.

3. Discover more about each other when you play relationship games that encourage you to talk openly about your love and life together. As we grow and mature, our attitudes, goals, desires and expectations change. When you play these games, you'll find new activities to do together. Some of the challenges may even seem difficult at the time, but they are excellent for bonding even closer together. You'll become more comfortable keeping your communication channels open, so you don't drift apart.

4. Playing fun, adult-themed, erotic games (sexual trivia, suggestive party games, etc.) with friends is a great way to gain new perspectives on how other people think and feel about sex. While gaining more sex knowledge to make you a better lover, you can also observe how your partner reacts to certain erotic subjects. With this insight, you will become a more understanding and sensitive lover too.

5. Bedroom games provide ways to randomly mix up and combine different types of sensual pleasure. Foreplay games allow you to playfully delay sex while you stimulate and arouse each other in new ways. These kinds of games encourage you both to experiment with a variety of sex positions and techniques – things you might not allow yourself to do if it wasn't part of the game. As you release your inhibitions and become more aware of what you both enjoy, you'll gain confidence in your creative lovemaking skills.

6. Amazing sex makes you feel happier and improves your outlook on life. Regular sex can even make you look years younger. More and better sex can help you live longer. It's been claimed that women can add up to eight years to their life span when they enjoy sex (quality counts). Recent studies have also shown that more frequent ejaculations help reduce the risk of prostate cancer in men. So make great sex a priority in your life.

7. Learn to satisfy your secret sexual desires as you explore wild fantasies and experiment with role-playing games. By pretending to be different characters acting out a passionate scene, you can release your inhibitions and explore hot sex with wild abandon. It's also great as a neurobic sex exercise. When you fully engage your emotions and all your senses (costumes, props, accents, different locations), role-playing can help keep your mind younger, healthier and more agile.

And, best of all, when you're both having fun satisfying your sexual desires with each other, you're both less tempted to stray and more likely to stay together.

Frisky Foreplay Activities

Frisky Foreplay is designed to use three different colored dice - say Red, White and Blue. The colors are not strictly important as long as they are distinct enough so they can be ordered in a sequence. This ordering provides 6*6*6 possible combinations, which means each dice roll can be mapped to one of 216 unique foreplay activities. It also allows the activities to be organized into 6 groups or levels of 36 each.

For example, if you are using Red, White and Blue dice in this order, the Red die would correspond to one of the 6 levels. The White/Blue combination would point to one of 36 pleasuring ideas within the level. In Frisky Foreplay, the Red die would indicate the intensity level (see below) with its own section in the book. Each section contains 36 activity ideas labeled with the complete dice sequence so you can identify which one to enjoy.

But, there's more! For even more variety, the foreplay ideas can be organized based on the gender of the player 'performing' the activity and the gender of the player 'receiving' the pleasure. The performer/receiver designation will change based on the type of game being played. It usually alternates by turn. For example, different body parts will be involved for a straight couple (one male and one female), and varied terminology is generally required to describe an activity. Only two sets of activities were provided in the original version of the game: Male_Female and Female_Male. In this book, we've developed ideas for 12 gender combinations to support straight, gay, lesbian and bisexual couples with or without extra intimate friends (threesomes or mixed couples):

Code	Players	Code	Players
MF	Male Female	FM	Female Male
MM	Male Male	FF	Female Female
MFF	Male Female Female	FMM	Female Male Male
MFM	Male Female Male	FMF	Female Male Female
MMM	Male Male Male	FFF	Female Female Female
MMF	Male Male Female	FFM	Female Female Male

Three interacting bodies can be complicated enough, so if you're playing with more, default to two players and arrange some way to randomly include a third. All others can enjoy watching.

Note the Code is added as a prefix to the roll numbers (e.g. FM246) to make the heading for each activity. This enables you to use the search feature in the Kindle/electronic version to quickly locate the specific item. In the book version, flip to the appropriate gender combination section, continue to the level subsection (first number) and visually search for the prefix/roll item.

Also, note that the order of the players is significant. The first player in the sequence is considered to be the primary Performer. The second player is designated as "Your Partner" in the activity description. Previous versions assumed a single couple and used the term "Your Lover". The optional third player is designated as "Your Assistant" in that they will be helping the Performer provide pleasure. When the active, performing player is reading the foreplay idea aloud, feel free to substitute in the names of the other players involved rather than these placeholders.

Foreplay Intensity Levels

As noted above, for each gender combination, the foreplay ideas are subdivided into 6 levels, each with 36 ideas. Higher levels include more explicit activities. Since Frisky Foreplay is also a stripping game, each level increase also assumes players are wearing fewer items of clothing. The titles and overviews of each level are provided below.

Warm & Loving

Start off with tender touching and kissing to get you both in the mood. The warm and loving ideas in this section are intended to awaken your desire for more sensual pleasures. Explore delicate and soft sensations. You'll be pleasantly surprised by how stimulating and arousing these foreplay ideas can be. But warm and loving foreplay level 1 is only the start.

Sensual Sensations

Explore new types of sensual sensations using a variety of techniques. Creatively stimulate all of your senses as you search and explore for new erogenous zones that you may not even be aware of yet. Experiment with arousing accessories in novel ways to experience subtle pleasures that'll make you both melt with desire. The sensual sensations in foreplay level 2 will get you hot, but there's more to come.

Intimate Intentions

There's no way you're holding back now. Clothing has been stripped off to reveal more than your desire to be naughty. Build the erotic tension as you revel in the seductive thrill of teasing and tantalizing each other. You'll start the passion fires burning, but there are even more ways to fan these flames.

Explicit, Erotic Passion

The gloves are off, and so are most of your clothes. Your passion is burning bright. You're both hot and horny as you lick, suck and play with each other. All your erogenous zones are explicitly available and throbbing with desire. The foreplay activities in level 4 will get your blood boiling with lust for each other. Are you willing to crank the heat up even more?

Lewd & Lascivious Loving

It's time to add more fuel to the sexual fire you started. But now, you need to be careful things don't explode prematurely. It's a delicate skill to know when enough is enough, but you're willing to push the limits. The foreplay activities in level 5 will encourage you to be lewd and lascivious as you demonstrate your burning love and lust for each other. But are you willing to play with a sexual wildfire?

Wild, Nasty, Kinky, Taboo

Now you've done it. Your sexual wildfires are burning in unexplored territory. You'll need a controlled burn to get these wild, nasty, kinky and taboo desires tamed. The extra hot foreplay activities in level 6 may be too intense. Handle each other with care.

How to Play Frisky Foreplay

Frisky Foreplay is a fun and exciting dice game for lovers that challenges you to perform erotic activities based on what you roll. It will lead you through an arousing sequence of foreplay activities that intensify toward a wild, explosive climax. The game encourages you to sample various types and intensities of stimulation for a total sensual experience.

You'll need three different colored dice (say red, white and blue) and five items each to use as free pass tokens (coins, condoms, cards, etc.). The order and numbers on the three dice correspond to one of 216 gender-specific foreplay ideas listed in the following sections of the book. For example, the red die indicates the intensity level. The white/blue combination would then point to one of 36 sexy activities in that level. (See Frisky Foreplay Activities for more details)

Players take turns rolling the dice and performing a corresponding foreplay activity. But of course, you don't just jump straight to the hardcore, kinky stuff. Instead, there are six progressively more intense levels of pleasure (shown below) to be unlocked as you play.

Intensity	Pleasuring Activity Type
1	Warm & Loving
2	Sensual Sensations
3	Intimate Intentions
4	Explicit, Erotic Passion
5	Lewd & Lascivious Loving
6	Wild, Nasty, Kinky, Taboo

So dim the lights, turn off the phone, find a comfy location and get down to it. You'll get lucky with every roll of the dice.

Setup & Preparation

Begin the game fully dressed with four or five items of clothing on. Stripping occurs at each level change. Agree on the sexual forfeits or reward for the winner. Each player is given five free pass tokens—the last player with a remaining token wins. You'll also need a way to record which level you're currently on.

How to Play

Start the game on the Warm & Loving intensity level 1. Record which level you're playing on as you go. Progress to the next level when someone rolls a special triple: all three dice match the current level.

Choose who goes first, then take turns. Roll all three dice each turn. If the red die is greater than the current level, adjust it to the number of the level you are on. After adjusting the red die, if necessary, look up and perform the corresponding foreplay activity.

If you don't have the required accessory to perform the activity, creatively adapt it to involve something you do have available. If you choose not to perform the activity, discard one of your free pass tokens and forfeit your turn. If your partner prefers not to participate in the activity, they must discard one of their free pass tokens.

If you rolled a special triple with all values matching the current level, advance to the next level. All players strip one article of clothing. Also, you get one of your partner's free pass tokens as a bonus.

Continue play until one player runs out of free pass tokens or you roll triple 6's while on level 6.

Special Note: When playing with three or more people, everyone takes turns being the active or performing player. If there is more than one potential 'receiving' player, flip a coin or roll a die to determine the partner of the performing player. And, if there are any potential 'assisting' players, flip a coin to see if a third will be participating as well.

Game Ideas in More Detail

Before you begin, mentally prepare yourself and each other for a fun, sensual experience. Take time to savor every pleasure-filled minute of the journey. This game is about sensual intimacy – sex is definitely on the menu.

The Frisky Foreplay game is intended to provide the creative spark to help you ignite your own passions together. Activity ideas corresponding to each dice roll are short and sweet, sour, tangy, spicy … all delicious. But they are only ideas. Perform them as creatively as you can. Tease and tantalize each other but resist the urge to go all the way until someone wins the game. The foreplay idea lists will encourage you to try new techniques, rarely used positions, unique accessories or even favorite sex toys in creative new ways. Take the chance to search for new erogenous zones and devise new ways to stimulate your favorites. You may roll the same activity multiple times. If so, perform it in a slightly different way each time. Inspire each other to go beyond the ordinary to make your adult playtime extra special.

Note that you are encouraged to mix in lower intensity activities. You can roll lower than the current level but never higher because the red die is capped and adjusted down if required. Effectively all the lower intensity activities are available as you progress up the levels. This rule ensures that you're warmed up with a full range of sensual pleasures before exploring foreplay activities in the higher intensity levels.

The activity lists include a broad spectrum of foreplay ideas that may not appeal to everyone. Although we recommend that you try each one, do not feel obligated to perform any activity – they are intended for mutual pleasure. If desired, feel free to creatively adapt any foreplay idea to your comfort level. There will, of course, be some activities that you are not prepared to do when you're playing the game. For instance, you may not have the appropriate accessories handy to perform it. You may even want to refuse to participate in an activity your partner is to perform. Regardless of your reason, you have five chances to pass on any activity without question. Indicate your preference and discard one of your free pass tokens.

However, to help encourage a bit of sexual exploration, each player only has a limited number of free pass tokens. If you use them all or your last token is rewarded away, the game ends. The winner should receive some reward for either being really lucky or daring to try something wild and new. So, before the game begins, agree on the sexual forfeits or sensual rewards for each of you. Choose ideas that will encourage a spirit of fun competition. This rule also helps to reduce any "hard feelings" that may occur if your partner passes on a foreplay idea. You'll know you're getting closer to receiving a bigger reward. And, of course, you can also win all the free pass tokens by rolling lots of triples.

When performing foreplay activities for each other as part of the game, you may want to use a timer set for 1-3 minutes. Sometimes the time pressure adds to the excitement. Other times you may want to enjoy the activity at a more leisurely pace until you feel it's time to move on.

More Game Ideas

With all the pleasure possibilities available (ranging from simple sensual foreplay to advanced Kama Sutra positions to sex toys to kinky fetishes), what do you want to do now, and how do you choose? Chances are, random acts of sex could be just what you need to shake things up in and out of the bedroom.

We believe enjoying random sex ideas as part of a game is a great way to spice up and enhance your relationship. For this reason, we organized this book so that you can select lots of different types of erotic ideas randomly using either cards or dice. We figured most people have a few decks of cards and some dice in their home. They are inexpensive, and you can get them almost anywhere. Dice and cards can also be easily packed in a suitcase with this book to take on a romantic vacation. With card and dice combinations, you can randomly select from a large number of different pleasuring ideas.

And, best of all, these items are used in many types of regular games that can easily be transformed for intimate play. Just select a few types of game events that occur fairly frequently but not necessarily every turn. Then adjust the rules so that when a player achieves or encounters a particular event, they either perform or receive a foreplay activity. The foreplay activity can be randomized or explicitly assigned to specific types of events.

You'll also want to include a stripping component if appropriate and escalate to more intense types of foreplay as the game progresses. For games that take longer to play, certain events naturally occur at later stages in the game. You can use these events as trigger points for stripping or foreplay level changes. For shorter games, play multiple times. Each win would be the trigger point to strip or advance to more intimate activities.

To add a bit more emotional 'color' to your game variation, adjust the game's concept to include a more erotic theme. The new theme could even tie in with the types of sexual forfeits and rewards you'll be playing for. Check out our book **Sex Games & Foreplay Ideas for Couples** for more game and random sex play ideas. A few of the games (slightly modified) have been included in the following sections as an example.

Note: Use the Card to Dice Key (page 15) to map playing cards to equivalent two dice combinations.

You can use random sex techniques to add a creative flair to your lovemaking style any time you desire. Keep your lover on their toes with anticipation not knowing what new pleasuring combinations you'll come up with. Even changing the sequence or combination of your normal bedroom activities can enhance your sex life. So get ready to introduce some random sex changes in your love life and start enjoying more frisky fun. There are hundreds of stimulating ideas in this book to pick from.

Even if you stick to less adventurous sensual activities, randomizing your regular lovemaking routine will create more interest and excitement. Even subtle changes in your sex routine can turn your everyday lovemaking into something extraordinary, spectacular, unique and memorable. It may not improve all aspects of your relationship, but stirring up the way you make love is bound to keep your sex life fresh and satisfying. So take a chance and enjoy random sex tonight!

Dominate Your Lover (Erotic Risk)

Here is a risque game of world conquest and domination for lovers. Pretend you're having the ultimate battle of the sexes. Uncover sensitive areas, break down any inhibiting defense and penetrate into restricted territory. Create your best-laid plans to strip away any will to resist your advances. Experiment with creative new techniques in unexpected zones. Play with their mind as you stimulate regions in different ways. See how they react and adjust your strategy. And when you triumph, revel in the spoils of war.

Add even more mystique to the game by pretending you're playing in historic times. Be an Egyptian queen, Caesar, Napoleon or any other character that might be interesting to roleplay. Include the personality of the characters in your sex play as well.

Objective

Win by conquering all the territories of the world. The victor receives the spoils of war and becomes the supreme ruler with corresponding rewards. Make the loser submit to all your desires - whatever pleasure you want.

The ultimate goal is to dominate each other with a burning passion and lust. Foreplay activities are performed when you capture territories from your rival. Take control of their privates and fulfill your secret desires. As the conflict escalates, so does the intensity of the foreplay. Your competition will strip everything to win. As they reveal themselves, gain intimate knowledge of their intentions. They will lay themselves bare before you, so take advantage when you can.

Setup & Preparation

You will need the regular board game of Risk. Setup as specified for the number of players. Start the game fully clothed. Negotiate a suitable sexual favor or fantasy reward that befits a supreme ruler such as yourself. You'll be using the Frisky Foreplay activity lists, so you'll each need a way to record which level you're on. All players start on intensity level 1.

How to Play

Use the standard rules from the original game of Risk with the following additions:

- If you capture at least one territory from another player, they must pleasure you at the end of your turn. They roll two dice and perform the corresponding foreplay activity from the Frisky Foreplay idea lists. The intensity set is based on your current level. Consider this a tribute or peace offering for halting your advance.

- Suppose a player successfully defends all their territories by the end of your turn. In that case, you must roll two dice and perform a foreplay activity for them using their current intensity level.

- When turning in a card set for extra armies, you must also remove an article of clothing if you have any left. You also increase to the next foreplay level.

- At any time, you may purchase 10 extra armies by stripping an article of clothing. You get to place them on any of your territories immediately.

Capture all other player territories to win. You then get to claim your victory reward.

More Than Two Players?

When more than two are playing, there may be situations where physical intimacy between specific pairs of players is not be desired. Rather than forfeiting the pleasuring tribute, assume you have a temporary alliance with another player and allow them to receive the reward while you get to watch. You could allow this type of alliance designation specifically to watch. The alliance rule can also apply in later stages of the game when the allied player has already been vanquished and is essentially out of play.

Also, if desired, three-player activities can be included when territories from two different players have been taken over. The first player losing territory will be considered the Performer, and the next will be the Assistant. Let the advancing player determine the style of tribute received and from whom:

- one single foreplay activity from one specific player
- multiple single foreplay activities from two or more players
- a single three-player foreplay activity from two other players

They should make the determination before looking up the activity.

Pleasure Monopoly

Here is a frisky variation of Monopoly for adults that allows you to buy happiness in the form of foreplay activities. It's a sensual game of sex and money for adults. You play the same game you know and love with a few erotic twists to the rules. For example, rather than renting houses, you build pleasure parlours. And instead of paying rent when you land on a property, you pay to receive pleasure.

You'll be playing as both the customer and the provider of sex for money. Your properties provide the base for your special erotic services. By adding more pleasure parlours (houses) and brothels (hotels), you can increase your fees. And, as you develop your properties, the services you offer become more explicit and sensually exciting. In this way, the game naturally starts off slow and becomes more intense near the end as more brothels are built.

Objective

Your objective is to build as many pleasure parlours as possible while providing top-notch "service" for your exceptional customer. Once you've obtained a sex monopoly in the business of pleasure, you'll be able to buy ultimate happiness in the form of a fantastic fantasy with your lover. In this erotic version of the game, you perform foreplay activities when a player lands on your properties and pays the fee. The types of sensual pleasuring you perform are based on the improvements you've made to your property (houses and hotels) and the increased cost of visiting. As the monetary stakes rise, more explicit or intense foreplay pleasures are provided. You win when other players have no money to pay for sex and must sell themselves to you.

Rather than playing as a land baron, you're trying to build a sex empire. You want to become the ultimate pleasure broker - the only one players can turn to for great sex.

Setup & Preparation

You will need the regular Monopoly board game with two different colored dice. Start the game fully clothed. Negotiate a suitable sexual favor or fantasy reward for winning. For example, you could write down a list of possible ideas, each with a price tag (earn as much dirty money as you can at the end of the game to pay for the really good stuff). You'll be using the Frisky Foreplay activity lists to determine what you're paying for during the game.

How to Play

Use the standard Monopoly rules with the following additions:

- When you land on a property owned by another player, pay the standard fee. However, they must perform a pleasuring task for you from the Frisky Foreplay activity lists.
- The foreplay intensity level is based on the number of houses built: bare properties (level 1), one to four pleasure parlours (level 2-5), brothel (level 6).
- The activity is selected based on the dice you rolled to get to the property. If the owner cannot or declines to provide the service, you get your money back. If you refuse to receive the service, they keep your fee.

When you spend all your money on pleasure, you eventually need to return the favor. The wealthiest player (either after a set time limit or by bankrupting everyone else) wins the game. Use your wealth to obtain pleasure from your rival sexpreneurs.

Make it a Stripping Game Too

To ensure everyone is prepared to get extra frisky later in the game, you'll want to add a stripping rule. Now, if you've ever played Monopoly with just one other player, you may have encountered a few frustrating elements. For example, when property sets get split between you and there's no way to start building houses. It can be a problem with more players as well unless you allow side deals. So here's a way to fix the problem and encourage some sexy stripping action too:

- If you land on a property owned by a rival and hold at least one of the matching properties, you can buy it from them.
- First, pay the regular fee and receive the pleasure you paid for. Then decide if you want to buy the place.
- If you want it, strip an item of clothing and pay the current owner triple the property value to take ownership.

- If you're already naked, take a chance with the level 6 activities. Roll one die to determine the level, then roll two dice to determine the foreplay activity. Perform the pleasuring, pay triple value and take ownership.

Here are some other ways to make this an excellent stripping game:

- When you land on Free Parking, receive bonus money when you take off an article of clothing. Make the value match the type of item being removed – say $500 for a shirt/pants, $1000 for underwear, and $1500 for a sexy dance if you're already naked.

- Assign a price tag for each piece of clothing that you're wearing. When you're short of money, strip and sell an article of clothing to a rival business owner for cash.

- When you roll 3 doubles in a row and get sent to Jail, strip one item of clothing.

- Select certain Community Chest and Chance cards and write on your own stripping-related instructions. For example, "You Win NUDE Beauty Contest, Collect $10(00), Strip Item of Clothing".

- When you build a brothel on all the properties in a color set, you must strip an item of clothing (get ready for special payments).

Use any or all of these extra stripping ideas in combination with the main one that gets you more profitable properties. The more ways to get naked means more incentive to get kinky when you really want to buy or need to sell one of those particular properties.

More Ways to Spice It Up

Here are a variety of ideas you can use to enhance your adult Monopoly gameplay and spice up the erotic fun even more:

- When either of you rolls doubles or land on the same location, passionately kiss each other

- Turn Just Visiting into a carnal visit – while standing, hug, kiss and fondle each other

- When you land on a railroad owned by your lover, you must "ride" them (you on top) for a minute per railroad owned

- When you land on Electric Company, use a vibrator to creatively stimulate your lover on any exposed erogenous zone

- When you land on Water Works, perform some manual pipe or tunnel work with your partner

- When sent to Jail, use actual bondage cuffs until released

- Use blank business cards to make your own erotically themed Chance and Community Chest decks with sexy challenges and sensual rewards

- For each roll to get out of Jail, perform the corresponding Frisky Foreplay activity starting with level 1 and increasing a level for each successive roll. If you opt to pay to get out of Jail, roll the dice and perform an activity from level 2

We hope these ideas have inspired you to pull out your old Monopoly game and enjoy some erotic fun together with the one you love.

Frisky Poker

Is your pleasure in good hands? Here is a variation of classic strip poker for intimate lovers willing to go all-in for pleasure. Play head to head with your partner and discover how to get pleasure with each hand.

This couples game is an erotic adaptation of Texas Hold'em Poker. It involves betting not just with chips but with special foreplay tokens or pleasure promise notes. Knowing how and when to use your hands will lead to stripping, sensual foreplay and passionate sex.

Objective

In this friendly game of no-limit poker, you want to literally bet the pants off your lover. You may need to put your ass on the line too. Having winning hands ensures that you receive as much pleasure as possible. Learn to read your lover's body language to get what you really want. Bet with chips and foreplay services valued as chips. The player who strips everything from their lover wins their favorite sex play activity or fantasy reward.

Setup & Preparation

Players should start fully dressed, wearing at least four or five items each. You'll need a standard deck of cards and 100 poker chips (50 each). Set the small and big blinds at 5 and 10 chips, respectively.

You could come up with your own set of foreplay forfeits or rewards to wager. However, in this version, you'll bet random activities from the Frisky Foreplay idea sets. Each set is valued at 10 times the intensity level (1-6). Choose a level based on the value of the bet you want or roll a single die to determine it randomly. Roll two dice to determine the activity if the bet is won. This adds an element of risk to the bet since you don't know what you'll need to do. You even risk having to strip - if the activity is something you can't or prefer not to do, strip an item of clothing instead. If you opt-out and you're already naked, you forfeit the game. If your partner refuses the activity, your bet is fulfilled.

How to Play

Play with the standard no-limit Texas Hold'em poker rules but apply the following enhanced strip poker rules:

- If you go all in and lose all your chips, strip off an article of clothing. If you are already naked, you lose the game. Each time you strip, the chips are redistributed evenly, and you start another round of erotic play.

- The player with the fewest chips may raise or call with a foreplay marker (either alone or with additional chips). Only one foreplay marker is allowed per hand. Once a foreplay bet is made, no further raises may be made for the hand. Progress to the showdown and see if either of you gets lucky. If you lose a foreplay bet, you are obliged to immediately perform the pleasuring activity for the winner.

The foreplay marker concept allows for an entirely open-ended variety to your foreplay games. Just create a new activity list with different types of erotic ideas. It also gives each player control over what they're willing to do throughout the game. Initially, you may try going all in using just chips (stripping off your outer clothing is "no big deal"). But, as you shed more clothing and the game heats up, you'll tend to wager more intense erotic activities as a way to avoid losing all your chips (and potentially losing the game). Also, if you have a really good hand, you may want to bet something really naughty. Since you're betting something your lover desires, they're more likely to call your bet. Or they might think you're luring them with temptation. This makes bluffing even more fun - just hope you can read your lover's body language.

Once a player is naked and runs out of chips again, the game is over. The winner receives a mutually pleasurable sexual reward agreed upon at the start.

Variations

Here are a few ways to enhance this foreplay game:

- Use XXX playing cards for visual stimulation.

- Each player writes out three pleasure promise notes and negotiates a value to assign to each one. The values do not need to be the same, and the totals do not need to be equal. When appropriate, bet with a pleasure promise note. Using one does not force a stop to the betting. Also, pleasure promises do not need to be performed immediately when won but do need to be honored on demand.

- Suppose you accept a foreplay bet into the pot by another player and lose the hand. Instead of passing on the pleasuring opportunity, you roll the dice and perform the activity for the winner.

- Pretend you're high-stakes poker players. Use multiple stacks of different colored chips with high monetary values. Play the game as part of a role-playing fantasy.

- Play with three or more intimate friends. Allow a max of two players to use foreplay bets and if a player wins both, use the three-player activities. Flip a coin to determine the Performing and Assistant player - the winner of the hand is the Receiving player. Use an activity from the highest level wagered.

Tied Up Foreplay

Bondage is optional in this erotic adaptation of the card game War. It's an easy bedroom game where tying each other leads to stripping, foreplay and amazing sex.

Objective

In this game, you want to *tie & beat* your lover as many times as you can - all tongue in cheek foreplay, of course. While attempting to dominate your lover with higher cards, you receive or perform foreplay activities whenever your cards match. The player who wins all the cards or has the most after a specified time limit wins a sexual favor or fantasy reward.

Setup & Preparation

Come up with a set of sex play activities to correspond to each of the 13 cards (Ace to King) in a deck. These will be the possible rewards for winning the game. You'll be using the Frisky Foreplay idea lists and the Card to Dice key to lookup pleasuring activities throughout the game. A full, standard deck of cards is used. Shuffle and deal out all the cards face down so that players get half the deck each (neatly stacked). Ensure no one sees what the cards are.

How to Play

Both players turn over the top card from their stack and place them face up next to each other. The player with the dominant card (higher card regardless of suit) wins both cards and puts them face down at the bottom of their stack. Aces are high, then kings, queens, jacks, etc.

When the two face-up cards are tied, each player counts out four cards to break the tie (first 3 face down and the fourth face-up). Count out loud in unison: 1, 2, 3, Foreplay! Again, the player with the higher card face-up wins the hand. But, they also receive the foreplay bonus corresponding to the two cards that tied. The losing player must perform the foreplay activity immediately before the game resumes. If another tie occurs, repeat with the winner receiving the Foreplay bonus for each matching set. Also, for every multiple foreplay tie, the losing player must remove an article of clothing.

Start at foreplay intensity level 1. Increase the level after each game, every 20 minutes or whenever a player is required to strip after a multi-set tie.

Play until someone wins all the cards or for a set time limit. The player with the most cards at the end wins and receives their sex play bonus corresponding to the last winning card.

Scoring

You score sexual favors from your partner based on how well you figuratively dominate or *tie & beat* them. Play as many times as you like. Once you play this game a few times, you'll come up with many of your own erotic variations to spice it up even more. There are many other variations of War available online that you can adapt similarly.

Variations

Here are a few ways to enhance this foreplay game even more:

- Use XXX playing cards for visual stimulation and distraction.
- Use two decks of cards combined for a longer game.
- Include Jokers in the mix. Jokers have a value of 1 (Two's beat them). If you win a Joker, strip an article of clothing.
- When playing with mixed genders, perform a female activity when a red match is found and male activity when a black match is found, both for red/black matches.
- Play with three people. If any cards match, all three play to resolve the tie. Perform an activity from the three-player lists: Winner is the Receiver, second highest card player is the Performer, and lowest card player is the Assistant.

Smack That!

Know of anyone in need of a royal spanking? Here is an erotic adaptation of the card game Slap Jack. It's for lovers who have been very naughty (or want to be). In this fast-paced and exciting bedroom game, you score with hot sex if you have quick hands. But if you're naughty and get caught red-handed, you may receive a few spankings to warm your butt. Regardless, your naughty behavior will result in some amazing sex.

Objective

In this game, the cards represent various naughty foreplay activities that the King and Queen may be engaged in. Be the first to catch them in the act (smack that King or Queen), and you get rewarded (paid off) with pleasure and a set of cards. Although fun, there are penalties if you get carried away with your smacking. The first player to win all the cards receives a special sex play bonus: the last nasty act you catch to be performed with your own King or Queen.

Setup & Preparation

You could make up your own set of foreplay activities to correspond to each of the 13 card values (Ace to King). Instead, for this version, use the Card to Dice key to look up Frisky Foreplay ideas. These represent the naughty activities the King and Queen will be performing throughout the game. Start off at level 1 and increase every 10 minutes or after a Joker has been played.

You may want to create a custom list of 13 possible sex play activities corresponding to each card value.

A complete, standard deck of cards is used with one or two Jokers included. Shuffle and deal out all the cards face down so that each player has half the deck each (neatly stacked). Ensure no one sees what the cards are.

How to Play

Players take turns placing their top card face up on a pile in the center. This continues until a King, Queen or Joker is turned up. Be the first player to smack that card, and you win the center pile of cards. But there's more:

- The card under the King or Queen corresponds to the foreplay reward you receive from your lover (to be performed immediately).
- Smacking a Joker means you give your lover an erotic spanking after they remove an article of clothing. Also, increase the intensity level of the Frisky Foreplay activities.

- If there are no cards beneath the King or Queen (masturbating?), the foreplay activity corresponds to this top card.

- When guys smack the Queen or girls smack the King first, you also get to give your lover a brief erotic spanking.

Suppose there is a dispute as to who smacked the card first. In that case, both players receive a spanking, both players must remove an article of clothing, and the center pile is shuffled and split between you. In this situation, no other foreplay activity is performed.

To make things fair, both of you should keep your dominant smacking hand equal distance away from the pile. If you're about to turn over a card, use your other hand and don't reveal it until it's over the pile. Then flip it over as quick as you can so you both have an equal chance to smack it first.

The cards you win should be shuffled into your stack after you determine the foreplay activity to perform. If a player runs out of cards, the other player keeps turning over cards. The player with no remaining cards must be the first to smack the King or Queen; otherwise, they lose the game. The winner receives their foreplay reward and gets a sex play bonus corresponding to the card below the King or Queen.

There are penalties if you smack the wrong card:

- You receive a brief erotic spanking from your lover.

- You must perform the foreplay activity corresponding to the card you smacked.

- Cards remain in the center, and play continues as if nothing happened.

Play until someone wins all the cards or for a set time limit. The player with the most cards at the end wins and receives their sex play bonus corresponding to the last winning card beneath the King or Queen.

Variations

Here are a few ways to enhance this foreplay game:

- Use XXX playing cards for visual stimulation and distraction.

- Use two decks of cards combined for a longer game.

- Turn it into a drinking game by having a player take a shot if they win 3 or more piles in a row (equal out the reaction times).

- Perform the female foreplay activity when a Queen is smacked and the male activity when a King is smacked regardless of who slaps the card first.

Manic Mood Match

In this erotic adaptation of the card game Snap, if you're both in the mood, don't hesitate. It's a fast-paced bedroom game where matching cards leads to stripping, sensual foreplay and passionate sex.

Objective

In this game, each card represents a foreplay activity that you're in the mood for. If your partner is also in the mood (a match), be the first one to "go for it". You'll receive sensual pleasuring and a set of cards. The player that wins the most cards gets a special sexual favor or reward - whatever you're in the mood for.

Setup & Preparation

Come up with a set of sex play activities to correspond to each of the 13 cards (Ace to King) in a deck. These will be the possible rewards for winning the game. You'll be using the Frisky Foreplay idea lists and the Card to Dice key to lookup pleasuring activities throughout the game. Start at any level you desire.

A complete, standard deck of cards is used. Shuffle and deal out all the cards face down so that each player has half the deck each (neatly stacked). Ensure no one sees what the cards are.

How to Play

At the same time, both players turn over the top card from their stack and place them face up next to each other. If the two top cards do not match, continue flipping cards in unison. If they do match, the first player to shout out the mood match wins the hand. But this isn't as simple as shouting "Snap":

- If both cards are red, call "**Lick**"

- If both cards are black, call "**Suck**"

- If the cards are red & black, call "**Fuck**"

If you're the first player to identify a mood match correctly, you get both piles of face-up cards (placed face down at the bottom of your deck). And, you receive the foreplay activity corresponding to the matching cards to be performed by your lover. If it's too close to call who was first, take each other's pile (swap), and both of you perform the corresponding foreplay activity for each other.

There are penalties if you call out a match incorrectly:

- If you call out the wrong type of match, you can either forfeit the cards to your lover or strip off one article of clothing and keep the cards. However, in either case, no one receives the corresponding foreplay. If you are currently naked, you must forfeit the cards.

- If you wrongly call out a match when there isn't one, the cards remain as is. But you must perform the foreplay activity corresponding to your lover's topmost card.

When you run out of face-down cards, take your face-up stack, shuffle and turn face down to continue. Play for a set time limit of 10-15 minutes per round or until someone wins most of the cards (5 or fewer cards remaining in a stack after it's used). The player with the most cards at the end wins. Increase the foreplay level after each round. The player winning the most rounds after level 6 receives their sex play reward corresponding to their last winning card.

Variations

Here are a few ways to enhance this bedroom game with even more foreplay:

- Use XXX playing cards for visual stimulation and distraction.
- Use two decks of cards combined for a longer game.
- For three players, use two decks of cards and call out any two-card matches. Use the three-player Frisky Foreplay idea sets. Flip a coin to determine which of the two other players are the Performer or Assistant for the activity.

You can also add another stripping element to the game by including Jokers in the mix. At the start of the game, give each player a Joker to shuffle into their stack. Matching Jokers with any other face card (J, Q, K) and being the first to shout "Strip" means the other player must remove an item of clothing.

To make the game even trickier, you can add different types of matching combinations and related activities:

- 6-9 shout "Sixty Nine" - mutual oral pleasuring
- Q-K shout "Screw" - intercourse or grinding together
- Q-J shout "Handjob" - manual pleasuring
- 8-J shout "Boobjob" - pleasuring involving breast play
- A-3 shout "Butt Plug" - ass play any way you feel

Any combination of different cards can be assigned a trigger word or phrase and a sexy activity.

Frisky Crazy Sex

Is wild & crazy sex in the cards for you tonight? Here is a quick and easy erotic adaptation of the card game Crazy Eights. Although simple to play, this foreplay game comes with some strategic opportunities to get what you really want: stripping, sensual foreplay and passionate sex.

Objective

The ultimate goal, of course, is to enjoy crazy sex that is wildly passionate. However, the sensual activities you perform are determined by the sequence of cards played as you try to be the first to get rid of all your cards. You score points in each of four (or more) games. The player with the highest total score wins their favorite sex play activity or fantasy.

Setup & Preparation

A complete, standard deck of cards is used. You'll be using the Frisky Foreplay idea lists and the Card to Dice key to lookup pleasuring activities throughout the game. Start at any level you desire. Agree on the sexual forfeits or rewards for winning. Choose a dealer. Shuffle and deal 8 cards to each player, then turn the next card face up in the center as the foreplay pile. The remaining deck is placed face down next to it.

How to Play

Choose who plays first. On your turn, attempt to place a card on the foreplay pile that is either the same suit or the same rank (a matching card of a different suit). If a match is made, you receive the foreplay activity corresponding to that card. The pleasuring activity should be performed by your lover immediately.

If you cannot follow suit, you must pick up cards one at a time until you find a card you can play. If, after picking up 3 or more cards, you still can't play a card, you have the option to strip off an article of clothing and pass or continue picking up cards until you can play one.

Since the game is related to crazy eights, eights are wild. You may place an 8 down anytime and declare both a suit and a rank for this wild card. The next player could, of course, match this wild card and receive their foreplay bonus. Note that an 8 will match another 8 even though it was declared as something else - you still get your foreplay bonus.

If the draw deck is exhausted (hopefully you aren't) before a player uses all their cards, the game is blocked. In this situation, the player with the lowest count scores the difference in value. Or, reshuffle the used cards in the foreplay pile (except for the top card) and continue playing.

If three or more are playing, the player making a match chooses their partner(s) and the foreplay idea set to use. If necessary, they also determine the Performer and Assistant for the activity.

Scoring

The first player to put down all their cards scores points for the unplayed cards in the other player's hands. Points are scored as follows:

- 25 points for each 8
- 10 points for face cards
- 1 point for each ace
- numeric value of other cards

Increase the foreplay level after each game. Play a set of games until you finish level 6, totaling the score in each game. The player with the highest total score is declared the winner and receives their special reward.

Variations

Here are a few more ways to enhance this foreplay game:

- Use XXX playing cards for visual stimulation
- Receive the corresponding foreplay for the last card when going out
- Use the last card played in the last game to determine a sex play activity for the winner
- Gameplay continues until one of you reaches a total score of 200 points

You can also assign extra penalty / bonus cards:

- Queen of Spades - next player picks up 5 cards or strips off one article of clothing
- Ace of Spades - next player chooses something kinky for you to do
- Any 2 - next player picks up 2 cards (doubles with each subsequent match)
- Any 4 - next player skips their turn

Remember Sex

In this erotic adaptation of the Memory card game, you can enjoy sex the way you remember it. Match cards and receive sensual foreplay. Match the most cards to win a special sexual favor or fantasy reward. It is a quick and easy bedroom game with stripping, sensual foreplay and passionate sex.

Objective

The ultimate goal, of course, is to have wildly passionate sex the way you remember it. However, the foreplay activities performed are determined by matching pairs of cards from a deck laid randomly face down. Attempt to find matches by turning over only two cards at a time. The player with the highest number of matches wins a special sexual favor or fantasy as their reward.

Setup & Preparation

You'll be using the Frisky Foreplay idea lists and the Card to Dice key to lookup pleasuring activities throughout the game. Start at any level you desire. Agree on the sexual forfeits or rewards for winning. You could create a list of 13 possible sex play activities corresponding to each card rank to randomize the prize.

A complete, standard deck of cards is used. Shuffle and place all the cards face down, so they don't overlap each other. Ensure no one sees what the cards are as they're being placed.

How to Play

Each player, in turn, attempts to find a matching pair of cards by turning over two at a time. If it is not a match, flip the cards back over face down again. If they are a match, then:

- If you match two cards of the same color, keep them and go again
- If you match a red and a black card, you keep them and receive the foreplay activity corresponding to the card

When you match a red and black card, perform the corresponding foreplay activity immediately. This makes remembering where the previously turned-up cards are just a little bit more difficult.

Play until there are 2 cards left. The final set of cards in the last game could determine the sex play activity the winner receives. For two players, leaving this one set out ensures that one player will have matched at least one more set than the other. Count up the number of matches you've found.

If three or more are playing, use multiple decks. Also, the player making a match chooses their partner(s) and the foreplay idea set to use. If necessary, they also determine the Performer and Assistant for the activity.

After each game, increase the Frisky Foreplay level. The winner also strips an item of clothing. Play until you finished at level 6.

Variations

Here are a few ways to enhance this foreplay game:

- Use XXX playing cards for visual stimulation and distraction.
- Include Jokers in the mix. Finding two Jokers means the other player removes an article of clothing.
- Perform female activity when a red match is found and male activity when a black match is found, none for mixed.
- For a single game, keep matched pairs in order. The winner receives the foreplay then sex play activities at the end of the game in sequence rather than as the game progresses. For each pair, roll a die to determine the activity level.

You can also use a timer (69 second timer if you can find one) and take turns trying to find the most matches. Use separate decks and keep the sequence of card matches found. For the player finding the most matches, perform the corresponding foreplay activities in sequence. Play a few rounds, then use the last match found to determine the sex play activity to perform.

Card to Dice Key

For card games like the examples in the previous sections, you could create your own list of pleasuring activities mapped to a deck of cards: 13 assigned to each rank, 26 assigned to rank and color, or 52 assigned to each individual card. However, since this book provides dice based activities for all two player, three player, straight, gay, lesbian and bi-sexual combinations, it is more practical to use these instead of creating new ones. The table below maps the 52 regular playing cards to 36 possible rolls of two ordered dice - there is some overlap. Assuming an intensity level (1-6) has been selected in some other way, look up the two other dice values using the card key then use the three numbers to look up a foreplay activity in the desired collection.

Card	♥	♦	♣	♠
A	1 1	2 1	3 5	4 6
2	1 2	2 2	3 6	5 1
3	1 3	2 3	4 1	5 2
4	1 4	2 4	4 2	5 3
5	1 5	2 5	4 3	5 4
6	1 6	2 6	4 4	5 5
7	2 1	3 1	4 5	5 6
8	2 2	3 2	4 6	6 1
9	2 3	3 3	5 1	6 2
10	2 4	3 4	5 2	6 3
J	2 5	3 5	5 3	6 4
Q	2 6	3 6	5 4	6 5
K	3 1	4 1	5 5	6 6

Male Female

Foreplay Activities

Male Female

Level 1 - Warm & Loving

MF111

Give feather-light kisses along Your Partner's neck and jawline. Breathe softly next to her ear to make her shiver with delight.

MF112

Massage Your Partner's head with the tips of your fingers. Stroke her hair.

MF113

Sit opposite each other. Place a hand on each other's chest, close your eyes and synchronize breathing slowly.

MF114

Kiss and lick Your Partner's wrist, inner arm and elbow.

MF115

Spider Walk your fingers delicately over parts of Your Partner's exposed body. Arouse her with a slow, light tickling and tapping motion.

MF116

From a book of fantasies or erotic letters, read a random one out loud to Your Partner.

MF121

Describe in detail a unique, romantic adventure involving both of you. Include elements of the love play you'll enjoy together.

MF122

Standing, hug and caress Your Partner from behind.

MF123

Write a pleasure promise note or coupon for Your Partner involving a relaxing, soothing massage to be redeemed later.

MF124

Kiss and lightly lick Your Partner's hand, palm and fingers. Choose her non-dominant hand.

MF125

Find a how-to article on a sex technique or activity that you have not yet experienced and read it together.

MF126

Use a feather or piece of silky material to tickle Your Partner's face, lips, ears and neck.

MF131

Delicately stroke Your Partner's hands and fingers with your fingertips. Swirl and circle as you explore and tickle every nerve to attention.

MF132

Apply cologne lightly to a few areas of your body. Choose a special one you know she loves.

MF133

Lovingly embrace Your Partner. Hug, caress and tenderly kiss each other.

MF134

Place soft, delicate kisses all over Your Partner's face – cheek, lips, nose, forehead, temples, chin. End with a tender, sensuous kiss.

MF135

Lick Your Partner's ear lobes and sensitive regions on her neck. Behind the ears and back of her neck are very sensitive. Whisper something deliciously sensual, loving or erotic.

MF136

Describe in detail a unique, novel or exotic place to make love. Include activities you would like to experience.

MF141

Gently kiss and lick Your Partner's inner arm – wrist to elbow.

MF142

Delicately lick around each of Your Partner's ears. Hot breaths in her ear will give her delightful shivers of pleasure.

MF143

Do something to set the mood. Play soft music, light a candle, pour a glass of wine, burn some incense, apply cologne, etc.

MF144

Dance embraced with Your Partner to one slow song. Kiss lovingly when it ends.

MF145

Massage one part of Your Partner's body (her choice). Experiment with a different type of technique.

MF146

Find and view some erotic art together - use books or the internet. Discuss what you like about it.

MF151

Erotically tickle any exposed erogenous zone. Creatively use your fingers, a feather, a soft paintbrush or your tongue.

MF152

Find an erotic edible and feed it to Your Partner sensually. Fruit, syrup, chocolate, oysters, liquor, etc.

MF153

Standing together, softly stroke and caress Your Partner's entire body. Lightly squeeze parts of her body that you find delightful.

MF154

Make up a fantasy scenario or roleplaying adventure for you and Your Partner. Include elements of a "real" fantasy – keep her guessing.

MF155

Both of you close your eyes. Delicately caress Your Partner's face. Trace your fingertips as lightly as you can. Explore every detail.

MF156

Remove one item of clothing erotically then slowly remove one item of clothing from Your Partner.

MF161

Massage Your Partner's toes one at a time.

MF162

Experiment with different types of kisses and kissing sensations. (upside down, open mouth, closed mouth, sideways, corner, firm, soft)

MF163

Tenderly kiss Your Partner with affection. Hold and caress her face with both hands.

MF164

Browse through a book with advanced or acrobatic sex positions with Your Partner. Choose one of them that you would like to experience together.

MF165

Browse an erotic book or magazine with Your Partner (her choice). Discuss pictures or images that appeal to you.

MF166

Give Your Partner a brief but relaxing massage the way you know she likes it.

Male Female

Level 2 - Sensual Sensations

MF211

Massage and fondle any part of Your Partner's body still clothed - do not touch any skin.

MF212

Massage Your Partner's feet and each toe with massage oil or lube.

MF213

Use a piece of fur, silk or satin to smoothly caress any/all exposed parts of Your Partner's body.

MF214

Lick, suck and lightly bite Your Partner's nipples. Blow on or suck in air around them to create warm and cool sensations.

MF215

Creatively use an ice cube to perk up sensitive regions on Your Partner's body. Follow each cold shock with a warm kiss or lick.

MF216

Gently suck each of Your Partner's nipples into your mouth. Add a vibrating sensation by humming or use a vibrator on your cheek.

MF221

Stroke and caress Your Partner's legs and inner thighs.

MF222

Put on any item to look, feel, smell or taste even more sexy for yourself and Your Partner.

MF223

Use a flavored lube or syrup on any rarely licked erogenous zone and entice Your Partner to lick it off.

MF224

Sensual Surprise – creatively stimulate Your Partner any way you desire.

MF225

Slowly and sensually lick and suck Your Partner's thumb. Stimulate every nerve with your twirling tongue.

MF226

Pleasure yourself as visual stimulation for Your Partner.

MF231

Fondle, rub and massage Your Partner's derriere.

MF232

Hug and passionately kiss each other.

MF233

Use a vibrator to delicately stimulate Your Partner's nipples.

MF234

Kneeling while Your Partner stands, kiss and lick her belly, hips and thighs. Kneed her buttocks gently.

MF235

Using massage oil, gently massage Your Partner's breasts. Circle but do not touch her nipples.

MF236

Apply a flavored lube to Your Partner's nipples. Tweak and tantalize them with your fingertips, then lick each nipple clean.

MF241

Kiss and lick the soft, sensitive skin behind Your Partner's knees.

MF242

Put an edible topping or liquor in Your Partner's navel and lick it out.

MF243

Whisper in Your Partner's ear how you want to pleasure her with your hot tongue.

MF244

Kiss, lick and suck each finger of Your Partner's non-dominant hand. Apply a flavored lube or syrup if you desire.

MF245

Stroke and caress Your Partner's breasts. Lightly circle her nipples.

MF246

Write a sex coupon for Your Partner involving an erotic massage to be redeemed later.

MF251

Expose and lightly lick Your Partner's lower back and side. Lightly bite and nibble her buttocks.

MF252

Creatively use a string of pearls or round beads to stimulate Your Partner in various ways.

MF253

Perform an erotic dance while removing an item of clothing. Play appropriate music if you desire.

MF254

Use an artist brush dipped in flavored lube to stimulate Your Partner's nipples. Apply delicate flicks and twirls then lick them clean.

MF255

Caress and lightly stroke any/all exposed parts of Your Partner's body.

MF256

Have Your Partner bend over your knee, expose her bum and allow you to administer a sensual spanking.

MF261

Lightly drag your fingernails down Your Partner's back, chest and tummy, legs or arms – your choice.

MF262

Whisper in Your Partner's ear how hard you are and how badly you want to be deep inside her.

MF263

Use a vibrator to stimulate Your Partner's toes and soles of her feet.

MF264

Write a sex coupon for Your Partner involving a night of uninterrupted intimate pleasuring to be redeemed later.

MF265

Use a soft artist or make-up brush to tickle and stimulate an exposed region of Your Partner's body.

MF266

Find and use an item with an interesting texture to stimulate and sensitize an exposed region of Your Partner's body. (soft, cold, rough, squishy, etc.)

Male Female

Level 3 - Intimate Intentions

MF311

Watch one scene of an XXX DVD with Your Partner. You choose the DVD or switch over to a free online porn site to watch a short video.

MF312

Suck one of Your Partner's fingers while manually pleasuring her pussy. (do not remove any clothing)

MF313

Dab some ice cream or smear a popsicle on Your Partner's nipples and lick them clean.

MF314

Put a glass or silicone dildo in the freezer to be enjoyed later.

MF315

Reveal an exotic roleplaying adventure you "may" be interested in experiencing with Your Partner. Include detailed, explicit content.

MF316

Kiss and lick Your Partner's breasts – all over except her nipples.

MF321

Look through an explicit pictorial magazine or book with Your Partner. Discuss what you consider erotic and arousing.

MF322

Look each other in the eyes while you both suck and lick the other person's middle finger. Use your tongues to swirl and stroke it.

MF323

Remove any clothing necessary for Your Partner to teasingly lick your inner thighs. Lay back and enjoy her tickling tongue.

MF324

Choose a position and a location other than on the bed to have sex later. Let your imagination run wild - be creative and adventurous.

MF325

Stroke Your Partner's tail bone and between her butt cheeks. Use your fingers, tongue, feather, spoon, string of beads, etc.

MF326

Expose the head of your penis (or cover the rest) and entice Your Partner to lick just the tip of it.

MF331

Standing, firmly cup Your Partner's pussy with one hand while you kiss passionately.

MF332

Expose and blow "raspberries" on Your Partner's butt cheeks.

MF333

Both you and Your Partner remove one item of clothing and dance while holding each other close to one slow song.

MF334

Caress Your Partner's bare feet with your bare feet.

MF335

Seductively read a short erotic passage or a dirty letter. Choose one that is very explicit and detailed.

MF336

Use a digital camera and play erotic photographer with Your Partner. View them together and delete afterward (unless you really like one to print).

MF341

Simulate a sex act of your choice with Your Partner.

MF342

Write a sex coupon for Your Partner involving you and a sex toy to be redeemed later. (her choice of sex toy)

MF343

Find and creatively use a non-sexual object to pleasure Your Partner.

MF344

Have Your Partner pulse her PC muscles as tightly and quickly as possible for a minute while you cup her crotch in one hand.

MF345

Describe in detail a design for an ultimate new sex toy or a creative new way to use one you already have.

MF346

Use an ice cube to cool then your lips and tongue to heat an exposed erogenous zone on Your Partner's body.

MF351

Using a flavored lube, massage a few of Your Partner's toes, then lick and suck them.

MF352

Express audible sounds of passion leading up to a fake orgasm. Use these same sounds of passion later when you have a real one.

MF353

Warm your mouth with a hot liquid (water, coffee, tea) swallow then kiss or lightly suck on one of Your Partner's exposed erogenous zones.

MF354

Use a vibrator to stimulate Your Partner's neck, chest and nipples.

MF355

Get into a 69 position with Your Partner (you on top) and nuzzle each other. Hum, purr or moan for an added thrill.

MF356

Select something sexy for Your Partner to wear (now and while making love later).

MF361

Write a sex coupon for Your Partner involving a quickie to be redeemed later.

MF362

Choose a sex toy that you'll use together with Your Partner while having sex later.

MF363

From a book or deck of cards with sex positions, choose a sex position you'll use later.

MF364

Write a sex coupon for Your Partner involving oral sex to be redeemed later.

MF365

Get Your Partner in a position to receive oral sex and simulate how you would perform it. Moan and hum with enthusiasm for added effect.

MF366

Hold a piece of frozen fruit (strawberry, mango, pineapple) in your mouth while you kiss Your Partner.

Male Female

Level 4 - Explicit & Erotic Passion

MF411

Sensuously demonstrate cunnilingus using an edible object (mango, peach, chocolate on Your Partner's fingers, etc.) – think juicy and messy.

MF412

Pleasure Your Partner's entire pussy orally. Use creative licking and sucking techniques.

MF413

Stimulate Your Partner with a sex toy. (Visual stimulation counts)

MF414

While Your Partner watches, demonstrate a technique you use to masturbate. Provide her visual stimulation without going all the way.

MF415

Expose, then pinch, tweak and twiddle your nipples. Use a lubricant if you desire. Then have Your Partner suck and bite them gently.

MF416

Use a piece of soft, juicy, sticky fruit to tickle Your Partner's clitoris then lick it clean.

MF421

Use a vibrator to tease Your Partner's pussy lips. Lightly circle her clitoris without directly touching it.

MF422

Creatively stimulate Your Partner with a vibrator. (Visual stimulation counts)

MF423

Apply some lube to the head of your cock and use it to stroke Your Partner's vaginal lips and clitoris – no penetration allowed.

MF424

In missionary or doggie position, penetrate Your Partner's vagina once as slowly and deeply as you can – she is not allowed to move.

MF425

Lightly squeeze and tug Your Partner's vaginal lips. Massage them delicately with moist fingertips.

MF426

Kiss and lick any exposed erogenous zone you desire on Your Partner's body.

MF431

Using lube and two fingers, massage Your Partner's pussy. Then penetrate her vagina with smooth, gliding strokes.

MF432

Insert a dildo of Your Partner's choice into her pussy while licking her clitoris. Move the dildo in slow, smooth strokes.

MF433

Lightly tug small amounts of pubic hair all around Your Partner's pussy. If she is shaved, stroke her mound softly.

MF434

In a doggie position, penetrate Your Partner slowly then give her 10 hard and fast thrusts before pulling out again.

MF435

Stand behind Your Partner in front of a mirror and watch each other as you stroke and fondle her body intimately.

MF436

In a missionary position, insert just the head of your cock into Your Partner's vagina. Use your hand to wiggle it back and forth and around.

MF441

Use broad tongue strokes to lick slowly up and down Your Partner's pussy. Use the underside of your tongue on her clitoris.

MF442

Pleasure Your Partner's clitoris orally using a warming, flavored lube.

MF443

Delicately flutter your tongue up, down and around Your Partner's pussy and inner thigh like a flickering flame always moving.

MF444

Look into Your Partner's eyes as you suck one of her fingers and manually pleasure her pussy.

MF445

Apply hot breaths on Your Partner's clitoris while playing with both her nipples. Avoid touching her pussy directly.

MF446

Insert one finger in Your Partner's vagina (moisten if necessary) and gently massage left, right, up, down and all around – no thrusting.

MF451

Simulate a sex act of your choice without involving Your Partner – she gets to watch as you pretend. Stimulate her desire.

MF452

Apply lube to Your Partner's nipples and stimulate them with the head of your cock.

MF453

Use an artist brush dipped in lube to delicately stimulate Your Partner's clitoris. Flick up, down and across - swirl in circles and zigzags.

MF454

Write a sex coupon for Your Partner involving a quickie in an unusual location to be redeemed later.

MF455

Find and creatively use a non-sexual object to pleasure Your Partner.

MF456

Apply lube between Your Partner's butt cheeks and slide your cock between them (no penetration).

MF461

Enjoy 30 seconds of intercourse standing, rear-entry with Your Partner facing up against a wall.

MF462

Nibble and suck on Your Partner's vaginal lips. Twirl your tongue inside her vagina – wiggle it in as deep as you can.

MF463

Enjoy 30 seconds of intercourse doggie style – no ejaculation allowed yet.

MF464

Use an ice cube and your lips and tongue to cool then heat Your Partner's nipples and her clitoris. Stimulate her pussy with hot and cold sensations.

MF465

Delicately massage Your Partner's clitoris and vaginal lips with a lubricant. Lovingly look into her eyes and discover how she responds to your touch.

MF466

Simulate a sex act of your choice as if you and Your Partner switched gender. Get her to use a dildo as a prop if desired.

Male Female

Level 5 - Sizzling, Sexual Stimulation

MF511

If you changed into a female for an hour and could have sex with any male, who would it be and what would you do. Describe the sex in detail.

MF512

Sit and have Your Partner straddle you (her back to your chest). Use your penis to tap and stroke her clitoris while playing with her nipples.

MF513

Write a sex coupon or promise note for Your Partner involving a quickie outside (moonlit night, beach, parked car, under a bridge, etc.).

MF514

While Your Partner stands, kneel behind her and nibble and bite her buttocks while playing with her pussy.

MF515

Remove all clothing on your upper bodies. Apply massage oil to your chests and bellies. Slither and slide against each other to one song.

MF516

Use an artist brush and lube to stimulate Your Partner's anus. Tickle it as you play with her clitoris or nipples.

MF521

With Your Partner standing, facing a wall, apply some lube to your cock and slide it between her butt cheeks – no penetration.

MF522

Gently suck Your Partner's clitoris in your mouth and create different vibrating sensations by humming, moaning, growling, etc.

MF523

Use the tip of a vibrator to tickle Your Partner's perineum and anus – no penetration.

MF524

Get into a doggie position with Your Partner. She is to remain still while you thrust to the left then right or wiggle sideways.

MF525

With Your Partner lying down, legs tight together, apply some lube between her butt cheeks and slide your cock between them – no penetration.

MF526

While Your Partner sits, perform an erotic dance for her to one song of your choice. Seductively entice her to caress and fondle your assets.

MF531

Gently suck and nibble on Your Partner's vaginal lips (labia) – one side then the other. Massage them with your lips and tongue.

MF532

With Your Partner lying on her back, legs raised and spread wide, watch closely as you ever so slowly insert a smooth dildo. Let her watch too.

MF533

Use a digital camera with a zoom lens to take very close-up and intimate shots of Your Partner's erogenous zones. Select one to print and frame.

MF534

While Your Partner uses her fingers to expose her clitoris for you, use only the soft underside of your tongue to delicately caress and stroke it.

MF535

Secretly select a sex toy or other accessory to be used in your sex play later. Keep it hidden to build the anticipation.

MF536

Play a favorite song and orally pleasure Your Partner to the rhythm – make it last the entire length of the song then stop.

MF541

Using lube, insert your two middle fingers with palm on her clitoris. Flutter your fingers up and down quickly. Trigger a G-Spot orgasm.

MF542

Use a dildo and some lube to demonstrate how you would like Your Partner to give you a hand-job.

MF543

Have Your Partner put on some "old" underwear and rip them off her (pre-cut the elastic band if necessary) then ravish her orally.

MF544

In a doggie position, penetrate Your Partner, grab a handful of her hair and pull her head back as you thrust vigorously for 10–20 seconds.

MF545

Lying down, have Your Partner straddle you and offer her breasts to you for oral pleasuring while you both "bump and grind" together.

MF546

Get into a 69 position with you on top. Pleasure each other orally.

MF551

Lube and pleasure Your Partner with a dildo or vibrator of her choice. Allow her to guide your hand or verbally coach you on technique.

MF552

Lube and pleasure Your Partner with the thinnest dildo or vibrator available.

MF553

Pleasure Your Partner with a dildo while you lick her clitoris and she plays with her nipples.

MF554

While lying down, have Your Partner straddle you facing your feet. As she grinds on your cock, give her a few slaps on her ass cheeks.

MF555

One minute of penetration in a position of your choice – No thrusting. Use your PC muscles to make your cock twitch and throb in her vagina.

MF556

Lying down so your head is hanging over an accessible edge (bed, table, sofa, etc.), orally pleasure Your Partner's pussy.

MF561

Warm or cool a glass or acrylic dildo and pleasure Your Partner with it.

MF562

With Your Partner standing, kneel before her and orally pleasure her pussy. Look up into her eyes as you enjoy her.

MF563

Spread Your Partner's butt cheeks wide and tickle her perineum and anus with a feather or piece of silky material.

MF564

Cup Your Partner's pubic mound with your palm just above her clitoris and press firmly. Slowly slide your hand back and forth or in circles.

MF565

Using a firm, pointed tongue, lick Your Partner's perineum using circles, swirls and zigzag strokes.

MF566

Go to a different location in your home with Your Partner and enjoy 30 seconds of intercourse in a creative position of your choice.

Male Female

Level 6 - Wild, Nasty, Kinky, Taboo

MF611

Use a dildo to demonstrate how you would like Your Partner to orally pleasure you.

MF612

In a missionary position, lift Your Partner's legs high and penetrate her deeply. Lick and suck on her toes to make her wiggle on your cock.

MF613

While lying down, have Your Partner straddle you facing your feet. As she grinds on your cock, anally stimulate her with a lubed finger.

MF614

If you changed into a lesbian female for an hour and could have sex with anyone, who would it be and what would you do. Describe the sex in detail.

MF615

Describe in detail a raunchy sex scenario or fantasy involving you and Your Partner in a threesome.

MF616

Ask Your Partner to select a sex toy to play Show and Tell. Demonstrate your self-pleasuring technique, eyes closed, while describing the sensations.

MF621

Make up a roleplay scenario with you as the master. Then sternly command your Love Slave to perform and service one of your desires.

MF622

Roleplaying as a Love Slave, submissively request then perform a sexual favor for your mistress.

MF623

Insert a lubed butt plug into Your Partner's anus and stimulate her with a dildo while she orally pleasures your cock.

MF624

Grab Your Partner and run to an unusual location in your house to have a quickie in a position of your choice – stop just before you orgasm.

MF625

Describe in detail the most extreme, weird or bizarre sexual activity you can think of (not that you want to do it, of course).

MF626

Sit in a comfortable chair with headphones on (favorite music playing), wearing a blindfold, legs spread while Your Partner orally pleasures you.

MF631

Erotically and passionately nibble and bite sensitive erogenous zones on Your Partner's body. Make her ache for you in a good way.

MF632

Describe in detail a raunchy S/M or bondage scenario involving you and Your Partner. Write Your Partner a sex coupon involving bondage for later.

MF633

Insert a lubed butt plug into Your Partner's anus and stimulate her with a dildo while you orally pleasure her clitoris.

MF634

Experiment with cross-dressing – have Your Partner select some of her lingerie (or other outfits) for you to model for her.

MF635

Pleasure Your Partner orally while also stimulating her anally with a lubed finger.

MF636

Using a double-ended anal dildo or silicone beads, both you and Your Partner get on all fours for a little "cheek to cheek" action.

MF641

Write a sex coupon for Your Partner involving anal sex to be redeemed later. Describe in detail what you intend to do together.

MF642

Kiss and lick Your Partner's feet then suck on her toes.

MF643

Creatively use a double-ended dildo with Your Partner.

MF644

Describe in detail how you would include a strap-on in a new sex position or activity. If Your Partner has one, entice her to get it on and have a bit of fun.

MF645

Drip hot wax on Your Partner's breasts or buttocks.

MF646

Apply a nipple clamp to one of Your Partner's nipples. (not for too long)

MF651

Allow Your Partner to masturbate you with a fake pussy (cock sleeve) - just to the brink - no orgasm allowed yet.

MF652

Pleasure yourself with an anal dildo or butt plug while Your Partner watches.

MF653

Use an implement of your choice to erotically spank Your Partner's bare ass until it radiates a sensual heat. Caress and stroke it between smacks.

MF654

Pleasure Your Partner with an edible dildo (cucumber, carrot, etc. of her choice - use a condom).

MF655

Stimulate Your Partner with a butt plug or anal dildo. (Visual stimulation counts)

MF656

Bend over and allow Your Partner to insert a lubricated butt plug – remove only when you are both finished playing.

MF661

With Your Partner propped in a mostly upside-down position, orally pleasure her.

MF662

Write a sex coupon for Your Partner involving role reversal or gender play to be redeemed later. Be explicit.

MF663

Describe in detail a new kinky activity that you "might" like to try (with or without Your Partner).

MF664

Give Your Partner a rim-job (oral-anal pleasuring). Use flavored lube if you wish.

MF665

Use one finger (and lube) to pleasure Your Partner anally. Use your thumb or a finger from the other hand to stimulate her vaginally.

MF666

STOP the Foreplay and START the Sex Play.

Female Male

Foreplay Activities

Female Male

Level 1 - Warm & Loving

FM111

From a book of fantasies or erotic letters, read a random one out loud to Your Partner.

FM112

Use a feather to tickle Your Partner's face, lips, ears and neck.

FM113

Kiss and nibble along Your Partner's neck and shoulder.

FM114

Standing, hug and caress Your Partner from behind.

FM115

Lovingly embrace Your Partner. Hug, caress and tenderly kiss each other.

FM116

Massage Your Partner's head with the tips of your fingers.

FM121

Find a how-to article on a sex technique or activity that you have not yet experienced and read it together.

FM122

Sit opposite and facing each other. Place a hand on each other's chest, close your eyes and synchronize breathing slowly.

FM123

Delicately lick around each of Your Partner's ears. Hot breaths in his ear will give him delightful shivers of pleasure.

FM124

Dance embraced with Your Partner to one slow song. Kiss each other lovingly when it ends.

FM125

Kiss and lick Your Partner's wrist, inner arm and elbow.

FM126

Apply perfume to a few areas of your body where you desire extra attention.

FM131

Describe in detail a unique, novel or exotic place to make love. Include activities you would like to experience.

FM132

Spider Walk your fingers delicately over parts of Your Partner's exposed body. Arouse him with a slow, light tickling and tapping motion.

FM133

Lick Your Partner's ear lobes and sensitive regions on his neck. Behind the ears and back of his neck are very sensitive. Whisper something deliciously sensual, loving or erotic.

FM134

Describe in detail a unique, romantic adventure involving both of you. Include elements of the love play you'll enjoy together.

FM135

Browse an erotic book or magazine with Your Partner (his choice). Discuss pictures or images that appeal to you.

FM136

Massage Your Partner's toes one at a time.

FM141

Tenderly kiss Your Partner with affection. Hold and caress his face with both hands.

FM142

Write a pleasure promise note or coupon for Your Partner involving a relaxing, soothing massage to be redeemed later.

FM143

Kiss and lightly lick Your Partner's hand, palm and fingers. Choose his non-dominant hand.

FM144

Place soft, delicate kisses all over Your Partner's face - cheek, lips, nose, forehead, temples, chin. End with a tender, sensuous kiss.

FM145

Experiment with different types of kisses and kissing sensations. (upside down, open mouth, closed mouth, sideways, corner, firm, soft)

FM146

Gently kiss and lick Your Partner's inner arm – wrist to elbow.

FM151

Both of you close your eyes. Delicately caress Your Partner's face. Trace your fingertips as lightly as you can as you explore every detail.

FM152

Do something to set the mood. Put on some soft music, light a candle, pour a glass of wine, burn some incense, spray some perfume, etc.

FM153

Give Your Partner a brief but relaxing massage the way you know he likes it.

FM154

Browse through a book with advanced or acrobatic sex positions with Your Partner. Choose one of them that you would like to experience together.

FM155

Find and view some erotic art together - use books or the internet. Discuss what you like about it.

FM156

Erotically tickle any exposed erogenous zone. Use your fingers, a feather, a soft paintbrush or your tongue. Be creative.

FM161

Find an erotic edible and feed it to Your Partner sensually. Fruit, syrup, chocolate, oysters, liquor, etc.

FM162

Standing together, softly stroke and caress Your Partner's entire body. Lightly squeeze parts of his body that you find delightful.

FM163

Make up a fantasy scenario or roleplaying adventure for you and Your Partner. Include elements of a "real" fantasy – but keep him guessing.

FM164

Massage one part of Your Partner's body (his choice). Experiment with a different type of technique.

Delicately stroke Your Partner's hands and fingers with your fingertips. Swirl and circle as you explore and tickle every nerve to attention.

FM166

Remove one item of clothing erotically then remove one item of clothing from Your Partner.

Female Male

Level 2 - Sensual Sensations

FM211

Slowly and sensually lick and suck Your Partner's thumb. Stimulate every nerve with your twirling tongue.

FM212

Have Your Partner get in any position you desire, expose his butt and allow you to administer a sensual spanking.

FM213

Use a vibrator to stimulate Your Partner's toes.

FM214

Expose and lightly lick Your Partner's lower back and side. Lightly bite and nibble his buttocks.

FM215

Lick the soft, sensitive skin behind Your Partner's knees.

FM216

Whisper in Your Partner's ear how wet you are and how you want his penis deep inside you.

FM221

Find and use an item with an interesting texture to stimulate/sensitize an exposed region of Your Partner's body. (soft, cold, rough, squishy, etc.)

FM222

Write a sex coupon for Your Partner involving a night of uninterrupted intimate pleasuring to be redeemed later.

FM223

Use a soft artist or make-up brush to tickle and stimulate an exposed region of Your Partner's body.

FM224

Put an edible topping or liquor in your navel and entice Your Partner to lick it out.

FM225

Kiss, lick and suck each finger of Your Partner's non-dominant hand. Apply a flavored lube or syrup if you desire.

FM226

Whisper in Your Partner's ear how you want to pleasure him with your warm, silky tongue.

FM231

Stroke and massage Your Partner's chest. Circle his nipples lightly.

FM232

Write a sex coupon for Your Partner involving an erotic massage to be redeemed later.

FM233

Perform an erotic dance while removing an item of clothing. Play appropriate music if you desire.

FM234

Creatively use a string of pearls or round beads to stimulate Your Partner in various ways.

FM235

Use an artist brush dipped in flavored lube to stimulate Your Partner's nipples. Apply delicate flicks and twirls. Then lick them clean.

FM236

Drag your fingernails down Your Partner's back, chest and tummy, legs or arms - your choice.

FM241

Caress and lightly stroke any exposed part of Your Partner's body.

FM242

Massage and fondle any part of Your Partner's body still covered with clothing - do not touch any skin.

FM243

Kneeling while Your Partner stands, kiss and lick his belly, hips and thighs. Kneed and massage his buttocks.

FM244

Massage Your Partner's feet and each toe with an oil or lube.

FM245

Hug and passionately kiss each other.

FM246

Use a piece of fur, silk or satin to smoothly caress any / all exposed parts of Your Partner's body.

FM251

Use a vibrator to delicately stimulate Your Partner's nipples.

FM252

Lick, suck and lightly bite Your Partner's nipples. Blow on or suck in air around them to create warm and cool sensations.

FM253

Apply a flavored lube to Your Partner's nipples. Tweak and tantalize them with your fingertips then lick each nipple clean.

FM254

Creatively use an ice cube to perk up sensitive regions on Your Partner's body. Follow each cold shock with a warm kiss or lick.

FM255

Put on a silky top and entice Your Partner to caress your breasts and circle your nipples through the fabric. Remove your bra if necessary.

FM256

Rub and massage Your Partner's crotch (through his clothing if he's still wearing any).

FM261

Redress into a new piece of visually and sensually erotic lingerie.

FM262

Put on any item to look, feel, smell or taste even more sexy for yourself and Your Partner.

FM263

Use a flavored lube or syrup on any rarely licked erogenous zone and entice Your Partner to lick it off.

FM264

Creatively stimulate Your Partner in any way you desire.

FM265

Pleasure yourself as visual stimulation for Your Partner.

FM266

Fondle, Rub and Massage Your Partner's buttocks.

Female Male

Level 3 - Intimate Intentions

FM311

Seductively read a short erotic passage or a dirty letter. Choose one that is very explicit and detailed.

FM312

Select something sexy for Your Partner to wear (now and while making love later).

FM313

Get Your Partner into a position to receive oral sex and simulate how you would perform it. Moan and hum for effect.

FM314

Express audible sounds of passion leading up to a fake orgasm.

FM315

Have Your Partner pulse his PC muscles as tightly and quickly as possible for a minute while you cup his crotch in one hand.

FM316

Use a vibrator to stimulate Your Partner's neck, chest and nipples.

FM321

Write a sex coupon for Your Partner involving you and a sex toy to be redeemed later. (his choice of sex toy)

FM322

Simulate a sex act of your choice with Your Partner.

FM323

Write a sex coupon for Your Partner involving oral sex to be redeemed later.

FM324

Find and creatively use a non-sexual object to pleasure Your Partner.

FM325

Write a sex coupon for Your Partner involving a quickie to be redeemed later.

FM326

Describe in detail a design for an ultimate new sex toy or a creative new way to use one you already have.

FM331

Choose a sex toy that you will use together with Your Partner while having sex later.

FM332

Use an ice cube to cool then your lips and tongue to heat an exposed erogenous zone on Your Partner's body.

FM333

Watch one scene of an XXX DVD with Your Partner. You choose the DVD or switch over to a free online porn site to watch a short video.

FM334

Reveal an exotic roleplaying adventure you "may" be interested in experiencing with Your Partner. Include detailed, explicit content.

FM335

Suck one of Your Partner's fingers while manually pleasuring his penis. (do not remove any clothing)

FM336

Dab some ice cream or smear a popsicle on your nipples and entice Your Partner to lick them clean.

FM341

Using flavored lube on a dildo, demonstrate your oral skills as a visual treat for Your Partner.

FM342

Get into a 69 position with Your Partner (you on top) and nuzzle each other. Hum, purr or moan for an added thrill.

FM343

Have Your Partner lay back while you caress his body with only your breasts. Brush sensitive regions with just your nipples.

FM344

Both you and Your Partner remove one item of clothing and dance while holding each other close to one slow song.

FM345

Hold a piece of frozen fruit (strawberry, mango, pineapple) in your mouth while you kiss Your Partner.

FM346

Warm your mouth with a hot liquid (water, coffee, tea) swallow then kiss or lightly suck on one of Your Partner's exposed erogenous zones.

FM351

Put a glass or silicone dildo in the freezer to be enjoyed later.

FM352

Look through an explicit pictorial magazine or book with Your Partner.

FM353

From a book or deck of cards with sex positions, choose a sex position you will use later.

FM354

Use a digital camera and play erotic photographer with Your Partner. View them together and delete afterward (unless you really like one to print).

FM355

Caress Your Partner's bare feet with your feet.

FM356

Look each other in the eyes while you both suck and lick the other person's middle finger. Use your tongues to swirl and stroke it.

FM361

Expose and blow "raspberries" on Your Partner's butt cheeks.

FM362

Dip a finger into your vagina and then let Your Partner savor your taste.

FM363

Remove any clothing necessary for Your Partner to teasingly lick your inner thighs. Lay back and enjoy his tickling tongue.

FM364

Choose a position and a location other than on the bed to have sex later. Let your imagination run wild - be creative and adventurous.

FM365

Standing, fondle Your Partner's penis and testicles while you kiss passionately.

FM366

Stroke Your Partner's tail bone and between his butt cheeks. Use your fingers, tongue, feather, spoon, string of beads, etc.

Female Male

Level 4 - Explicit & Erotic Passion

FM411

Lightly squeeze and tug Your Partner's scrotum. Gently play with his testicles.

FM412

Lightly tug small amounts of pubic hair all around Your Partner's genital region.

FM413

Apply lube to Your Partner's penis and rub your nipples with it. Finish by squeezing his penis between your breasts.

FM414

Lubricate Your Partner's penis and slide it between your butt cheeks. Sensuously wiggle and rub it with your derriere – no penetration.

FM415

Gently pull the skin of Your Partner's penis taut with one hand. Use your fingertips of your other hand to stroke and massage the head.

FM416

Use an artist brush dipped in oil or lube to stimulate the head of Your Partner's penis. Flick the frenulum and swirl around the corona.

FM421

With broad, luscious tongue strokes, lick all around the shaft of Your Partner's penis. Put the head in your mouth and suck it briefly.

FM422

Take one or both of Your Partner's testicles in your mouth and lick them tenderly.

FM423

Pleasure the head of Your Partner's penis orally with a mint, some liquor or dab of toothpaste in your mouth. Warming flavored lube is good too.

FM424

Tickle Your Partner's testicles, inner thighs and perineum with your tongue. Flutter your tongue like a flickering flame.

FM425

Massage Your Partner's penis with lube - use creative stroking techniques. Lovingly look in his eyes and discover how he responds to your touch.

FM426

Look into Your Partner's eyes as you suck one of his fingers and manually pleasure his penis.

FM431

Express audible sounds of passion leading up to a fake orgasm. Use these same sounds of passion later when you have a real one.

FM432

Simulate a creative new sex act of your choice.

FM433

Simulate a sex act of your choice as if you and Your Partner switched gender. Use a dildo as a prop if you desire.

FM434

Use an ice cube and your lips and tongue to cool then heat Your Partner's penis and testicles. Alternate cooling one area as you warm another.

FM435

Write a sex coupon for Your Partner involving a quickie.

FM436

Find and creatively use a non-sexual item to pleasure Your Partner.

FM441

Have 30 seconds of intercourse standing, rear-entry with you facing up against a wall.

FM442

Have 30 seconds of intercourse doggie style.

FM443

Sensuously demonstrate fellatio using a sex toy or edible object. Close your eyes and pretend it's the real thing.

FM444

Pleasure Your Partner's entire penis and testicles orally. Use creative licking and sucking techniques.

FM445

Stimulate Your Partner with a vibrator. (Visual stimulation counts)

FM446

Stimulate Your Partner with a sex toy. (Visual stimulation counts)

FM451

While Your Partner watches, masturbate any way you desire. Provide him visual stimulation. Go all the way if you desire.

FM452

Kiss and lick any exposed erogenous zone you desire.

FM453

Expose, then pinch, tweak and twiddle your nipples. Use lube if desired. Then have Your Partner suck and bite them gently.

FM454

Use a piece of soft, juicy, sticky fruit. Rub it on Your Partner's penis then lick it clean.

FM455

Use a vibrator to tease Your Partner's scrotum and perineum.

FM456

Apply some lube to the head of Your Partner's penis. Straddle him and use his penis to rub your vaginal lips and clitoris – no penetration allowed.

FM461

Using lube in your palms, wrap your hands around Your Partner's penis and stimulate him by twisting them in opposite directions.

FM462

In a missionary position, have Your Partner insert just the head of his penis into your vagina. Wiggle and twist your pelvis.

FM463

Straddle Your Partner in a way that allows you to slide his penis deep inside your vagina once as slowly as you can – he is not allowed to move.

FM464

Lovingly kiss Your Partner's penis and use it to stroke your lips, cheek and neck. Wrap it with your hair.

FM465

Sit on Your Partner's lap facing him, guide his penis inside you and wrap your legs around him. Kiss each other passionately – no thrusting.

FM466

Stand behind Your Partner in front of a mirror and watch each other as you stroke and fondle his body intimately.

Female Male

Level 5 - Sizzling, Sexual Stimulation

FM511

Manually stimulate Your Partner's penis with one hand and his perineum with the other.

FM512

Have Your Partner hold a dildo while you demonstrate how you would give him a foot-job. Use lube if you desire.

FM513

Use a dildo and some lube to demonstrate how you would give Your Partner a creative hand-job.

FM514

Pleasure yourself with a glass or acrylic dildo for Your Partner's visual pleasure. Be as lewd as you dare.

FM515

Give Your Partner a foot-job. Apply lube and use your toes and the soles of your feet to stimulate his penis.

FM516

Lube and pleasure yourself with the thickest dildo you own. Provide Your Partner with a good show for his visual pleasure.

FM521

Put on a piece of clothing or accessory (leather, stockings, boots, high heels, etc.) that you know will drive Your Partner crazy with desire.

FM522

While Your Partner stands, kneel before him and orally pleasure his penis just to the brink of ejaculation – then stop.

FM523

Laying down so your head is hanging over an accessible edge (bed, table, sofa, etc.), orally pleasure Your Partner's penis.

FM524

Get into a "69" position with you on top. Pleasure each other orally.

FM525

Straddle Your Partner's face and allow him to lick your pussy. Play with his nipples or his penis as he orally pleasures you.

FM526

Lube and pleasure yourself with the largest dildo available. Insert it slowly so that Your Partner can see every detail.

FM531

Using a suction cup dildo (or one held in place by Your Partner), stimulate your self without using your hands.

FM532

One minute of penetration in a position of your choice – No thrusting. Use your PC muscles to squeeze and pulse around his penis.

FM533

If you changed into a male for an hour and could have sex with any female, who would it be and what would you do. Describe the sex in detail.

FM534

Spread Your Partner's butt cheeks wide and tickle his perineum and surrounding erogenous zones with a feather or piece of silky material.

FM535

Write a sex coupon or promise note for Your Partner involving a quickie outside.

FM536

Use an artist brush and lube to stimulate Your Partner's perineum and surrounding erogenous zones. Tickle it as you play with his testicles.

FM541

Circle Your Partner's scrotum just above his testicles with your thumb and index finger. Pull down gently until taut and lick his testicles.

FM542

Using a firm, pointed tongue, lick Your Partner's perineum and base of his scrotum using circles, swirls and zigzag strokes.

FM543

Go to a different location in your home with Your Partner and enjoy 30 seconds of intercourse in a creative position of your choice.

FM544

Secretly select a sex toy or other accessory to be used in your sex play later. Keep it hidden to build the anticipation.

FM545

Use the tip of a vibrator to tickle Your Partner's perineum and surrounding erogenous zones – no penetration.

FM546

Get into a doggie position with Your Partner. He is to remain still while you wiggle and circle your pelvis against him.

FM551

With Your Partner sitting, straddle him with your back to his chest. Use his penis to tap and stroke your clitoris while playing with his testicles.

FM552

While Your Partner stands, kneel behind him and nibble and bite his buttocks while playing with his penis and testicles.

FM553

Apply some lube between your butt cheeks. With Your Partner standing up against a wall, rub and stroke his penis between your ass.

FM554

Squeeze and stroke Your Partner's penis between your breasts. Lick the head every now and then and blow cool air on it.

FM555

With Your Partner lying on his back, straddle him (no penetration). Rub his penis with your pussy while playing with your nipples and clitoris.

FM556

Remove all clothing on your upper bodies. Apply massage oil to your chests and bellies. Slither and slide against each other to one song.

FM561

Play a favorite song and orally pleasure Your Partner to the rhythm. Make it last the entire length of the song then stop.

FM562

Take Your Partner's penis in your mouth and create different vibrating sensations by humming, purring, growling, etc.

FM563

While Your Partner sits, perform a lap dance for him to one song of your choice. Seductively rub and grind yourself on him.

FM564

Suck on the shaft of Your Partner's penis. Slide your lips up and down the sides of his erection as you lick and flick with your tongue.

FM565

Use only the soft underside of your tongue to lick the head of Your Partner's penis.

FM566

Use a digital camera with a zoom lens to take very close-up and intimate shots of Your Partner's erogenous zones. Select one to print and frame.

Female Male

Level 6 - Wild, Nasty, Kinky, Taboo

FM611

Give Your Partner a rim-job (oral-anal pleasuring). Use flavored lube if you wish.

FM612

If you changed into a gay male for an hour and could have sex with anyone, who would it be and what would you do. Describe the sex in detail.

FM613

Your choice of Nasty, Kinky or Taboo foreplay activity – surprise him with your wild side.

FM614

Write a sex coupon for Your Partner involving role reversal or gender play to be redeemed later. Describe in detail what you intend to do together.

FM615

Kiss and lick Your Partner's feet then suck on his toes.

FM616

Creatively use a double-ended dildo with Your Partner.

FM621

Write a sex coupon for Your Partner involving a taboo sex activity to be redeemed later. Describe in detail what you intend to do together.

FM622

Describe in detail how you would like to include a strap-on in a new sex position or activity. If you have one, get it on and have a bit of fun.

FM623

Describe in detail a new kinky activity that you "might" like to try (with or without Your Partner).

FM624

Drip hot wax on Your Partner's chest or buttocks.

FM625

Apply a nipple clamp (or clothes peg) to one of Your Partner's nipples. (not for too long)

FM626

With a fake pussy (penis sleeve), masturbate Your Partner just to the brink then stop.

FM631

Use your fingers and lube to pleasure Your Partner anyway you desire.

FM632

Pleasure yourself with a dildo or butt plug while Your Partner watches.

FM633

Use an implement of your choice to erotically spank Your Partner's bare bum until it radiates a sensual heat. Caress and stroke it between smacks.

FM634

Pleasure yourself with an edible dildo (cucumber, carrot, etc. - use a condom) while Your Partner watches.

FM635

Stimulate Your Partner with a butt plug or dildo. (Visual stimulation counts)

FM636

With Your Partner propped in a mostly upside-down position, orally pleasure him.

FM641

Describe in detail a raunchy sex scenario or fantasy involving you and Your Partner in a threesome.

FM642

Using a double-ended dildo or silicone beads, both you and Your Partner get on all fours for a little "cheek to cheek" action.

FM643

Pleasure Your Partner orally while also stimulating an "Alternate" erogenous zone with a lubed finger.

FM644

Use a butt plug or dildo to stimulate yourself while Your Partner orally pleasures your clitoris.

FM645

Creatively explore a pleasurable combination of a dildo and his penis at the same time. He is not allowed to thrust – but you can.

FM646

Experiment with cross-dressing – select some appropriate lingerie for Your Partner to wear.

FM651

Use a dildo or butt plug and orally pleasure Your Partner at the same time while he also stimulates your pussy with a vibrator.

FM652

Ask Your Partner to select a sex toy to play Show and Tell. Demonstrate your self-pleasuring technique, eyes closed, while describing the sensations.

FM653

Roleplaying as a strict mistress, sternly command your Love Slave to perform and service one of your desires.

FM654

Describe in detail a raunchy S/M or bondage scenario involving you and Your Partner. Write Your Partner a sex coupon involving bondage for later.

FM655

Roleplaying as a Love Slave, submissively request of then perform a sexual favor for your master.

FM656

Experience Aural Sex with Your Partner. Call a phone sex line together – or listen to an erotic CD, porn soundtrack (no watching), or tell a story.

FM661

Change or redress into a sexy roleplaying outfit – slutty vixen, cheerleader, horny executive, genie, dominatrix – let yourself go wild.

FM662

Grab Your Partner and run to an unusual location in your house to have a quickie in a position of your choice – stop just before Your Partner has an orgasm.

FM663

Describe in detail the most extreme, weird or bizarre sexual activity you can think of (not that you want to do it, of course).

FM664

Sit in a comfortable chair with headphones on (favorite music playing), wearing a blindfold, legs spread while Your Partner orally pleasures you.

FM665

Erotically and passionately nibble and bite sensitive erogenous zones on Your Partner's body. Make him ache for you in a good way.

FM666

STOP the Foreplay and START the Sex Play.

Male Male

Foreplay Activities

Male Male

Level 1 - Warm & Loving

MM111

From a book of fantasies or erotic letters, read a random one out loud to Your Partner.

MM112

Use a feather to tickle Your Partner's face, lips, ears and neck.

MM113

Kiss and nibble along Your Partner's neck and shoulder.

MM114

Standing, hug and caress Your Partner from behind.

MM115

Lovingly embrace Your Partner. Hug, caress and tenderly kiss each other.

MM116

Massage Your Partner's head with the tips of your fingers.

MM121

Find a how-to article on a sex technique or activity that you have not yet experienced and read it together.

MM122

Sit opposite and facing each other. Place a hand on each other's chest, close your eyes and synchronize breathing slowly.

MM123

Delicately lick around each of Your Partner's ears. Hot breaths in his ear will give him delightful shivers of pleasure.

MM124

Dance embraced with Your Partner to one slow song. Kiss each other lovingly when it ends.

MM125

Kiss and lick Your Partner's wrist, inner arm and elbow.

MM126

Apply cologne to a few areas of your body where you desire extra attention.

MM131

Describe in detail a unique, novel or exotic place to make love. Include activities you would like to experience.

MM132

Spider Walk your fingers delicately over parts of Your Partner's exposed body. Arouse him with a slow, light tickling and tapping motion.

MM133

Lick Your Partner's ear lobes and sensitive regions on his neck. Behind the ears and back of his neck are very sensitive. Whisper something deliciously sensual, loving or erotic.

MM134

Describe in detail a unique, romantic adventure involving both of you. Include elements of the love play you'll enjoy together.

MM135

Browse an erotic book or magazine with Your Partner (his choice). Discuss pictures or images that appeal to you.

MM136

Massage Your Partner's toes one at a time.

MM141

Tenderly kiss Your Partner with affection. Hold and caress his face with both hands.

MM142

Write a pleasure promise note or coupon for Your Partner involving a relaxing, soothing massage to be redeemed later.

MM143

Kiss and lightly lick Your Partner's hand, palm and fingers. Choose his non-dominant hand.

MM144

Place soft, delicate kisses all over Your Partner's face - cheek, lips, nose, forehead, temples, chin. End with a tender, sensuous kiss.

MM145

Experiment with different types of kisses and kissing sensations. (upside down, open mouth, closed mouth, sideways, corner, firm, soft)

MM146

Gently kiss and lick Your Partner's inner arm – wrist to elbow.

MM151

Both of you close your eyes. Delicately caress Your Partner's face. Trace your fingertips as lightly as you can as you explore every detail.

MM152

Do something to set the mood. Put on some soft music, light a candle, pour a glass of wine, burn some incense, spray some cologne, etc.

MM153

Give Your Partner a brief but relaxing massage the way you know he likes it.

MM154

Browse through a book with advanced or acrobatic sex positions with Your Partner. Choose one of them that you would like to experience together.

MM155

Find and view some erotic art together - use books or the internet. Discuss what you like about it.

MM156

Erotically tickle any exposed erogenous zone. Creatively use your fingers, a feather, a soft paintbrush or your tongue.

MM161

Find an erotic edible and feed it to Your Partner sensually. Fruit, syrup, chocolate, oysters, liquor, etc.

MM162

Standing together, softly stroke and caress Your Partner's entire body. Lightly squeeze parts of his body that you find delightful.

MM163

Make up a fantasy scenario or roleplaying adventure for you and Your Partner. Include elements of a "real" fantasy – but keep him guessing.

MM164

Massage one part of Your Partner's body (his choice). Experiment with a different type of technique.

MM165

Delicately stroke Your Partner's hands and fingers with your fingertips. Swirl and circle as you explore and tickle every nerve to attention.

MM166

Remove one item of clothing erotically then remove one item of clothing from Your Partner.

Male Male

Level 2 - Sensual Sensations

MM211

Slowly and sensually lick and suck Your Partner's thumb. Stimulate every nerve with your twirling tongue.

MM212

Have Your Partner get in any position you desire, expose his butt and allow you to administer a sensual spanking.

MM213

Use a vibrator to stimulate Your Partner's toes and soles of his feet.

MM214

Expose and lightly lick Your Partner's lower back and side. Lightly bite and nibble his buttocks.

MM215

Lick the soft, sensitive skin behind Your Partner's knees.

MM216

Whisper in Your Partner's ear how horny you are and how you want his penis deep inside you.

MM221

Find and use an item with an interesting texture to stimulate/sensitize an exposed region of Your Partner's body. (soft, cold, rough, squishy, etc.)

MM222

Write a sex coupon for Your Partner involving a night of uninterrupted intimate pleasuring to be redeemed later.

MM223

Use a soft artist or make-up brush to tickle and stimulate an exposed region of Your Partner's body.

MM224

Put an edible topping or liquor in your navel and entice Your Partner to lick it out.

MM225

Kiss, lick and suck each finger of Your Partner's non-dominant hand. Apply a flavored lube or syrup if you desire.

MM226

Whisper in Your Partner's ear how you want to pleasure him with your hot, slick tongue.

MM231

Stroke and massage Your Partner's chest. Circle his nipples lightly.

MM232

Write a sex coupon for Your Partner involving an erotic massage to be redeemed later.

MM233

Perform an erotic dance while removing an item of clothing. Play appropriate music if you desire.

MM234

Creatively use something round and smooth to stimulate Your Partner in various ways.

MM235

Use an artist brush dipped in flavored lube to stimulate Your Partner's nipples. Apply delicate flicks and twirls. Then lick them clean.

MM236

Drag your fingernails down Your Partner's back, chest and tummy, legs or arms - your choice.

MM241

Caress and lightly stroke any exposed part of Your Partner's body.

MM242

Massage and fondle any part of Your Partner's body still covered with clothing - do not touch any skin.

MM243

Kneeling while Your Partner stands, kiss and lick his belly, hips and thighs. Kneed and massage his buttocks.

MM244

Massage Your Partner's feet and each toe with an oil or lube.

MM245

Hug and passionately kiss each other.

MM246

Use a piece of fur, silk or satin to smoothly caress any / all exposed parts of Your Partner's body.

MM251

Use a vibrator to delicately stimulate Your Partner's nipples.

MM252

Lick, suck and lightly bite Your Partner's nipples. Blow on or suck in air around them to create warm and cool sensations.

MM253

Apply a flavored lube to Your Partner's nipples. Tweak and tantalize them with your fingertips, then lick each nipple clean.

MM254

Creatively use an ice cube to perk up sensitive regions on Your Partner's body. Follow each cold shock with a warm kiss or lick.

MM255

Put on a tight top that shows off your chest. Entice Your Partner to caress your chest and circle your nipples through the fabric.

MM256

Rub and massage Your Partner's crotch (through his clothing if he's still wearing any).

MM261

Sensually lick exposed regions of Your Partner's body. Search out rarely explored erogenous zones.

MM262

Put on any item to look, feel, smell or taste even more sexy for yourself and Your Partner.

MM263

Use a flavored lube or syrup on any rarely licked erogenous zone and entice Your Partner to lick it off.

MM264

Creatively stimulate Your Partner any way you desire.

MM265

Pleasure yourself as visual stimulation for Your Partner.

MM266

Fondle, Rub and Massage Your Partner's buttocks.

Male Male

Level 3 - Intimate Intentions

MM311

Seductively read a short erotic passage or a dirty letter. Choose one that is very explicit and detailed.

MM312

Select something sexy for Your Partner to wear (now and while making love later).

MM313

Get Your Partner into a position to receive oral sex and simulate how you would perform it. Moan and hum for effect.

MM314

Have Your Partner lay on his stomach, apply massage oil to his back and provide him a creative, erotic massage.

MM315

Have Your Partner pulse his PC muscles as tightly and quickly as possible for a minute while you cup his crotch in one hand.

MM316

Use a vibrator to stimulate Your Partner's neck, chest and nipples.

MM321

Write a sex coupon for Your Partner involving you and a pleasuring accessory to be redeemed later. (his choice of sex toy)

MM322

Simulate a sex act of your choice with Your Partner.

MM323

Tell Your Partner a dirty, explicitly erotic story involving a few sexy elements of his choice. Be a graphic as possible.

MM324

Find and creatively use a non-sexual object to pleasure Your Partner.

MM325

Describe in detail a raunchy S/M or bondage scenario involving you and Your Partner. Write Your Partner a sex coupon involving bondage for later.

MM326

Describe in detail a design for an ultimate new sex toy or a creative new way to use one you already have.

MM331

Choose a pleasuring accessory that you will use together with Your Partner while having sex later.

MM332

Use an ice cube to cool, then your lips and tongue to heat an exposed erogenous zone on Your Partner's body.

MM333

Watch one scene of an XXX DVD with Your Partner. You choose the DVD or switch over to a free online porn site to watch a short video.

MM334

Reveal an exotic roleplaying adventure you "may" be interested in experiencing with Your Partner. Include detailed, explicit content.

MM335

Suck one of Your Partner's fingers while manually pleasuring his penis. (do not remove any clothing)

MM336

Dab some ice cream or smear a popsicle on your nipples and entice Your Partner to lick them clean.

MM341

Using flavored lube on a dildo, demonstrate your oral skills as a visual treat for Your Partner.

MM342

Get into a 69 position with Your Partner (you on top) and nuzzle each other. Hum, purr or moan for an added thrill.

MM343

In a doggie position, grab a handful of Your Partner's hair and pull his head back as you thrust vigorously against him for 10–20 seconds.

MM344

Both you and Your Partner remove one item of clothing and dance while holding each other close to one slow song.

MM345

Hold a piece of frozen fruit (strawberry, mango, pineapple) in your mouth while you kiss Your Partner.

MM346

Warm your mouth with a hot liquid (water, coffee, tea) swallow then kiss or lightly suck on one of Your Partner's exposed erogenous zones.

MM351

Standing, mutually grope and fondle each other (under or over clothing).

MM352

Look through an explicit pictorial magazine or book with Your Partner.

MM353

From a book or deck of cards with sex positions, choose a sex position you will use later.

MM354

Use a digital camera and play erotic photographer with Your Partner. View them together and delete afterward (unless you really like one to print).

MM355

Caress Your Partner's bare feet with your feet.

MM356

Look each other in the eyes while you both suck and lick the other person's middle finger. Use your tongues to swirl and stroke it.

MM361

Expose and blow "raspberries" on Your Partner's butt cheeks.

MM362

Have Your Partner put on some "old" underwear and rip them off him (pre-cut the elastic band if necessary) then ravish him orally.

MM363

Remove any clothing necessary for Your Partner to teasingly lick your inner thighs. Lay back and enjoy his tickling tongue.

MM364

Choose a position and a location other than on the bed to have sex later. Let your imagination run wild - be creative and adventurous.

MM365

Standing, fondle Your Partner's penis and testicles while you kiss passionately.

MM366

Stroke Your Partner's tail bone and between his butt cheeks. Use your fingers, tongue, feather, spoon, string of beads, etc.

Male Male

Level 4 - Explicit & Erotic Passion

MM411

Lightly squeeze and tug Your Partner's scrotum. Gently play with his testicles.

MM412

Lightly tug small amounts of pubic hair all around Your Partner's genital region.

MM413

Apply lube to Your Partner's penis and rub your nipples with it.

MM414

Lubricate Your Partner's penis and slide it between your butt cheeks. Sensuously wiggle and rub it with your derriere – no penetration.

MM415

Gently pull the skin of Your Partner's penis taut with one hand. Use your fingertips of your other hand to stroke and massage the head.

MM416

Use an artist brush dipped in oil or lube to stimulate the head of Your Partner's penis. Flick the frenulum and swirl around the corona.

MM421

With broad, luscious tongue strokes, lick all around the shaft of Your Partner's penis. Put the head in your mouth and suck it briefly.

MM422

Take one or both of Your Partner's testicles in your mouth and lick them tenderly.

MM423

Pleasure the head of Your Partner's penis orally with a mint, some liquor or dab of toothpaste in your mouth. Warming flavored lube is good too.

MM424

Tickle Your Partner's testicles, inner thighs and perineum with your tongue. Flutter your tongue like a flickering flame.

MM425

Massage Your Partner's penis with lube - use creative stroking techniques. Lovingly look in his eyes and discover how he responds to your touch.

MM426

Look into Your Partner's eyes as you suck one of his fingers and manually pleasure his penis.

MM431

Express audible sounds of passion leading up to a fake orgasm. Use these same sounds of passion later when you have a real one.

MM432

Simulate a creative new sex act of your choice.

MM433

Simulate a sex act of your choice as if you or Your Partner switched gender.

MM434

Use an ice cube and your lips and tongue to cool then heat Your Partner's penis and testicles. Alternate cooling one area as you warm another.

MM435

Write a sex coupon for Your Partner involving a quickie somewhere risque.

MM436

Find and creatively use a non-sexual item to pleasure Your Partner.

MM441

Have 30 seconds of femoral coitus (non-penetrative intercourse) standing, rear-entry with you facing up against a wall.

MM442

Have 30 seconds of femoral coitus (non-penetrative intercourse) doggie style.

MM443

Sensuously demonstrate fellatio using a sex toy or edible object. Close your eyes and pretend it's the real thing.

MM444

Pleasure Your Partner's entire penis and testicles orally. Use creative licking and sucking techniques.

MM445

Stimulate Your Partner with a vibrator. (Visual stimulation counts)

MM446

Stimulate Your Partner with a sex toy. (Visual stimulation counts)

MM451

While Your Partner watches, masturbate any way you desire. Provide him visual stimulation. Edge yourself if you wish.

MM452

Kiss and lick any exposed erogenous zone you desire.

MM453

Expose then pinch, tweak and twiddle your nipples. Use lube if desired. Then have Your Partner suck and bite them gently.

MM454

Use a piece of soft, juicy, sticky fruit. Rub it on Your Partner's penis then lick it clean.

MM455

Use a vibrator to tease Your Partner's scrotum and perineum.

MM456

Apply some lube to the head of Your Partner's penis. Straddle him and use his penis to massage your perineum – no penetration allowed.

MM461

Using lube in your palms, wrap your hands around Your Partner's penis and stimulate him by twisting them in opposite directions.

MM462

In a missionary position, have Your Partner press the head of his penis against your anus. Wiggle and twist your pelvis.

MM463

Straddle Your Partner in a way that allows you to slide his penis over your anus as slowly and sensually as you can – he is not allowed to move.

MM464

Lovingly kiss Your Partner's penis and use it to stroke your lips, cheek and neck.

MM465

Sit on Your Partner's lap facing him, guide his cock between your butt cheeks and wrap your legs around him. Kiss each other passionately – no thrusting.

MM466

Stand behind Your Partner in front of a mirror and watch each other as you stroke and fondle his body intimately.

Male Male

Level 5 - Sizzling, Sexual Stimulation

MM511

Manually stimulate Your Partner's cock with one hand and his perineum with the other.

MM512

Have Your Partner hold a dildo while you demonstrate how you would give him a foot-job. Use lube if you desire.

MM513

Use a dildo and some lube to demonstrate how you would give Your Partner a creative hand-job.

MM514

Pleasure yourself with a glass or acrylic dildo for Your Partner's visual pleasure. Be as lewd as you dare.

MM515

Give Your Partner a foot-job. Apply lube and use your toes and the soles of your feet to stimulate his penis.

MM516

Lube and pleasure yourself with the thickest dildo or buttplug you own. Provide Your Partner with a good show for his visual pleasure.

MM521

Put on a piece of clothing or accessory (leather, stockings, boots, heels, collar etc.) that you know will drive Your Partner crazy with desire.

MM522

While Your Partner stands, kneel before him and orally pleasure his penis just to the brink of ejaculation – then stop.

MM523

Laying down so your head is hanging over an accessible edge (bed, table, sofa, etc.), orally pleasure Your Partner's penis.

MM524

Get into a "69" position with you on top. Pleasure each other orally.

MM525

Straddle Your Partner's face and allow him to lick your scrotum and perineum. Play with his nipples or his penis as he orally pleasures you.

MM526

Lube and pleasure yourself with the largest dildo available. Insert it slowly so that Your Partner can see every detail.

MM531

Using a suction cup dildo (or one held in place by Your Partner), stimulate your self without using your hands.

MM532

One minute of penetration in a position of your choice – No thrusting. Use your PC muscles to squeeze and pulse around Your Partner's penis.

MM533

If you changed into a female for an hour and could have sex with any other guy, who would it be and what would you do. Describe the sex in detail.

MM534

Spread Your Partner's butt cheeks wide and tickle his perineum and surrounding erogenous zones with a feather or piece of silky material.

MM535

Using lube and one or two fingers, massage Your Partner's perineum. Then penetrate his anus with smooth, gliding strokes.

MM536

Use an artist brush and lube to stimulate Your Partner's perineum and surrounding erogenous zones. Tickle it as you play with his testicles.

MM541

Circle Your Partner's scrotum just above his testicles with your thumb and index finger. Pull down gently until taut and lick his testicles.

MM542

Using a firm, pointed tongue, lick Your Partner's perineum and base of his scrotum using circles, swirls and zigzag strokes.

MM543

Go to a different location in your home with Your Partner and enjoy 30 seconds of femoral coitus (non-penetrative intercourse) in a creative position of your choice.

MM544

In a missionary position, lift Your Partner's legs high, pressing your penis on his. Lick and suck on his toes to make him wiggle on your cock.

MM545

Use the tip of a vibrator to tickle Your Partner's perineum and surrounding erogenous zones – no penetration.

Get into a doggie position with Your Partner. He is to remain still while you wiggle and circle your pelvis against him.

MM551

With Your Partner sitting, straddle him with your back to his chest. Use his penis to tap and stroke your cock while playing with his testicles.

MM552

While Your Partner stands, kneel behind him and nibble and bite his buttocks while playing with his penis and testicles.

MM553

Apply some lube between your butt cheeks. With Your Partner standing up against a wall, rub and stroke his penis between your ass.

MM554

Apply some lube between Your Partner's butt cheeks. With him standing up facing against a wall, rub and stroke your penis between his ass.

MM555

With Your Partner laying on his back, straddle him (no penetration). Rub his penis with your ass while playing with your nipples and cock.

MM556

Remove all clothing on your upper bodies. Apply massage oil to your chests and bellies. Slither and slide against each other to one song.

MM561

Play a favorite song and orally pleasure Your Partner to the rhythm. Make it last the entire length of the song then stop.

MM562

Take Your Partner's penis in your mouth and create different vibrating sensations by humming, purring, growling, etc.

MM563

While Your Partner sits, perform a lap dance for him to one song of your choice. Seductively rub and grind yourself on him.

MM564

Suck on the shaft of Your Partner's penis. Slide your lips up and down the sides of his erection as you lick and flick with your tongue.

MM565

Use only the soft underside of your tongue to lick the head of Your Partner's penis.

MM566

Use a digital camera with a zoom lens to take very close-up and intimate shots of Your Partner's erogenous zones. Select one to print and frame.

Male Male

Level 6 - Wild, Nasty, Kinky, Taboo

MM611

orally pleasure Your Partner's anus in a position of your choice.

MM612

Visit a sex store website with exotic fetish gear. Choose an item and discuss how you would enjoy playing with it.

MM613

Your choice of Nasty, Kinky or Taboo foreplay activity – surprise him with your wild side.

MM614

Write a sex coupon for Your Partner involving role reversal or gender play to be redeemed later. Describe in detail what you intend to do together.

MM615

Kiss and lick Your Partner's feet then suck on his toes.

MM616

Creatively use a double-ended dildo with Your Partner.

MM621

Write a sex coupon for Your Partner involving a taboo sex activity to be redeemed later. Describe in detail what you intend to do together.

MM622

Insert one lubed finger in Your Partner's anus and gently massage left, right, up, down and all around – no thrusting.

MM623

Describe in detail a new kinky, fantasy activity that you "might" like to try (with or without Your Partner).

MM624

Drip hot wax on Your Partner's chest or buttocks.

MM625

Apply a nipple clamp (or clothes peg) to one of Your Partner's nipples. (not for too long)

MM626

With a fake pussy (penis sleeve), masturbate Your Partner just to the brink then stop.

MM631

Use your fingers and lube to pleasure Your Partner anyway you desire.

MM632

Pleasure yourself with a dildo or butt plug while Your Partner watches.

MM633

Use an implement of your choice to erotically spank Your Partner's bare bum until it radiates a sensual heat. Caress and stroke it between smacks.

MM634

Use the tip of a vibrator to tickle Your Partner's perineum and anus – no penetration.

MM635

Stimulate Your Partner with a buttplug or dildo. (Visual stimulation counts)

MM636

With Your Partner propped in a mostly upside-down position, orally pleasure him.

MM641

While Your Partner pleasures you orally, anally stimulate him with a vibrator, dildo or buttplug.

MM642

Using a double-ended dildo or silicone beads, both you and Your Partner get on all fours for a little "cheek to cheek" action.

MM643

Pleasure Your Partner orally while also stimulating him anally with a lubed finger.

MM644

Use a buttplug or dildo to stimulate yourself while Your Partner orally pleasures your cock.

MM645

Creatively explore a pleasurable combination of a dildo and his penis at the same time.

MM646

Experiment with cross-dressing – select some appropriate feminine wear for Your Partner to wear.

MM651

Pleasure Your Partner orally while he also stimulates you with a vibrator, dildo or buttplug.

MM652

Ask Your Partner to select a sex toy to play Show and Tell. Demonstrate your self-pleasuring technique, eyes closed, while describing the sensations.

MM653

Roleplaying as a strict master, sternly command your Love Slave to perform and service one of your desires.

MM654

While lying down, have Your Partner straddle you facing your feet. As he grinds on your cock with his, give him a few slaps on his ass cheeks.

MM655

Roleplaying as a Love Slave, submissively request of then perform a sexual favor for your master.

MM656

Experience Aural Sex with Your Partner. Call a phone sex line together – or listen to an erotic CD, porn soundtrack (no watching), or tell a story.

MM661

Change or redress into a sexy roleplaying outfit – horny executive, slutty vixen, genie, dungeon master, officer – let yourself go wild.

MM662

Grab Your Partner and run to an unusual location in your house to have a quickie in a position of your choice – stop just before either of you have an orgasm.

MM663

Describe in detail the most extreme, weird or bizarre sexual activity you can think of (not that you want to do it, of course).

MM664

Sit in a comfortable chair with headphones on (favorite music playing), wearing a blindfold, legs spread while Your Partner orally pleasures you.

MM665

Erotically and passionately nibble and bite sensitive erogenous zones on Your Partner's body. Make him ache for you in a good way.

MM666

STOP the Foreplay and START the Sex Play.

Female Female

Foreplay Activities

Female Female

Level 1 - Warm & Loving

FF111

Give feather-light kisses along Your Partner's neck and jawline. Breathe softly next to her ear to make her shiver with delight.

FF112

Massage Your Partner's head with the tips of your fingers. Stroke her hair.

FF113

Sit opposite each other. Place a hand on each other's chest, close your eyes and synchronize breathing slowly.

FF114

Kiss and lick Your Partner's wrist, inner arm and elbow.

FF115

Spider Walk your fingers delicately over parts of Your Partner's exposed body. Arouse her with a slow, light tickling and tapping motion.

FF116

From a book of fantasies or erotic letters, read a random one out loud to Your Partner.

FF121

Describe in detail a unique, romantic adventure involving both of you. Include elements of the love play you'll enjoy together.

FF122

Standing, hug and caress Your Partner from behind.

FF123

Write a pleasure promise note or coupon for Your Partner involving a relaxing, soothing or erotic massage to be redeemed later.

FF124

Kiss and lightly lick Your Partner's hand, palm and fingers. Choose her non-dominant hand.

FF125

Find a how-to article on a sex technique or activity that you have not yet experienced and read it together.

FF126

Use a feather or piece of silky material to tickle Your Partner's face, lips, ears and neck.

FF131

Delicately stroke Your Partner's hands and fingers with your fingertips. Swirl and circle as you explore and tickle every nerve to attention.

FF132

Apply perfume lightly to a few areas of your body. Choose a special one you know she loves.

FF133

Lovingly embrace Your Partner. Hug, caress and tenderly kiss each other.

FF134

Place soft, delicate kisses all over Your Partner's face – cheek, lips, nose, forehead, temples, chin. End with a tender, sensuous kiss.

FF135

Lick Your Partner's ear lobes and sensitive regions on her neck. Behind the ears and back of her neck are very sensitive. Whisper something deliciously sensual, loving or erotic.

FF136

Describe in detail a unique, novel or exotic place to make love. Include activities you would like to experience.

FF141

Gently kiss and lick Your Partner's inner arm – wrist to elbow.

FF142

Delicately lick around each of Your Partner's ears. Hot breaths in her ear will give her delightful shivers of pleasure.

FF143

Do something to set the mood. Play soft music, light a candle, pour a glass of wine, burn some incense, apply perfume, etc.

FF144

Dance embraced with Your Partner to one slow song. Kiss her lovingly when it ends.

FF145

Massage one part of Your Partner's body (her choice). Experiment with a different type of technique.

FF146

Find and view some erotic art together - use books or the internet. Discuss what you like about it.

FF151

Erotically tickle any exposed erogenous zone. Creatively use your fingers, a feather, a soft paintbrush or your tongue.

FF152

Find an erotic edible and feed it to Your Partner sensually. Fruit, syrup, chocolate, oysters, liquor, etc.

FF153

Standing together, softly stroke and caress Your Partner's entire body. Lightly squeeze parts of her body that you find delightful.

FF154

Make up a fantasy scenario or roleplaying adventure for you and Your Partner. Include elements of a "real" fantasy – keep her guessing.

FF155

Both of you close your eyes. Delicately caress Your Partner's face. Trace your fingertips as lightly as you can. Explore every detail.

FF156

Remove one item of clothing erotically then slowly remove one item of clothing from Your Partner.

FF161

Massage Your Partner's toes one at a time.

FF162

Experiment with different types of kisses and kissing sensations. (upside down, open mouth, closed mouth, sideways, corner, firm, soft)

FF163

Tenderly kiss Your Partner with affection. Hold and caress her face with both hands.

FF164

Browse through a book with advanced or acrobatic sex positions with Your Partner. Choose one of them that you would like to experience together.

FF165

Browse an erotic book or magazine with Your Partner (her choice). Discuss pictures or images that appeal to you.

FF166

Give Your Partner a brief but relaxing massage the way you know she likes it.

Female Female

Level 2 - Sensual Sensations

FF211

Massage and fondle any part of Your Partner's body still clothed - do not touch any skin.

FF212

Massage Your Partner's feet and each toe with massage oil or lube.

FF213

Use a piece of fur, silk or satin to smoothly caress any/all exposed parts of Your Partner's body.

FF214

Lick, suck and lightly bite Your Partner's nipples. Blow on or suck in air around them to create warm and cool sensations.

FF215

Creatively use an ice cube to perk up sensitive regions on Your Partner's body. Follow each cold shock with a warm kiss or lick.

FF216

Gently suck each of Your Partner's nipples into your mouth. Add a vibrating sensation by humming or use a vibrator on your cheek.

FF221

Stroke and caress Your Partner's legs and inner thighs.

FF222

Put on any item to look, feel, smell or taste even more sexy for yourself and Your Partner.

FF223

Use a flavored lube or syrup on any rarely licked erogenous zone and entice Your Partner to lick it off.

FF224

Sensual Surprise – creatively stimulate Your Partner any way you desire.

FF225

Slowly and sensually lick and suck Your Partner's thumb. Stimulate every nerve with your twirling tongue.

FF226

Pleasure yourself as visual stimulation for Your Partner.

FF231

Fondle, rub and massage Your Partner's derriere.

FF232

Hug and passionately kiss each other.

FF233

Use a vibrator to delicately stimulate Your Partner's nipples.

FF234

Kneeling while Your Partner stands, kiss and lick her belly, hips and thighs. Kneed her buttocks gently.

FF235

Using massage oil, gently massage Your Partner's breasts. Circle but do not touch her nipples.

FF236

Apply a flavored lube to Your Partner's nipples. Tweak and tantalize them with your fingertips, then lick each nipple clean.

FF241

Kiss and lick the soft, sensitive skin behind Your Partner's knees.

FF242

Put an edible topping or liquor in Your Partner's navel and lick it out.

FF243

Whisper in Your Partner's ear how you want to pleasure her with your hot tongue.

FF244

Kiss, lick and suck each finger of Your Partner's non-dominant hand. Apply a flavored lube or syrup if you desire.

FF245

Stroke and caress Your Partner's breasts. Lightly circle her nipples.

FF246

Put on a silky top and entice Your Partner to caress your breasts and circle your nipples through the fabric. Remove your bra if necessary.

FF251

Expose and lightly lick Your Partner's lower back and side. Lightly bite and nibble her buttocks.

FF252

Creatively use a string of pearls or round beads to stimulate Your Partner in various ways.

FF253

Perform an erotic dance while removing an item of clothing. Play appropriate music if you desire.

FF254

Use an artist brush dipped in flavored lube to stimulate Your Partner's nipples. Apply delicate flicks and twirls then lick them clean.

FF255

Caress and lightly stroke any/all exposed parts of Your Partner's body.

FF256

Have Your Partner bend over your knee, expose her bum and allow you to administer a sensual spanking.

FF261

Lightly drag your fingernails down Your Partner's back, chest and tummy, legs or arms – your choice.

FF262

Whisper in Your Partner's ear how horny you are and how badly you want your fingers and tongue deep inside her.

FF263

Use a vibrator to stimulate Your Partner's toes and soles of her feet.

FF264

Have Your Partner lay back while you caress her body with only your breasts. Brush sensitive regions with just your nipples.

FF265

Use a soft artist or make-up brush to tickle and stimulate an exposed region of Your Partner's body.

FF266

Find and use an item with an interesting texture to stimulate and sensitize an exposed region of Your Partner's body. (soft, cold, rough, squishy, etc.)

Female Female

Level 3 - Intimate Intentions

FF311

Watch one scene of an XXX DVD with Your Partner. You choose the DVD or switch over to a free online porn site to watch a short video.

FF312

Suck one of Your Partner's fingers while manually pleasuring her pussy. (do not remove any clothing)

FF313

Dab some ice cream or smear a popsicle on Your Partner's nipples and lick them clean.

FF314

Put a glass or silicone dildo in the freezer to be enjoyed later.

FF315

Reveal an exotic roleplaying adventure you "may" be interested in experiencing with Your Partner. Include detailed, explicit content.

FF316

Kiss and lick Your Partner's breasts – all over except her nipples.

FF321

Look through an explicit pictorial magazine or book with Your Partner. Discuss what you consider erotic and arousing.

FF322

Look each other in the eyes while you both suck and lick the other person's middle finger. Use your tongues to swirl and stroke it.

FF323

Remove any clothing necessary for Your Partner to teasingly lick your inner thighs. Lay back and enjoy her tickling tongue.

FF324

Describe in detail how you would like to include a strap-on in a new sex position or activity.

FF325

Stroke Your Partner's tail bone and between her butt cheeks. Use your fingers, tongue, feather, spoon, string of beads, etc.

FF326

Expose the head of your pretend penis and entice Your Partner to lick just the tip of it.

FF331

Standing, firmly cup Your Partner's pussy with one hand while you kiss passionately.

FF332

Expose and blow "raspberries" on Your Partner's butt cheeks.

FF333

Both you and Your Partner remove one item of clothing and dance while holding each other close to one slow song.

FF334

Caress Your Partner's bare feet with your bare feet.

FF335

Seductively read a short erotic passage or a dirty letter. Choose one that is very explicit and detailed.

FF336

Use a digital camera and play erotic photographer with Your Partner. View them together and delete afterward (unless you really like one to print).

FF341

Simulate a heterosexual sex act of your choice with Your Partner. Thrust and grind against each other vigorously. Use a dildo as a prop if desired.

FF342

Write a sex coupon for Your Partner involving you and a pleasuring accessory to be redeemed later. (her choice of sex toy)

FF343

Find and creatively use a non-sexual object to pleasure Your Partner.

FF344

Have Your Partner pulse her PC muscles as tightly and quickly as possible for a minute while you cup her crotch in one hand.

FF345

Dip a finger into your vagina and then let Your Partner savor your taste.

FF346

Use an ice cube to cool then your lips and tongue to heat an exposed erogenous zone on Your Partner's body.

FF351

Using a flavored lube, massage a few of Your Partner's toes, then lick and suck them.

FF352

Express audible sounds of passion leading up to a fake orgasm. Use these same sounds of passion later when you have a real one.

FF353

Warm your mouth with a hot liquid (water, coffee, tea) swallow then kiss or lightly suck on one of Your Partner's exposed erogenous zones.

FF354

Use a vibrator to stimulate Your Partner's neck, chest and nipples.

FF355

Get into a 69 position with Your Partner (you on top) and nuzzle each other. Hum, purr or moan for an added thrill.

FF356

Select something sexy for Your Partner to wear (now and while making love later).

FF361

Tell Your Partner a dirty, explicitly erotic story involving a few sexy elements of her choice. Be a graphic as possible.

FF362

Choose a sex toy that you'll use together with Your Partner while having sex later.

FF363

From a book or deck of cards with sex positions, choose a sex position you'll use later.

FF364

Standing, mutually grope and fondle each other (under or over clothing).

FF365

Get Your Partner in a position to receive oral sex and simulate how you would perform it. Moan and hum with enthusiasm for added effect.

FF366

Hold a piece of frozen fruit (strawberry, mango, pineapple) in your mouth while you kiss Your Partner.

Female Female

Level 4 - Explicit & Erotic Passion

FF411

Sensuously demonstrate cunnilingus using an edible object (mango, peach, chocolate on Your Partner's fingers, etc.) – think juicy and messy.

FF412

Pleasure Your Partner's entire pussy orally. Use creative licking and sucking techniques.

FF413

Stimulate Your Partner with a sex toy. (Visual stimulation counts)

FF414

While Your Partner watches, demonstrate a technique you use to masturbate. Provide her visual stimulation to orgasm if desired.

FF415

Expose, then pinch, tweak and twiddle your nipples. Use a flavored lube if desired. Then have Your Partner suck and bite them gently.

FF416

Use a piece of soft, juicy, sticky fruit to tickle Your Partner's clitoris then lick it clean.

FF421

Use a vibrator to tease Your Partner's pussy lips. Lightly circle her clitoris without directly touching it.

FF422

Creatively stimulate Your Partner with a vibrator. (Visual stimulation counts)

FF423

Apply some lube to the head of your pretend cock. In a position of your choice, use it to stroke Your Partner's vaginal lips and clitoris – no penetration allowed.

FF424

Using a strap-on in missionary or doggie position, penetrate Your Partner's vagina once as slowly and deeply as you can.

Grind against her.

FF425

Lightly squeeze and tug Your Partner's vaginal lips. Massage them delicately with moist fingertips.

FF426

Kiss and lick any exposed erogenous zone you desire on Your Partner's body.

FF431

Using lube and two fingers, massage Your Partner's pussy. Then penetrate her vagina with smooth, gliding strokes.

FF432

Insert a dildo of Your Partner's choice into her pussy while licking her clitoris. Move the dildo in slow, smooth strokes.

FF433

Lightly tug small amounts of pubic hair all around Your Partner's pussy. If she is shaved, stroke her mound softly.

FF434

Sit and have Your Partner straddle your leg. Encourage her to grind her pussy hard as you lick, suck and nibble on her breasts.

FF435

Stand behind Your Partner in front of a mirror and watch each other as you stroke and fondle her body intimately.

FF436

Wearing a strapless strap-on in a missionary position, insert just the head of your cock into Your Partner's vagina. Use your hand to wiggle it back and forth and around.

FF441

Use broad tongue strokes to lick slowly up and down Your Partner's pussy. Use the underside of your tongue on her clitoris.

FF442

Pleasure Your Partner's clitoris orally using a warming, flavored lube.

FF443

Delicately flutter your tongue up, down and around Your Partner's pussy and inner thigh like a flickering flame always moving.

FF444

Look into Your Partner's eyes as you suck one of her fingers and manually pleasure her pussy.

FF445

Apply hot breaths on Your Partner's clitoris while playing with both her nipples. Avoid touching her pussy directly.

FF446

Insert one or two fingers in Your Partner's vagina (moisten if necessary) and gently massage left, right, up, down and all around – no thrusting.

FF451

Simulate a sex act of your choice without involving Your Partner – she gets to watch as you pretend. Stimulate her desire.

FF452

Apply lube to Your Partner's nipples and your own, then rub, circle and flick them together.

FF453

Use an artist brush dipped in lube to delicately stimulate Your Partner's clitoris. Flick up, down and across - swirl in circles and zigzags.

FF454

Using a suction cup dildo, masturbate yourself hands-free while Your Partner watches and plays with herself.

FF455

Find and creatively use a non-sexual object to pleasure Your Partner.

FF456

With Your Partner in a missionary position, legs spread wide, slide your pussy over hers slowly and gently at first, then with more pressure and speed.

FF461

Apply massage oil or lube to your breasts and stimulate any of Your Partner's exposed erogenous zones.

FF462

Nibble and suck on Your Partner's vaginal lips. Twirl your tongue inside her vagina – wiggle it in as deep as you can.

FF463

Describe in explicit detail a BDSM scenario you would like to experience with Your Partner.

FF464

Use an ice cube and your lips and tongue to cool then heat Your Partner's nipples and her clitoris. Stimulate her pussy with hot and cold sensations.

FF465

Delicately massage Your Partner's clitoris and vaginal lips with a lubricant. Lovingly look into her eyes and discover how she responds to your touch.

FF466

Simulate a sex act of your choice as if you or Your Partner switched gender. Get her to use a dildo as a prop if desired.

Female Female

Level 5 - Sizzling, Sexual Stimulation

FF511

If you changed into a male and had to have sex with any other person to change back, who would it be and what would you do. Describe the sex in detail.

FF512

Sit and have Your Partner straddle you (her back to your chest). Stroke her clitoris while playing with her nipples.

FF513

Use a dildo or butt plug and orally pleasure Your Partner at the same time while she also stimulates your pussy with a vibrator or dildo.

FF514

While Your Partner stands, kneel behind her and nibble and bite her buttocks while playing with her pussy.

FF515

Remove all clothing on your upper bodies. Apply massage oil to your chests and bellies. Slither and slide against each other to one song.

FF516

Use an artist brush and lube to stimulate Your Partner's anus. Tickle it as you play with her clitoris or nipples.

FF521

With Your Partner standing, facing a wall, press hard against her, kissing her neck and fingering her pussy.

FF522

Gently suck Your Partner's clitoris in your mouth and create different vibrating sensations by humming, moaning, growling, etc.

FF523

Use the tip of a vibrator to tickle Your Partner's perineum and anus – no penetration.

FF524

With Your Partner lying on her back, straddle her face so she can orally pleasure your pussy.

FF525

Experiment with a new, creative "scissoring" position.

FF526

While Your Partner sits, perform an erotic dance for her to one song of your choice. Seductively entice her to caress and fondle your assets.

FF531

Gently suck and nibble on Your Partner's vaginal lips (labia) – one side then the other. Massage them with your lips and tongue.

FF532

With Your Partner lying on her back, legs raised and spread wide, watch closely as you ever so slowly insert a smooth dildo. Let her watch too.

FF533

Use a digital camera with a zoom lens to take very close-up and intimate shots of Your Partner's erogenous zones. Select one to print and frame.

FF534

While Your Partner uses her fingers to expose her clitoris for you, use only the soft underside of your tongue to delicately caress and stroke it.

FF535

Secretly select a sex toy or other accessory to be used in your sex play later. Keep it hidden to build the anticipation.

FF536

Play a favorite song and orally pleasure Your Partner to the rhythm – make it last the entire length of the song then stop.

FF541

Using lube, insert your two middle fingers with palm on her clitoris. Flutter your fingers up and down quickly. Trigger a G-Spot orgasm or come close.

FF542

With Your Partner using a dildo or strap-on as a fake cock, demonstrate your best blowjob technique in a position of her choice.

FF543

Have Your Partner put on some "old" underwear and rip them off her (pre-cut the elastic band if necessary) then ravish her orally.

FF544

In a doggie position with a strap-on or handheld dildo, penetrate Your Partner, grab a handful of her hair and pull her head back as you thrust vigorously for 10–20 seconds.

FF545

Laying down, have Your Partner straddle you and offer her breasts to you for oral pleasuring while you both "bump and grind" together.

FF546

Get into a 69 position with you on top. Pleasure each other orally.

FF551

Lube and pleasure Your Partner with a dildo or vibrator of her choice. Allow her to guide your hand or verbally coach you on technique.

FF552

Lube and pleasure Your Partner with the thinnest dildo or vibrator available.

FF553

Pleasure Your Partner with a dildo while you lick her clitoris and she plays with her nipples.

FF554

While lying down, have Your Partner straddle you facing your feet. Insert two or more fingers in her vagina and stroke her clitoris with your thumb. As she grinds on your fingers, give her a few slaps on her ass cheeks.

FF555

Research and Discuss the possibility of fisting.

FF556

Laying down so your head is hanging over an accessible edge (bed, table, sofa, etc.), orally pleasure Your Partner's pussy.

FF561

Warm or cool a glass or acrylic dildo and pleasure Your Partner with it.

FF562

With Your Partner standing, kneel before her and orally pleasure her pussy. Look up into her eyes as you enjoy her.

FF563

Spread Your Partner's butt cheeks wide and tickle her perineum and anus with a feather or piece of silky material.

FF564

Cup Your Partner's pubic mound with your palm just above her clitoris and press firmly. Slowly slide your hand back and forth or in circles.

FF565

Using a firm, pointed tongue, lick Your Partner's perineum using circles, swirls and zigzag strokes.

FF566

With Your Partner in a missionary position, legs spread wide, provide her an amazing rim-job.

Female Female

Level 6 - Wild, Nasty, Kinky, Taboo

FF611

Use a dildo to demonstrate how you would like Your Partner to orally pleasure you if you had a real penis.

FF612

Using a strap-on in a missionary position, lift Your Partner's legs high and penetrate her deeply. Lick and suck on her toes to make her wiggle on your "cock".

FF613

While lying down, have Your Partner straddle you facing your feet. As she grinds her pussy on your body, anally stimulate her with a lubed finger.

FF614

If you changed into a gay man for an hour and could have sex with anyone, who would it be and what would you do. Describe the sex in detail.

FF615

Describe in detail a raunchy sex scenario or fantasy involving you and Your Partner in a threesome.

FF616

Ask Your Partner to select a sex toy to play Show and Tell. Demonstrate your self-pleasuring technique, eyes closed, while describing the sensations.

FF621

Make up a roleplay scenario with you as the Mistress. Then sternly command your Love Slave to perform and service one of your desires.

FF622

Roleplaying as a Love Slave, submissively request then perform a sexual favor for your Mistress.

FF623

Insert a lubed butt plug into Your Partner's anus and stimulate her with a dildo while she orally pleasures you.

FF624

Give Your Partner a G-Spot orgasm using your fingers (palm on clitoris, three fingers inserted, quick fluttering motion, strong pressure). Try to make her squirt.

FF625

Describe in detail the most extreme, weird or bizarre sexual activity you can think of (not that you want to do it, of course).

FF626

Sit in a comfortable chair with headphones on (favorite music playing), wearing a blindfold, legs spread while Your Partner orally pleasures you.

FF631

Erotically and passionately nibble and bite sensitive erogenous zones on Your Partner's body. Make her ache for you in a good way.

FF632

Describe in detail a raunchy S/M or bondage scenario involving you and Your Partner. Write Your Partner a sex coupon involving bondage for later.

FF633

Insert a lubed butt plug into Your Partner's anus and stimulate her with a dildo while you orally pleasure her clitoris.

FF634

Using a double-ended dildo, enjoy mutual intercourse in a position of Your Partner's choice.

FF635

Pleasure Your Partner orally while also stimulating her anally with a lubed finger.

FF636

Using a double-ended anal dildo or silicone beads, both you and Your Partner get on all fours for a little "cheek to cheek" action.

FF641

Write a sex coupon for Your Partner involving anal sex to be redeemed later. Describe in detail what you intend to do together.

FF642

Kiss and lick Your Partner's feet then suck on her toes.

FF643

Creatively use a double-ended dildo with Your Partner.

FF644

Using a strap-on with lube, perform anal intercourse in a position of Your Partner's choice.

FF645

Drip hot wax on Your Partner's breasts or buttocks.

FF646

Apply a nipple clamp (or clothes peg) to one of Your Partner's nipples. (not for too long)

FF651

Allow Your Partner to masturbate you with the largest, most realistic dildo you own.

FF652

Pleasure yourself with an anal dildo or butt plug while Your Partner watches.

FF653

Use an implement of your choice to erotically spank Your Partner's bare ass until it radiates a sensual heat. Caress and stroke it between smacks.

FF654

Pleasure Your Partner with an edible dildo (cucumber, carrot, etc. of her choice - use a condom).

FF655

Stimulate Your Partner with a butt plug or anal dildo. (Visual stimulation counts)

FF656

Bend over and allow Your Partner to insert a lubricated butt plug – remove only when you are both finished playing.

FF661

With Your Partner propped in a mostly upside-down position, orally pleasure her.

FF662

Write a sex coupon for Your Partner involving a role reversal or gender play scenario to be redeemed later. Describe your intended activities in detail.

FF663

Describe in detail a new kinky activity that you "might" like to try (with or without Your Partner).

FF664

Give Your Partner a rim-job (oral-anal pleasuring). Use flavored lube if you wish.

FF665

Use one finger (and lube) to pleasure Your Partner anally. Use your thumb or a finger from the other hand to stimulate her vaginally.

FF666

STOP the Foreplay and START the Sex Play.

Female Female Female

Foreplay Activities

Female Female Female

Level 1 - Warm & Loving

FFF111

Both you and Your Assistant give feather-light kisses along Your Partner's neck and jawline. Breathe softly next to her ear to make her shiver with delight.

FFF112

Massage Your Partner's head with the tips of your fingers. Stroke her hair. She follows your lead to massage Your Assistant's head in the same way.

FFF113

Sit opposite and facing each other. Place a hand on each other's chest, close your eyes and synchronize breathing slowly.

FFF114

Kiss and lick Your Partner's wrist, inner arm and elbow. Your Assistant does the same on her other arm.

FFF115

Both you and Your Assistant spider Walk your fingers delicately over parts of Your Partner's exposed body. Arouse her with a slow, light tickling and tapping motion.

FFF116

From a book of fantasies or erotic letters, read a random one out loud to Your Partner while she kisses Your Assistant.

FFF121

Describe in detail a new erotic adventure involving the three of you. Include elements of the love play you'll enjoy together.

FFF122

Standing, hug and caress Your Partner from behind. Your Assistant kneels in front and caresses her lower region.

FFF123

Kiss and nibble along Your Partner's neck and shoulder while Your Assistant does the same to you from behind.

FFF124

Kiss and lightly lick Your Partner's hand, palm and fingers. Choose her non-dominant hand. She matches your actions on Your Assistant's hand.

FFF125

Find a how-to article on a sex technique or activity that you have not yet experienced and read it together.

FFF126

While sensually kissing Your Partner, allow Your Assistant to tickle both of you with a feather (face, lips, ears and neck).

FFF131

Both you and Your Assistant delicately stroke each of Your Partner's hands and fingers with your fingertips. Swirl and circle as you explore and tickle every nerve to attention.

FFF132

While Your Partner and Your Assistant kiss, apply perfume to a few areas of your body where you desire extra attention.

FFF133

Lovingly embrace Your Partner and Your Assistant. Hug, caress and tenderly kiss each other.

FFF134

Place soft, delicate kisses all over Your Partner's face - cheek, lips, nose, forehead, temples, chin. End with a tender,

sensuous kiss. Repeat for Your Assistant.

FFF135

Both you and Your Assistant lick Your Partner's ear lobes and sensitive regions on her neck. Behind the ears and back of her neck are very sensitive. Whisper something deliciously sensual, loving or erotic.

FFF136

Describe in detail a unique, novel or exotic place to make love. Include activities you would like to experience.

FFF141

Gently kiss and lick Your Partner's inner arm – wrist to elbow. Your Assistant does the same for her other arm.

FFF142

Delicately lick around one of Your Partner's ears. Your Assistant does the same on the other one. Hot breaths in her ear will give her delightful shivers of pleasure.

FFF143

While Your Partner and Your Assistant kiss, do something to set the mood. Play soft music, light a candle, pour a glass of wine, burn some incense, apply perfume, etc.

FFF144

Dance embraced with Your Partner and Your Assistant to one slow song. Kiss each of them lovingly when it ends.

FFF145

Stand still and allow Your Partner and Your Assistant to both caress and stroke your body.

FFF146

Find and view some erotic art together - use books or the internet. Discuss what you each like about it.

FFF151

Both you and Your Assistant erotically tickle any of Your Partner's exposed erogenous zones. Creatively use your fingers, a feather, a soft paintbrush or your tongues.

FFF152

Find an erotic edible and feed it to Your Partner and Your Assistant sensually. Fruit, syrup, chocolate, oysters, liquor, etc. Encourage them to savor the treats at the same time.

FFF153

Standing together, both you and Your Assistant softly stroke and caress Your Partner's entire body. Lightly squeeze parts of her body that you find delightful.

FFF154

Make up a fantasy scenario or roleplaying adventure for Your Partner and Your Assistant that they might perform for your erotic pleasure.

FFF155

All three of you close your eyes. Delicately caress Your Partner's and Your Assistant's faces, each with one hand. Trace your fingertips as lightly as you can as you explore every detail.

FFF156

Remove one item of clothing erotically then remove one item of clothing from both Your Partner and Your Assistant.

FFF161

Massage Your Partner's toes one at a time. Your Assistant does the same, starting with the other foot.

FFF162

Experiment with different types of kisses and kissing sensations - (upside down, open mouth, closed mouth, sideways, corner, firm, soft). Alternate between Your Partner and Your Assistant.

FFF163

Tenderly kiss Your Partner with affection. Hold and caress her face with both hands. Then kiss Your Assistant with the same affection.

FFF164

Browse through a book with advanced or acrobatic sex positions together. Choose one of them for Your Partner and Your Assistant to try out (simulate the sex play for now).

FFF165

All browse an erotic book or magazine with Your Partner (her choice). Discuss pictures or images that appeal to each of you.

FFF166

Both you and Your Assistant give Your Partner a brief but relaxing massage the way she likes it.

Female Female Female

Level 2 - Sensual Sensations

FFF211

Both you and Your Assistant massage and fondle any part of Your Partner's body still clothed - do not touch any skin.

FFF212

With Your Partner and Your Assistant positioned so their feet are barely touching, massage their feet and each toe with an oil or lube. They then stroke their feet together.

FFF213

Both you and Your Assistant each use a piece of fur, silk or satin to smoothly caress any/all exposed parts of Your Partner's body.

FFF214

Lick, suck and lightly bite Your Partner's nipples. Blow on or suck in air around them to create warm and cool sensations. Alternate with Your Assistant's nipples.

FFF215

Creatively use an ice cube to perk up sensitive regions on Your Partner's body. Your Assistant follows each cold shock with a warm kiss or lick.

FFF216

Both you and Your Assistant each gently suck one of Your Partner's nipples into your mouth at the same time. Add a vibrating sensation by humming or use a vibrator on your cheek.

FFF221

Both you and Your Partner stroke and caress Your Assistant's legs and inner thighs.

FFF222

Both you and Your Assistant sensually lick exposed regions of Your Partner's body. Search out rarely explored erogenous zones.

FFF223

Use a flavored lube or syrup on any rarely licked erogenous zone and entice both Your Partner and Your Assistant to lick it off together.

FFF224

Instruct Your Assistant to creatively stimulate Your Partner any way you desire.

FFF225

Slowly and sensually lick and suck Your Partner's thumb. Your Assistant does the same for her other thumb. Stimulate every nerve with your twirling tongues.

FFF226

Fondle, rub and massage both Your Partner's pussy and Your Assistant's pussy at the same time (through their clothing if they are still wearing any).

FFF231

While Your Partner and Your Assistant stand together and kiss, kneel next to them and fondle, rub and massage their buttocks.

FFF232

Enjoy a threeway kiss with Your Partner and Your Assistant.

FFF233

Use a vibrator to delicately stimulate Your Partner's nipples. She repeats your technique on Your Assistant's nipples.

FFF234

Kneeling while Your Partner stands, kiss and lick her belly, hips and thighs. Kneed her buttocks gently. Your Assistant stands behind her and fondles her breasts.

FFF235

Using massage oil, both you and Your Assistant gently each massage one of Your Partner's breasts. Circle but do not touch her nipples.

FFF236

Apply a flavored lube to Your Partner's nipples. Tweak and tantalize them with your fingertips, then let Your Assistant lick each nipple clean.

FFF241

Both you and Your Assistant each lick the soft, sensitive skin behind Your Partner's knees at the same time.

FFF242

Put an edible topping or liquor in your navel and entice Your Partner and Your Assistant to lick it out together.

FFF243

Whisper in Your Partner's ear how you want to pleasure her with your hot tongue. Do the same for Your Assistant.

FFF244

Kiss, lick and suck each finger of Your Partner's non-dominant hand. Apply a flavored lube or syrup if you desire. She matches your actions on Your Assistant's hand.

FFF245

Both you and Your Assistant stroke and caress Your Partner's breasts. Lightly circle her nipples.

FFF246

Put on a silky top and entice both Your Partner and Your Assistant to caress your breasts and circle your nipples through the fabric. Remove your bra if necessary.

FFF251

Both you and Your Assistant expose and lightly lick Your Partner's lower back and side. Lightly bite and nibble her buttocks.

FFF252

Creatively use a string of pearls or round beads to stimulate Your Partner in various ways. Repeat for Your Assistant.

FFF253

Both you and Your Assistant perform an erotic dance together while removing an item of clothing each. Play appropriate music if desired.

FFF254

Use an artist brush dipped in flavored lube to stimulate Your Partner's nipples. Apply delicate flicks and twirls. Your Assistant gets to lick them clean.

FFF255

Both you and Your Assistant caress and lightly stroke any/all exposed parts of Your Partner's body.

FFF256

Have Your Partner get in any position you desire, expose her butt and allow both you and Your Assistant to give her a sensual spanking.

FFF261

Lightly drag your fingernails down Your Partner's back, chest and tummy, legs or arms – your choice. Do the same for Your Assistant.

FFF262

Both you and Your Assistant whisper in Your Partner's ear how horny you are and how badly you want your fingers and tongue deep inside her.

FFF263

With Your Partner and Your Assistant positioned so their feet are barely touching, use a vibrator to stimulate their toes and soles of their feet.

FFF264

Have Your Partner lay back while you caress her body with only your breasts. Brush sensitive regions with just your nipples. Repeat for Your Assistant.

FFF265

While Your Partner and Your Assistant kiss, use a soft artist or make-up brush to tickle and stimulate exposed erogenous zones on their bodies.

FFF266

Find and use an item with an interesting texture to stimulate/sensitize an exposed region of Your Partner's body. (soft, cold, rough, squishy, etc.) Then pleasure Your Assistant in a similar way.

Female Female Female

Level 3 - Intimate Intentions

FFF311

Watch one scene of an explicit video with Your Partner and Your Assistant. You choose the DVD or switch over to a free online porn site.

FFF312

Suck one of Your Partner's fingers while manually pleasuring her pussy (do not remove any clothing). Your Assistant does the same for you.

FFF313

Dab some ice cream or smear a popsicle on your nipples and entice Your Partner and Your Assistant to lick them clean.

FFF314

Both you and Your Assistant massage a different symmetrical part of Your Partner's body (legs, arms, breasts, shoulders, etc.). Experiment with a different type of technique.

FFF315

Have Your Partner lay on her stomach. Both you and Your Assistant apply massage oil to her back and provide her a creative, erotic massage while kissing each other.

FFF316

Both you and Your Assistant each kiss and lick one of Your Partner's breasts at the same time – all over except her nipples.

FFF321

Look through an explicit pictorial magazine or book together. Discuss what you each consider erotic and arousing.

FFF322

Close your eyes while each of you sucks and licks the other person's middle finger. Use your tongues to swirl and stroke them.

FFF323

Remove any clothing necessary for Your Partner and Your Assistant to teasingly lick your inner thighs. Lay back and enjoy their tickling tongues.

FFF324

Describe in detail how you would like to include one or more strap-ons in a new sex position or activity involving Your Partner and Your Assistant.

FFF325

Stroke both Your Partner's and Your Assistant's tail bone and between their butt cheeks. Use your fingers, tongue, feather, spoon, string of beads, etc. - alternate as required to stimulate both of them equally.

FFF326

Using a realistic dildo, get in a position for Your Partner and Your Assistant to lick and suck your fake cock at the same time.

FFF331

Standing, fondle both Your Partner's and Your Assistant's pussy while you alternate kissing them passionately.

FFF332

Both you and Your Assistant expose and blow "raspberries" on Your Partner's butt cheeks.

FFF333

Remove one item of clothing from Your Partner and Your Assistant. Choose a slow song for them to dance to while holding each other close.

FFF334

Both you and Your Assistant each caress one of Your Partner's bare feet with your bare feet.

FFF335

While Your Partner and Your Assistant kiss, seductively read a short erotic passage or a dirty letter. Choose one that is very explicit and detailed.

FFF336

Use a digital camera and play erotic photographer with Your Partner and Your Assistant as your models. View them together and delete afterward (unless you really like one to print).

FFF341

Have Your Partner and Your Assistant simulate a sex act of your choice. Encourage them to thrust and grind against each other as vigorously as you want. Have them use a dildo or two as a prop if desired.

FFF342

Describe in detail a pleasuring accessory you have in mind for Your Partner and Your Assistant and how you would like it used in your sex play.

FFF343

Find and creatively use a non-sexual object to pleasure both Your Partner and Your Assistant (not necessarily at the same time).

FFF344

With one hand cupping Your Partner's pussy and the other cupping Your Assistant's pussy (palm pressing on clitoris), gently insert one finger. Once comfortable, have them both pulse their PC muscles as tightly and quickly as possible for one minute.

FFF345

Dip a finger into your vagina and then let Your Partner savor your taste. Both you and Your Partner do the same for Your Assistant.

FFF346

Use an ice cube to cool, then your lips and tongue to heat an exposed erogenous zone on Your Partner's body. Your Assistant does the same.

FFF351

Using a flavored lube, massage each of Your Partner's toes on one foot, then lick and suck them clean. Your Assistant does the same for the other foot at the same time.

FFF352

In turn, starting with Your Assistant, express audible sounds of passion leading up to a fake orgasm. Each rate the most convincing.

FFF353

Both you and Your Assistant warm your mouth with a hot liquid (water, coffee, tea) swallow then kiss or lightly suck on one of Your Partner's exposed erogenous zones.

FFF354

Use a vibrator to stimulate Your Partner's neck, chest and nipples while Your Assistant nuzzles her pussy.

FFF355

Get into a threeway 69 position with Your Partner and Your Assistant and nuzzle each other. Hum, purr or moan for an added thrill.

FFF356

Pretend you're a porn director/star. Get Your Partner and Your Assistant into a novel, creative position to perform/simulate a sex act. Detail how you want the scene to play out. Provide props if desired.

FFF361

Tell a dirty, explicitly erotic story involving two sexy elements provided by Your Partner and Your Assistant. Be as graphic as possible.

FFF362

Sit, legs spread, so Your Partner and Your Assistant can both grind their pussy on one of your thighs at the same time while facing you. Fondle both their breasts and alternate kissing each of them passionately.

FFF363

While Your Partner and Your Assistant stand together kissing and grinding their pussy on each other's thigh, kneel next to them and fondle, rub and massage their buttocks.

FFF364

Standing, mutually grope and fondle each other (under or over clothing).

FFF365

Remove any clothing necessary for Your Partner and Your Assistant to teasingly lick your belly. Lay back and enjoy their tickling tongues.

FFF366

Both you and Your Partner hold a piece of frozen fruit (strawberry, mango, pineapple) in your mouth while you alternate kissing Your Assistant.

Female Female Female

Level 4 - Explicit & Erotic Passion

FFF411

Sensuously demonstrate cunnilingus using an edible object (mango, peach, chocolate on Your Partner's fingers, etc.) – think juicy and messy. At the same time, Your Assistant sensuously demonstrates fellatio using a sex toy or edible object.

FFF412

Pleasure Your Partner's entire pussy orally. Your Assistant orally pleasures her nipple. Both use creative licking and sucking techniques.

FFF413

Stimulate Your Partner with a sex toy that Your Assistant chooses. (Visual stimulation counts)

FFF414

Have Your Partner hold a large dildo while you and Your Assistant demonstrate how you would perform a foot-job together. Use lube if desired.

FFF415

Expose, then pinch, tweak and twiddle your nipples. Use a flavored lube if desired. Then have Your Partner and Your Assistant each suck and bite them as hard as you like.

FFF416

Use a piece of soft, juicy, sticky fruit to tickle Your Partner's clitoris then have Your Assistant lick it clean. Repeat as often as you want.

FFF421

Get in a threeway position that enables you each to use a vibrator to tease one another's pussy lips and vaginal entrance. Lightly circle the clitoris without directly touching it.

FFF422

Creatively stimulate Your Partner and Your Assistant, each with a different vibrator at the same time.

FFF423

Apply some lube to the head of your pretend cock. In a position of your choice, use it to stroke Your Partner's vaginal lips and clitoris – no penetration allowed. Repeat for Your Assistant.

FFF424

Using a strap-on in missionary or doggie position, penetrate Your Partner's vagina once as slowly and deeply as you can. Grind against her. Repeat for Your Assistant.

FFF425

Lightly squeeze and tug Your Partner's vaginal lips. Massage them delicately with moist fingertips. At the same time,

Your Assistant uses lubed fingers to stimulate her nipples.

FFF426

Both you and Your Assistant kiss and lick any exposed erogenous zone you desire on Your Partner's body.

FFF431

Using lube and two fingers, massage Your Partner's pussy. Then penetrate her vagina with smooth, gliding strokes. Use your other hand to mirror your actions for Your Assistant's pleasure.

FFF432

Insert a dildo of Your Partner's choice into her vagina while Your Assistant licks her clitoris. Move the dildo in slow, smooth strokes.

FFF433

While Your Assistant tickles her tummy with her tongue, lightly tug small amounts of pubic hair all around Your Partner's pussy. If she is shaved, stroke her mound softly.

FFF434

Sit, legs spread, so Your Partner and Your Assistant can both rub their pussy on one of your thighs at the same time while facing you. Encourage them to grind hard as you lick, suck and nibble on their breasts.

FFF435

Both you and Your Assistant stand beside Your Partner in front of a mirror and watch each other as you stroke and fondle her body intimately.

FFF436

Wearing a strapless strap-on in a missionary position, insert just the head of your cock into Your Partner's vagina. Allow Your Assistant to use her hand to wiggle it back and forth and around.

FFF441

Use broad tongue strokes to lick slowly up and down Your Partner's pussy. Use the underside of your tongue on her clitoris. Repeat for Your Assistant.

FFF442

Pleasure Your Partner orally while Your Assistant kisses her passionately and plays with her tits.

FFF443

With Your Partner laying on her back, legs spread wide, both you and Your Assistant delicately flutter your tongues up, down and around her pussy and inner thigh like a flickering flame always moving.

FFF444

Your Partner and Your Assistant both kneel doggie style and look into each other's eyes while sucking one finger of the other woman. Kneel behind them and manually pleasure their pussies.

FFF445

Apply hot (slow) and cool (faster) breaths on Your Partner's clitoris. Moisten with your tongue and suck in air for more cooling sensations. Your Assistant does the same on both her nipples.

FFF446

Insert one or two fingers in Your Partner's vagina (moisten if necessary) and gently massage left, right, up, down and all around – no thrusting. Your Assistant does the same for you.

FFF451

Wearing a strap-on in a missionary position (you on top push up style), insert just the head of your cock into Your Partner's vagina. Allow Your Assistant to sensually spank your ass. Resist plunging deeper as long as you can.

FFF452

Apply lube to Your Partner's nipples and your own, then rub, circle and flick them together. Your Assistant repeats with her, then you.

FFF453

Use an artist brush dipped in lube to delicately stimulate Your Partner's clitoris. Flick up, down and across - swirl in circles and zigzags. Your Assistant uses another brush to stimulate her nipples in a similar way at the same time.

FFF454

Using a suction cup dildo, masturbate yourself hands-free while Your Partner watches and plays with herself. Orally pleasure Your Assistant at the same time.

FFF455

Find and creatively use a non-sexual object to pleasure both Your Partner and Your Assistant (not necessarily at the same time).

FFF456

With Your Partner in a missionary position, legs spread wide, slide your pussy over hers slowly and gently at first, then with more pressure and speed. Your Assistant strokes you both from behind.

FFF461

Both you and Your Assistant apply massage oil or lube to your breasts and use them to stimulate any of Your Partner's exposed erogenous zones.

FFF462

Nibble and suck on Your Partner's vaginal lips. Twirl your tongue inside her vagina – wiggle it in as deep as you can. Repeat for Your Assistant.

FFF463

Describe in detail a raunchy S/M or bondage scenario involving Your Partner and Your Assistant.

FFF464

Use an ice cube to cool followed by Your Assistant's lips and tongue to heat Your Partner's nipples and clitoris. Stimulate various erogenous zones with hot and cold sensations.

FFF465

Delicately massage Your Partner's clitoris and vaginal lips with a flavored lube. Your Assistant follows with sensual licking and sucking.

FFF466

Using a realistic dildo or strap-on, both you and Your Assistant lovingly kiss Your Partner's penis together and use it to stroke your lips, cheek and neck.

Female Female Female

Level 5 - Sizzling, Sexual Stimulation

FFF511

Insert one lubed finger in Your Partner's anus and gently massage left, right, up, down and all around – no thrusting. Your Assistant does the same for you.

FFF512

Sit and have Your Partner straddle you (her back to your chest). Play with her nipples while Your Assistant orally pleasures both of you.

FFF513

Use a dildo or buttplug and orally pleasure Your Partner at the same time while she also stimulates Your Assistant's pussy with a vibrator or dildo.

FFF514

While Your Partner orally pleasures Your Assistant, nibble and bite her buttocks while playing with her pussy.

FFF515

All three remove all clothing on your upper bodies. Apply massage oil to your chests and bellies. Slither and slide against each other to one song.

FFF516

Use an artist brush and lube to stimulate Your Partner's anus. Tickle it as Your Assistant plays with her clitoris or nipples.

FFF521

With Your Partner standing, facing a wall, press hard against her, kissing her neck and fingering her pussy. Your Assistant joins from the rear stimulating you in a similar way.

FFF522

Gently suck Your Partner's clitoris in your mouth and create different vibrating sensations by humming, moaning, growling, etc. Your Partner follows your lead pleasuring Your Assistant in the same way.

FFF523

Use the tip of a vibrator to tickle Your Partner's perineum and anus – no penetration. At the same time, Your Assistant offers her pussy or nipples for Your Partner to lick and suck.

FFF524

With Your Partner lying on her back, straddle her face so she can orally pleasure your pussy. Your Assistant uses a vibrator, dildo or buttplug to pleasure her at the same time.

FFF525

Experiment with a new, creative "scissoring" position with Your Partner that allows Your Assistant to stimulate both of you with a vibrator.

FFF526

While Your Partner sits, both you and Your Assistant perform an erotic lap dance for her to one song of your choice. Seductively rub and grind yourselves on her. Seductively entice her to caress and fondle your assets.

FFF531

Gently suck and nibble on Your Partner's vaginal lips (labia) – one side then the other. Massage them with your lips and tongue. Your Assistant offers her nipples for Your Partner to lick and suck.

FFF532

With Your Partner lying on her back, legs raised and spread wide, watch closely as you ever so slowly insert a dildo. Your Assistant holds a mirror so she can see how her pussy engulfs the fake cock.

FFF533

Use a digital camera with a zoom lens to take very close-up and intimate shots of Your Partner and Your Assistant in various explicit poses. Select one to print and frame.

FFF534

While Your Partner uses her fingers to expose her clitoris for you, use only the soft underside of your tongue to delicately caress and stroke it. Repeat for Your Assistant.

FFF535

While Your Partner stands, kneel behind her. Nibble and bite her buttocks while stroking her thighs. Your Assistant kneels in front and orally pleasures her.

FFF536

Select two sex toys for Your Partner and Your Assistant to play Show and Tell. In turn, they are to demonstrate their self-pleasuring technique, eyes closed, while describing the sensations.

FFF541

Using lube, insert your two middle fingers in Your Partner's vagina with palm on her clitoris. Flutter your fingers up and down quickly. Trigger a G-Spot orgasm or come close. Using your other hand, do the same for Your Assistant.

FFF542

With Your Partner using a realistic dildo or strap-on as a fake cock, both you and Your Assistant demonstrate your best blowjob technique in a position of her choice.

FFF543

Have Your Partner put on some "old" underwear. Let Your Assistant rip them off her (pre-cut the elastic band if necessary) so you can ravish her orally.

FFF544

In a doggie position with a strap-on or handheld dildo, penetrate Your Partner, grab a handful of her hair and pull her head back as you thrust vigorously for 10–20 seconds. Repeat for Your Assistant.

FFF545

Sitting, legs spread, hold a dildo on each thigh. Your Partner and Your Assistant both mount one of the toys and grind against you while kissing each other. At the same time, both fondle your tits and/or pussy.

FFF546

Get into a threeway 69 position and pleasure each other orally.

FFF551

Lube and pleasure Your Partner with a dildo or vibrator of her choice. Allow her to guide your hand or verbally coach you on technique. Repeat for Your Assistant.

FFF552

Pleasure Your Partner with the thinnest dildo or smallest vibrator available. At the same time, Your Assistant uses a similar toy to pleasure you.

FFF553

Pleasure Your Partner with a dildo while you lick her clitoris and Your Assistant plays with her nipples.

FFF554

While lying down, have Your Partner straddle you facing your feet. Insert two or more fingers in her vagina and stroke her clitoris with your thumb. As she grinds on your fingers, Your Assistant gives her a few slaps on her ass cheeks.

FFF555

Research and Discuss the possibility of fisting. Plan how/when you might do it and identify each of your roles in the activity.

FFF556

Laying down so your head is hanging over an accessible edge (bed, table, sofa, etc.), orally pleasure Your Partner's pussy. At the same time, Your Assistant manually pleasures your vagina with fluttering fingers (G-Spot stimulation).

FFF561

While Your Partner and Your Assistant stroke each other's clitoris, pleasure yourself with a glass or acrylic dildo for their visual pleasure. Be as lewd as you dare.

FFF562

With Your Partner standing, kneel before her and orally pleasure her pussy. Your Assistant joins doggie style using her hands to caress you any way she desires.

FFF563

Spread Your Partner's butt cheeks wide and tickle her perineum and anus with a feather or piece of silky material. Your

Assistant stimulates you in a similar way.

FFF564

Use your fingers and lube to pleasure Your Partner anyway you desire. Stimulate Your Assistant using your other hand in the same way at the same time.

FFF565

Using a firm, pointed tongue, lick Your Partner's perineum using circles, swirls and zigzag strokes. Your Assistant sucks on her nipples at the same time.

FFF566

Get into a threeway '69' position and give each other a rim-job.

Female Female Female

Level 6 - Wild, Nasty, Kinky, Taboo

FFF611

Using your fingers or any other sex toys of your choice, stimulate Your Partner anally and Your Assistant vaginally at the same time.

FFF612

Using a strap-on in a missionary position, lift Your Partner's legs high and penetrate her deeply. Both you and Your Assistant lick and suck her toes to make her wiggle on your "cock".

FFF613

While lying down, have Your Partner straddle you facing your feet. As she grinds her pussy on your body, anally stimulate her with a lubed finger. Your Assistant sensually spanks her for added sensation.

FFF614

Orally pleasure Your Partner's anus in a position of your choice. Your Assistant orally pleasures her clitoris at the same time.

FFF615

While Your Partner lies between Your Assistant's legs missionary style, both kissing passionately, use a strap-on for vigorous rear-entry intercourse with her. Pull her hair while Your Assistant holds her tight.

FFF616

Describe in detail a BDSM activity for Your Partner and Your Assistant to perform for your erotic amusement.

FFF621

Roleplaying as a strict Mistress, sternly command your Love Slaves to perform and service one of your desires.

FFF622

Laying down so your head is hanging over an accessible edge (bed, table, sofa, etc.), orally pleasure Your Partner's pussy. At the same time, Your Assistant uses a strap-on for missionary intercourse.

FFF623

Insert a lubed buttplug into Your Partner's anus and stimulate her with a dildo while she orally pleasures you. Your Assistant sensually spanks any available ass cheeks.

FFF624

Attempt to give both Your Partner and Your Assistant a simultaneous G-Spot orgasm using your fingers (palm on clitoris, three fingers inserted, quick fluttering motion, strong pressure). Try to make both of them squirt.

FFF625

Using two suction cup dildos stuck to the floor, both you and Your Partner squat on them while kissing and thrusting in unison. Your Assistant uses a vibrator to motivate both of you.

FFF626

Using two strapless strap-ons or double dildos or one of each, enjoy threeway doggie-style anal intercourse.

FFF631

Both you and Your Assistant erotically and passionately nibble and bite sensitive erogenous zones on Your Partner's body. Make her ache for you in a good way.

FFF632

Describe in detail an extreme BDSM scenario/fantasy involving all three of you. Set the stage and let Your Partner and Your Assistant add to the story in turn.

FFF633

Insert a lubed buttplug into Your Partner's anus and stimulate her with a dildo while you orally pleasure her clitoris. Your Assistant sucks on her tits at the same time.

FFF634

Using a double-ended dildo, enjoy mutual intercourse in a position of Your Partner's choice. Your Assistant uses a strap-on and chooses one of you to perform fellatio or receive anal intercourse at the same time.

FFF635

Pleasure Your Partner orally while also stimulating her anally with a lubed finger. Your Assistant offers her tits for licking and sucking.

FFF636

Using a double-ended anal dildo or silicone beads, both you and Your Partner get on all fours for a little "cheek to cheek" action. At the same time, Your Assistant uses a vibrator to stimulate either or both of you.

FFF641

Your choice of Nasty, Kinky or Taboo foreplay activity for Your Partner and Your Assistant to perform for you – surprise them with your wild side.

FFF642

Have Your Partner lay on her back, legs raised. Use a dildo to pleasure her vaginally while Your Assistant squats over her mouth for oral pleasuring. At the same time, both kiss, lick and suck on Your Partner's toes.

FFF643

Creatively use a double-ended dildo with Your Partner. Allow Your Assistant to hold and manipulate it as desired.

FFF644

Using a strap-on with lube, perform anal intercourse in a position of Your Partner's choice. At the same time, Your Assistant uses a vibrator to stimulate either or both of you.

FFF645

Drip hot wax on both Your Partner and Your Assistant (breasts, thighs or buttocks) while they lay next to each other.

FFF646

While Your Partner and Your Assistant kiss, apply nipple clamps (or clothes pegs) to their nipples. Remove when one of them breaks their kiss.

FFF651

Allow Your Partner to masturbate you with the largest, most realistic dildo you own in a position of her choice. Your Assistant positions herself to receive your oral pleasuring at the same time.

FFF652

Both you and Your Partner pleasure yourself with an anal dildo or butt plug while Your Assistant watches, stroking herself.

FFF653

Use an implement of your choice to erotically spank Your Partner's bare ass until it radiates a sensual heat. Let Your Assistant caress and stroke it between smacks.

FFF654

With you and Your Partner each wearing a strap-on, position Your Assistant to experience double penetration.

FFF655

Stimulate Your Partner and Your Assistant each with a different buttplug or dildo at the same time.

FFF656

Both you and Your Assistant bend over and allow Your Partner to insert lubricated buttplugs (one for each including herself) – remove only when you are both finished playing or other activities require.

FFF661

With Your Partner propped in a mostly upside-down position, orally pleasure her pussy. Your Assistant helps hold her up while giving her a rim-job.

FFF662

Using one or more strapless strap-ons or suction cup dildos, your choice of sex position involving all three of you engaging in oral and/or anal/vaginal intercourse at the same time.

FFF663

Describe in detail an extreme BDSM scenario/fantasy involving all three of you. Set the stage and let Your Partner and Your Assistant add to the story in turn.

FFF664

Orally pleasure Your Partner's anus in a missionary position, legs spread wide. While holding her legs for balance, Your Assistant squats over her face so she can lick and suck pussy at the same time.

FFF665

Use one finger (and lube) to pleasure Your Partner anally. Use your thumb or fingers from the other hand to stimulate her vaginally. Your Assistant does the same for you.

FFF666

STOP the Foreplay and START the Sex Play.

Female Female Male

Foreplay Activities

Female Female Male

Level 1 - Warm & Loving

FFM111

Both you and Your Assistant give feather-light kisses along Your Partner's neck and jawline. Breathe softly next to her ear to make her shiver with delight.

FFM112

Massage Your Partner's head with the tips of your fingers. Stroke her hair. She follows your lead to massage Your Assistant's head in the same way.

FFM113

Sit opposite and facing each other. Place a hand on each other's chest, close your eyes and synchronize breathing slowly.

FFM114

Kiss and lick Your Partner's wrist, inner arm and elbow. Your Assistant does the same on her other arm.

FFM115

Both you and Your Assistant spider Walk your fingers delicately over parts of Your Partner's exposed body. Arouse her with a slow, light tickling and tapping motion.

FFM116

From a book of fantasies or erotic letters, read a random one out loud to Your Partner while she kisses Your Assistant.

FFM121

Describe in detail a new erotic adventure involving the three of you. Include elements of the love play you'll enjoy together.

FFM122

Standing, hug and caress Your Partner from behind. Your Assistant kneels in front and caresses her lower region.

FFM123

Kiss and nibble along Your Partner's neck and shoulder while Your Assistant does the same to you from behind.

FFM124

Kiss and lightly lick Your Partner's hand, palm and fingers. Choose her non-dominant hand. She matches your actions on Your Assistant's hand.

FFM125

Find a how-to article on a sex technique or activity that you have not yet experienced and read it together.

FFM126

While sensually kissing Your Partner, allow Your Assistant to tickle both of you with a feather (face, lips, ears and neck).

FFM131

Both you and Your Assistant delicately stroke each of Your Partner's hands and fingers with your fingertips. Swirl and circle as you explore and tickle every nerve to attention.

FFM132

While Your Partner and Your Assistant kiss, apply perfume to a few areas of your body where you desire extra attention.

FFM133

Lovingly embrace Your Partner and Your Assistant. Hug, caress and tenderly kiss each other.

FFM134

Place soft, delicate kisses all over Your Partner's face - cheek, lips, nose, forehead, temples, chin. End with a tender,

sensuous kiss. Repeat for Your Assistant.

FFM135

Both you and Your Assistant lick Your Partner's ear lobes and sensitive regions on her neck. Behind the ears and back of her neck are very sensitive. Whisper something deliciously sensual, loving or erotic.

FFM136

Describe in detail a unique, novel or exotic place to make love. Include activities you would like to experience.

FFM141

Gently kiss and lick Your Partner's inner arm – wrist to elbow. Your Assistant does the same for her other arm.

FFM142

Delicately lick around one of Your Partner's ears. Your Assistant does the same on the other one. Hot breaths in her ear will give her delightful shivers of pleasure.

FFM143

While Your Partner and Your Assistant kiss, do something to set the mood. Play soft music, light a candle, pour a glass of wine, burn some incense, apply perfume, etc.

FFM144

Dance embraced with Your Partner and Your Assistant to one slow song. Kiss each of them lovingly when it ends.

FFM145

Stand still and allow Your Partner and Your Assistant to both caress and stroke your body.

FFM146

Find and view some erotic art together - use books or the internet. Discuss what you each like about it.

FFM151

Both you and Your Assistant erotically tickle any of Your Partner's exposed erogenous zones. Creatively use your fingers, a feather, a soft paintbrush or your tongues.

FFM152

Find an erotic edible and feed it to Your Partner and Your Assistant sensually. Fruit, syrup, chocolate, oysters, liquor, etc. Encourage them to savor the treats at the same time.

FFM153

Standing together, both you and Your Assistant softly stroke and caress Your Partner's entire body. Lightly squeeze parts of her body that you find delightful.

FFM154

Make up a fantasy scenario or roleplaying adventure for Your Partner and Your Assistant that they might perform for your erotic pleasure.

FFM155

All three of you close your eyes. Delicately caress Your Partner's and Your Assistant's faces, each with one hand. Trace your fingertips as lightly as you can as you explore every detail.

FFM156

Remove one item of clothing erotically then remove one item of clothing from both Your Partner and Your Assistant.

FFM161

Massage Your Partner's toes one at a time. Your Assistant does the same, starting with the other foot.

FFM162

Experiment with different types of kisses and kissing sensations - (upside down, open mouth, closed mouth, sideways, corner, firm, soft). Alternate between Your Partner and Your Assistant.

FFM163

Tenderly kiss Your Partner with affection. Hold and caress her face with both hands. Then kiss Your Assistant with the same affection.

FFM164

Browse through a book with advanced or acrobatic sex positions together. Choose one of them for Your Partner and Your Assistant to try out (simulate the sex play for now).

FFM165

All browse an erotic book or magazine with Your Partner (her choice). Discuss pictures or images that appeal to each of you.

FFM166

Both you and Your Assistant give Your Partner a brief but relaxing massage the way she likes it.

Female Female Male

Level 2 - Sensual Sensations

FFM211

Both you and Your Assistant massage and fondle any part of Your Partner's body still clothed - do not touch any skin.

FFM212

With Your Partner and Your Assistant positioned so their feet are barely touching, massage their feet and each toe with an oil or lube. They then stroke their feet together.

FFM213

Both you and Your Assistant each use a piece of fur, silk or satin to smoothly caress any/all exposed parts of Your Partner's body.

FFM214

Lick, suck and lightly bite Your Partner's nipples. Blow on or suck in air around them to create warm and cool sensations. Alternate with Your Assistant's nipples.

FFM215

Creatively use an ice cube to perk up sensitive regions on Your Partner's body. Your Assistant follows each cold shock with a warm kiss or lick.

FFM216

Both you and Your Assistant each gently suck one of Your Partner's nipples into your mouth at the same time. Add a vibrating sensation by humming or use a vibrator on your cheek.

FFM221

Both you and Your Partner stroke and caress Your Assistant's legs and inner thighs.

FFM222

Both you and Your Assistant sensually lick exposed regions of Your Partner's body. Search out rarely explored erogenous zones.

FFM223

Apply a flavored lube or syrup on any rarely licked erogenous zone and entice both Your Partner and Your Assistant to lick it off together.

FFM224

Instruct Your Assistant to creatively stimulate Your Partner any way you desire.

FFM225

Slowly and sensually lick and suck Your Partner's thumb. Your Assistant does the same for her other thumb. Stimulate every nerve with your twirling tongues.

FFM226

Fondle, rub and massage both Your Partner's pussy and Your Assistant's penis at the same time (through their clothing if they are still wearing any).

FFM231

While Your Partner and Your Assistant stand together and kiss, kneel next to them and fondle, rub and massage their buttocks.

FFM232

Enjoy a threeway kiss with Your Partner and Your Assistant.

FFM233

Use a vibrator to delicately stimulate Your Partner's nipples. She repeats your technique on Your Assistant's nipples.

FFM234

Kneeling while Your Partner stands, kiss and lick her belly, hips and thighs. Kneed her buttocks gently. Your Assistant stands behind her and fondles her breasts.

FFM235

Using massage oil, both you and Your Assistant gently each massage one of Your Partner's breasts. Circle but do not touch her nipples.

FFM236

Apply a flavored lube to Your Partner's nipples. Tweak and tantalize them with your fingertips, then let Your Assistant lick each nipple clean.

FFM241

Both you and Your Assistant each lick the soft, sensitive skin behind Your Partner's knees at the same time.

FFM242

Put an edible topping or liquor in your navel and entice Your Partner and Your Assistant to lick it out together.

FFM243

Whisper in Your Partner's ear how you want to pleasure her with your hot tongue. Do the same for Your Assistant.

FFM244

Kiss, lick and suck each finger of Your Partner's non-dominant hand. Apply a flavored lube or syrup if you desire. She matches your actions on Your Assistant's hand.

FFM245

Both you and Your Assistant stroke and caress Your Partner's breasts. Lightly circle her nipples.

FFM246

Put on a silky top and entice both Your Partner and Your Assistant to caress your breasts and circle your nipples through the fabric. Remove your bra if necessary.

FFM251

Both you and Your Assistant expose and lightly lick Your Partner's lower back and side. Lightly bite and nibble her buttocks.

FFM252

Creatively use a string of pearls or round beads to stimulate Your Partner in various ways. Repeat for Your Assistant.

FFM253

Both you and Your Assistant perform an erotic dance together while removing an item of clothing each. Play appropriate music if desired.

FFM254

Use an artist brush dipped in flavored lube to stimulate Your Partner's nipples. Apply delicate flicks and twirls. Your Assistant gets to lick them clean.

FFM255

Both you and Your Assistant caress and lightly stroke any/all exposed parts of Your Partner's body.

FFM256

Have Your Partner get in any position you desire, expose her butt and allow both you and Your Assistant to administer a sensual spanking.

FFM261

Lightly drag your fingernails down Your Partner's back, chest and tummy, legs or arms – your choice. Do the same for Your Assistant.

FFM262

Both you and Your Assistant whisper in Your Partner's ear how horny you are and how badly you want your fingers and tongue deep inside her.

FFM263

With Your Partner and Your Assistant positioned so their feet are barely touching, use a vibrator to stimulate their toes and soles of their feet.

FFM264

Have Your Partner lay back while you caress her body with only your breasts. Brush sensitive regions with just your nipples. Repeat for Your Assistant.

FFM265

While Your Partner and Your Assistant kiss, use a soft artist or make-up brush to tickle and stimulate exposed erogenous zones on their bodies.

FFM266

Find and use an item with an interesting texture to stimulate/sensitize an exposed region of Your Partner's body. (soft, cold, rough, squishy, etc.) Then pleasure Your Assistant in a similar way.

Female Female Male

Level 3 - Intimate Intentions

FFM311

Watch one scene of an explicit video with Your Partner and Your Assistant. You choose the DVD or switch over to a free online porn site.

FFM312

Suck one of Your Partner's fingers while manually pleasuring her pussy (do not remove any clothing). Your Assistant does the same for you.

FFM313

Dab some ice cream or smear a popsicle on your nipples and entice Your Partner and Your Assistant to lick them clean.

FFM314

Both you and Your Assistant massage a different symmetrical part of Your Partner's body (legs, arms, breasts, shoulders, etc.). Experiment with a different type of technique.

FFM315

Have Your Partner lay on her stomach. Both you and Your Assistant apply massage oil to her back and provide her a creative, erotic massage while kissing each other.

FFM316

Both you and Your Assistant each kiss and lick one of Your Partner's breasts at the same time – all over except her nipples.

FFM321

Look through an explicit pictorial magazine or book together. Discuss what you each consider erotic and arousing.

FFM322

Close your eyes while each of you sucks and licks the other person's middle finger. Use your tongues to swirl and stroke them.

FFM323

Remove any clothing necessary for Your Partner and Your Assistant to teasingly lick your inner thighs. Lay back and enjoy their tickling tongues.

FFM324

Describe in detail how you would like to include one or more strap-ons in a new sex position or activity involving all three of you.

FFM325

Stroke both Your Partner's and Your Assistant's tail bone and between their butt cheeks. Use your fingers, tongue, feather, spoon, string of beads, etc. - alternate as required to stimulate both of them equally.

FFM326

Using a realistic dildo, get in a position for Your Partner and Your Assistant to lick and suck your fake cock at the same time.

FFM331

Standing, fondle both Your Partner's pussy and Your Assistant's penis while you alternate kissing them passionately.

FFM332

Both you and Your Assistant expose and blow "raspberries" on Your Partner's butt cheeks.

FFM333

Remove one item of clothing from Your Partner and Your Assistant. Choose a slow song for them to dance to while holding each other close.

FFM334

Both you and Your Assistant each caress one of Your Partner's bare feet with your bare feet.

FFM335

While Your Partner and Your Assistant kiss, seductively read a short erotic passage or a dirty letter. Choose one that is very explicit and detailed.

FFM336

Use a digital camera and play erotic photographer with Your Partner and Your Assistant as your models. View them together and delete afterward (unless you really like one to print).

FFM341

You and Your Partner simulate a sex act of Your Assistant's choice - he encourages you to thrust and grind against each other as vigorously as he wants. Use a dildo or two as a prop if desired.

FFM342

Describe in detail a pleasuring accessory you have in mind for Your Partner and Your Assistant and how you would like it used in your sex play.

FFM343

Find and creatively use a non-sexual object to pleasure both Your Partner and Your Assistant (not necessarily at the same time).

FFM344

With one hand cupping Your Partner's pussy and the other cupping your pussy (palm pressing on clitoris), Your Assistant gently inserts one finger for each of you. Once comfortable, both pulse your PC muscles as tightly and quickly as you can for one minute.

FFM345

Dip a finger into your vagina and then let Your Partner savor your taste. She repeats for you, then both of you do the same for Your Assistant.

FFM346

Use an ice cube to cool, then your lips and tongue to heat an exposed erogenous zone on Your Partner's body. Your Assistant does the same.

FFM351

Using a flavored lube, massage each of Your Partner's toes on one foot, then lick and suck them clean. Your Assistant does the same for the other foot at the same time.

FFM352

In turn starting with Your Assistant, express audible sounds of passion leading up to a fake orgasm. Each rate the most convincing.

FFM353

Both you and Your Assistant warm your mouth with a hot liquid (water, coffee, tea) swallow then kiss or lightly suck on one of Your Partner's exposed erogenous zones.

FFM354

Use a vibrator to stimulate Your Partner's neck, chest and nipples while Your Assistant nuzzles her pussy.

FFM355

Get into a threeway 69 position with Your Partner and Your Assistant and nuzzle each other. Hum, purr or moan for an added thrill.

FFM356

Pretend you're a porn director/star. Get Your Partner and Your Assistant into a novel, creative position to perform/simulate a sex act. Detail how you want the scene to play out. Provide props if desired.

FFM361

Tell a dirty, explicitly erotic story involving two sexy elements provided by Your Partner and Your Assistant. Be as graphic as possible.

FFM362

Your Assistant sits, legs spread, so you and Your Partner can both grind your pussy on one of his thighs at the same time while facing him. He fondles both your breasts and alternates kissing each of you passionately.

FFM363

While Your Partner and Your Assistant stand together kissing and grinding their crotch on each other's thigh, kneel next to them and fondle, rub and massage their buttocks.

FFM364

Standing, mutually grope and fondle each other (under or over clothing).

FFM365

Remove any clothing necessary for Your Partner and Your Assistant to teasingly lick your belly. Enjoy their tickling tongues.

FFM366

Both you and Your Partner hold a piece of frozen fruit (strawberry, mango, pineapple) in your mouth while you alternate kissing Your Assistant.

Female Female Male

Level 4 - Explicit & Erotic Passion

FFM411

Your Assistant sensuously demonstrates cunnilingus using an edible object (mango, peach, chocolate on Your Partner's fingers, etc.) – think juicy and messy. At the same time, you sensuously demonstrate fellatio using a sex toy or edible object.

FFM412

Pleasure Your Partner's entire pussy orally. Your Assistant orally pleasures her nipple. Both use creative licking and sucking techniques.

FFM413

Stimulate Your Partner with a sex toy that Your Assistant chooses. (Visual stimulation counts)

FFM414

Have Your Assistant hold a large dildo while you and Your Partner demonstrate how you would perform a foot-job together. Use lube if desired.

FFM415

Expose, then pinch, tweak and twiddle your nipples. Use a flavored lube if desired. Then have Your Partner and Your Assistant each suck and bite them as hard as you like.

FFM416

Use a piece of soft, juicy, sticky fruit to tickle Your Partner's clitoris then have Your Assistant lick it clean. Repeat as often as you want.

FFM421

You and Your Partner get in a position that enables Your Assistant to use two vibrators to tease both of your pussy lips and vaginal entrances at the same time. He must lightly circle each clitoris without directly touching it.

FFM422

Creatively stimulate Your Partner and Your Assistant, each with a different vibrator at the same time.

FFM423

Apply some lube to the head of Your Assistant's cock. Have him get in a position of your choice, use it to stroke Your Partner's vaginal lips and clitoris – no penetration allowed.

FFM424

Using a strap-on in missionary or doggie position, penetrate Your Partner's vagina once as slowly and deeply as you can. Grind against her. Your Assistant follows your lead with his own equipment.

FFM425

Lightly squeeze and tug Your Partner's vaginal lips. Massage them delicately with moist fingertips. At the same time, Your Assistant uses lubed fingers to stimulate her nipples.

FFM426

Both you and Your Assistant kiss and lick any exposed erogenous zone you desire on Your Partner's body.

FFM431

Using lube and two fingers, massage Your Partner's pussy. Then penetrate her vagina with smooth, gliding strokes. Your Assistant watches up close then pleasures you in the same way.

FFM432

Insert a dildo of Your Partner's choice into her vagina while Your Assistant licks her clitoris. Move the dildo in slow, smooth strokes.

FFM433

While Your Assistant tickles her tummy with his tongue, lightly tug small amounts of pubic hair all around Your Partner's pussy. If she is shaved, stroke her mound softly.

FFM434

Your Assistant sits, legs spread, so you and Your Partner can both rub your pussy on one of his thighs at the same time while facing him. Both of you grind hard as he licks, sucks and nibbles on your breasts.

FFM435

Both you and Your Assistant stand beside Your Partner in front of a mirror and watch each other as you stroke and fondle her body intimately.

FFM436

Wearing a strapless strap-on in a missionary position, insert just the head of your cock into Your Partner's vagina. Allow Your Assistant to use his hand to wiggle it back and forth and around.

FFM441

Use broad tongue strokes to lick slowly up and down Your Partner's pussy. Use the underside of your tongue on her clitoris. Repeat in a similar way for Your Assistant's pleasure.

FFM442

Pleasure Your Partner orally while Your Assistant kisses her passionately and plays with her tits.

FFM443

With Your Partner laying on her back, legs spread wide, both you and Your Assistant delicately flutter your tongues up, down and around her pussy and inner thigh like a flickering flame always moving.

FFM444

You and Your Partner both kneel doggie style and look into each other's eyes while each sucking one finger of the other woman. Your Assistant kneels behind you and manually pleasures both of your pussies at the same time.

FFM445

Apply hot (slow) and cool (faster) breaths on Your Partner's clitoris. Moisten with your tongue and suck in air for more cooling sensations. Your Assistant does the same on both her nipples.

FFM446

Insert one or two fingers in Your Partner's vagina (moisten if necessary) and gently massage left, right, up, down and all around – no thrusting. Your Assistant does the same for you.

FFM451

Wearing a strap-on in a missionary position (you on top push up style), insert just the head of your cock into Your Partner's vagina. Allow Your Assistant to sensually spank your ass. Resist plunging deeper as long as you can.

FFM452

Apply lube to Your Partner's nipples and your own, then rub, circle and flick them together. Both of you then rub your nipples on Your Assistant to stimulate any of his exposed erogenous zones.

FFM453

Use an artist brush dipped in lube to delicately stimulate Your Partner's clitoris. Flick up, down and across - swirl in circles and zigzags. Your Assistant uses another brush to stimulate her nipples in a similar way at the same time.

FFM454

Using a suction cup dildo, masturbate yourself hands free while Your Partner watches and plays with herself. Orally pleasure Your Assistant at the same time.

FFM455

Find and creatively use a non-sexual object to pleasure both Your Partner and Your Assistant (not necessarily at the same time).

FFM456

With Your Partner in a missionary position, legs spread wide, slide your pussy over hers slowly and gently at first, then with more pressure and speed. Your Assistant strokes you both from behind.

FFM461

Both you and Your Partner apply massage oil or lube to your breasts and use them to stimulate any of Your Assistant's exposed erogenous zones.

FFM462

Nibble and suck on Your Partner's vaginal lips. Twirl your tongue inside her vagina – wiggle it in as deep as you can. Your Assistant follows and does the same for her.

FFM463

Describe in detail a raunchy S/M or bondage scenario involving Your Partner and Your Assistant.

FFM464

Use an ice cube to cool followed by Your Assistant's lips and tongue to heat Your Partner's nipples and clitoris. Stimulate various erogenous zones with hot and cold sensations.

FFM465

Delicately massage Your Partner's clitoris and vaginal lips with a flavored lube. Your Assistant follows with sensual licking and sucking.

FFM466

Both you and Your Partner lovingly kiss Your Assistant's penis together and use it to stroke your lips, cheek and neck.

Female Female Male

Level 5 - Sizzling, Sexual Stimulation

FFM511

Insert one lubed finger in Your Partner's anus and gently massage left, right, up, down and all around – no thrusting. Your Assistant does the same for you.

FFM512

Sit and have Your Partner straddle you (her back to your chest). Play with her nipples while Your Assistant orally pleasures both of you.

FFM513

Use a dildo or buttplug and orally pleasure Your Partner at the same time while she also orally pleasures Your Assistant.

FFM514

While Your Partner orally pleasures Your Assistant, nibble and bite her buttocks while playing with her pussy.

FFM515

All three remove all clothing on your upper bodies. Apply massage oil to your chests and bellies. Slither and slide against each other to one song.

FFM516

Use an artist brush and lube to stimulate Your Partner's anus. Tickle it as Your Assistant plays with her clitoris or nipples.

FFM521

With Your Partner standing, facing a wall, press hard against her, kissing her neck and fingering her pussy. Your Assistant joins from the rear stimulating you in a similar way.

FFM522

Gently suck Your Partner's clitoris in your mouth and create different vibrating sensations by humming, moaning, growling, etc. Your Partner follows your lead pleasuring Your Assistant in a similar way.

FFM523

Use the tip of a vibrator to tickle Your Partner's perineum and anus – no penetration. At the same time, Your Assistant offers his penis or nipples for Your Partner to lick and suck (her choice).

FFM524

With Your Partner laying on her back, straddle her face so she can orally pleasure your pussy. Your Assistant uses a vibrator, dildo or buttplug to pleasure her at the same time.

FFM525

Experiment with a new, creative "scissoring" position with Your Partner that allows Your Assistant to stimulate both of you with a vibrator.

FFM526

While Your Partner sits, both you and Your Assistant perform an erotic lap dance for her to one song of your choice. Seductively rub and grind yourselves on her. Seductively entice her to caress and fondle your assets.

FFM531

Gently suck and nibble on Your Partner's vaginal lips (labia) – one side then the other. Massage them with your lips and tongue. Your Assistant licks and sucks her nipples at the same time.

FFM532

With Your Partner lying on her back, legs raised and spread wide, watch closely as you ever so slowly insert a dildo. Your Assistant holds a mirror so she can see how her pussy engulfs the fake cock.

FFM533

Use a digital camera with a zoom lens to take very close-up and intimate shots of Your Partner and Your Assistant in various explicit poses. Select one to print and frame.

FFM534

While Your Partner uses her fingers to expose her clitoris for you, use only the soft underside of your tongue to delicately caress and stroke it. Your Assistant follows and pleasures her in the same way.

FFM535

While Your Partner stands, kneel behind her. Nibble and bite her buttocks while stroking her thighs. Your Assistant kneels in front and orally pleasures her.

FFM536

Select two sex toys for Your Partner and Your Assistant to play Show and Tell. In turn, they are to demonstrate their self-pleasuring technique, eyes closed, while describing the sensations.

FFM541

Using lube, insert your two middle fingers in Your Partner's vagina with palm on her clitoris. Flutter your fingers up and down quickly. Trigger a G-Spot orgasm or come close. Your Assistant then does the same for you.

FFM542

With Your Partner using a realistic dildo or strap-on as a fake cock, both you and Your Assistant demonstrate your best blowjob technique in a position of her choice.

FFM543

Have Your Partner put on some "old" underwear. Let Your Assistant rip them off her (pre-cut the elastic band if necessary) so you can ravish her orally.

FFM544

In a doggie position with a strap-on or handheld dildo, penetrate Your Partner, grab a handful of her hair and pull her head back as you thrust vigorously for 10–20 seconds. Your Assistant offers her his penis to suck at the same time.

FFM545

Your Assistant sits, legs spread, holding a dildo on each thigh. You and Your Partner both mount one of the toys and grind against him while kissing each other and fondling his body together.

FFM546

Get into a threeway 69 position and pleasure each other orally.

FFM551

Lube and pleasure Your Partner with a dildo or vibrator of her choice. Allow her to guide your hand or verbally coach you on technique. Your Assistant then does the same for you.

FFM552

Pleasure Your Partner with the thinnest dildo or smallest vibrator available. At the same time, Your Assistant uses a similar toy to pleasure you.

FFM553

Pleasure Your Partner with a dildo while you lick her clitoris and Your Assistant plays with her nipples.

FFM554

While lying down, have Your Partner straddle you facing your feet. Insert two or more fingers in her vagina and stroke her clitoris with your thumb. As she grinds on your fingers, Your Assistant gives her a few slaps on her ass cheeks.

FFM555

Research and Discuss the possibility of fisting. Plan how/when you might do it and identify each of your roles in the activity.

FFM556

Laying down so your head is hanging over an accessible edge (bed, table, sofa, etc.), orally pleasure Your Partner's pussy. At the same time, Your Assistant manually pleasures your vagina with fluttering fingers (G-Spot stimulation).

FFM561

While Your Partner and Your Assistant stroke each other, pleasure yourself with a glass or acrylic dildo for their visual pleasure. Be as lewd as you dare.

FFM562

With Your Partner standing, kneel before her and orally pleasure her pussy. Your Assistant joins doggie style using his hands to caress you any way he desires.

FFM563

Spread Your Partner's butt cheeks wide and tickle her perineum and anus with a feather or piece of silky material. Your Assistant stimulates you in a similar way.

FFM564

Use your fingers and lube to pleasure Your Partner anyway you desire. Stimulate Your Assistant using your other hand in a similar way at the same time.

FFM565

Using a firm, pointed tongue, lick Your Partner's perineum using circles, swirls and zigzag strokes. Your Assistant sucks on her nipples at the same time.

FFM566

Get into a threeway '69' position and give each other a rim-job.

Female Female Male

Level 6 - Wild, Nasty, Kinky, Taboo

FFM611

Using your fingers or any other sex toys of your choice, stimulate Your Assistant anally and Your Partner vaginally at the same time.

FFM612

Using a strap-on in a missionary position, lift Your Partner's legs high and penetrate her deeply. Both you and Your Assistant lick and suck her toes to make her wiggle on your "cock".

FFM613

While lying down, have Your Partner straddle you facing your feet. As she grinds her pussy on your body, anally stimulate her with a lubed finger. Your Assistant sensually spanks her for added sensation.

FFM614

Orally pleasure Your Partner's anus in a position of your choice. Your Assistant orally pleasures her clitoris at the same time.

FFM615

While Your Partner lies between your legs missionary style, kissing each other passionately, Your Assistant pleasures her with 30 seconds of vigorous rear-entry intercourse. He pulls her hair while you hold her tight.

FFM616

Describe in detail a BDSM activity for Your Partner and Your Assistant to perform for your erotic amusement.

FFM621

Roleplaying as a strict Mistress, sternly command your Love Slaves to perform and service one of your desires.

FFM622

Laying down so your head is hanging over an accessible edge (bed, table, sofa, etc.), orally pleasure Your Partner's pussy. At the same time, Your Assistant pleasures you with slow missionary intercourse.

FFM623

Insert a lubed buttplug into Your Partner's anus and stimulate her with a dildo while she orally pleasures you. Your Assistant sensually spanks any available ass cheeks.

FFM624

Your Assistant will attempt to give both you and Your Partner a simultaneous G-Spot orgasm using his fingers (palm on clitoris, two or three fingers inserted, quick fluttering motion, strong pressure). Try to make both women squirt.

FFM625

Using two suction cup dildos stuck to the floor, both you and Your Partner squat on them while kissing and thrusting in unison. Your Assistant uses a vibrator to motivate both of you.

FFM626

Using one or two strapless strap-ons or double dildos or one of each, enjoy threeway doggie-style anal intercourse.

FFM631

Both you and Your Assistant erotically and passionately nibble and bite sensitive erogenous zones on Your Partner's body. Make her ache for you in a good way.

FFM632

Describe in detail an extreme BDSM scenario/fantasy involving all three of you. Set the stage and let Your Partner and Your Assistant add to the story in turn.

FFM633

Insert a lubed buttplug into Your Partner's anus and stimulate her with a dildo while you orally pleasure her clitoris. Your Assistant sucks on her tits at the same time.

FFM634

Using a double-ended dildo, enjoy mutual intercourse in a position of Your Partner's choice. Your Assistant chooses one of you to perform fellatio or receive anal intercourse at the same time.

FFM635

Pleasure Your Partner orally while also stimulating her anally with a lubed finger. Your Assistant offers his cock for licking and sucking.

FFM636

Using a double-ended anal dildo or silicone beads, both you and Your Partner get on all fours for a little "cheek to cheek" action. At the same time, Your Assistant uses a vibrator to stimulate either or both of you.

FFM641

Your choice of Nasty, Kinky or Taboo foreplay activity for Your Partner and Your Assistant to perform for you – surprise them with your wild side.

FFM642

Have Your Partner lay on her back, legs raised. Your Assistant uses a dildo to pleasure her vaginally while you squat over her mouth for oral pleasuring. At the same time, both kiss, lick and suck on Your Partner's toes.

FFM643

Creatively use a double-ended dildo with Your Partner. Allow Your Assistant to hold and manipulate it as desired.

FFM644

Using a strap-on with lube, perform anal intercourse in a position of Your Partner's choice. At the same time, Your Assistant uses a vibrator to stimulate either or both of you.

FFM645

Drip hot wax on both Your Partner and Your Assistant (chest, thighs or buttocks) while they lay next to each other.

FFM646

While you and Your Partner kiss, Your Assistant applies nipple clamps (or clothes pegs) to your nipples. Remove when one of you breaks your kiss.

FFM651

Allow Your Partner to masturbate you with the largest, most realistic dildo you own in a position of her choice. Your Assistant positions himself to receive your oral pleasuring at the same time.

FFM652

Both you and Your Partner pleasure yourself with an anal dildo or butt plug while Your Assistant watches, stroking himself.

FFM653

Use an implement of your choice to erotically spank Your Partner's bare ass until it radiates a sensual heat. Let Your Assistant caress and stroke it between smacks.

FFM654

With you wearing a strap-on, Your Partner gets to experience double penetration with you and Your Assistant in a position of her choice.

FFM655

Stimulate Your Partner and Your Assistant each with a different buttplug or dildo at the same time.

FFM656

Both you and Your Assistant bend over and allow Your Partner to insert lubricated buttplugs (one for each including herself) – remove only when you are both finished playing or other activities require.

FFM661

With Your Partner propped in a mostly upside-down position, orally pleasure her pussy. Your Assistant helps hold her up while giving her a rim-job.

FFM662

Using one or more strapless strap-ons or suction cup dildos, your choice of sex position involving all three of you engaging in oral and/or anal/vaginal intercourse at the same time.

FFM663

While Your Assistant lays on his back, you or Your Partner squats on his cock while the other squats over his mouth. Both of you hold still kissing each other while he licks and thrusts.

FFM664

Your Assistant orally pleasures Your Partner in a missionary position, legs spread wide. While holding her legs for balance, you squat over her face so she can lick and suck pussy at the same time.

FFM665

Use one finger (and lube) to pleasure Your Partner anally. Use your thumb or fingers from your other hand to stimulate her vaginally. Your Assistant does the same for you.

FFM666

STOP the Foreplay and START the Sex Play.

Female Male Female

Foreplay Activities

Female Male Female

Level 1 - Warm & Loving

FMF111

From a book of fantasies or erotic letters, read a random one out loud to Your Partner while he kisses Your Assistant.

FMF112

While sensually kissing Your Partner, allow Your Assistant to tickle both of you with a feather (face, lips, ears and neck).

FMF113

Kiss and nibble along Your Partner's neck and shoulder while Your Assistant does the same to you from behind.

FMF114

Standing, hug and caress Your Partner from behind. Your Assistant kneels in front of him and strokes his lower region.

FMF115

Lovingly embrace Your Partner and Your Assistant. Hug, caress and tenderly kiss each other.

FMF116

Massage Your Partner's head with the tips of your fingers. He follows your lead to massage Your Assistant's head in the same way.

FMF121

Find a how-to article on a sex technique or activity that you have not yet experienced and read it together.

FMF122

Sit opposite and facing each other. Place a hand on each other's chest, close your eyes and synchronize breathing slowly.

FMF123

Delicately lick around one of Your Partner's ears. Your Assistant does the same on the other one. Hot breaths in his ear will give him delightful shivers of pleasure.

FMF124

Dance embraced with Your Partner and Your Assistant to one slow song. Kiss each of them lovingly when it ends.

FMF125

Kiss and lick Your Partner's wrist, inner arm and elbow. Your Assistant does the same on his other arm.

FMF126

While Your Partner and Your Assistant kiss, apply perfume to a few areas of your body where you desire extra attention.

FMF131

Describe in detail a unique, novel or exotic place to make love. Include activities you would like to experience.

FMF132

Both you and Your Assistant spider Walk your fingers delicately over parts of Your Partner's exposed body. Arouse him with a slow, light tickling and tapping motion.

FMF133

Both you and Your Assistant lick Your Partner's ear lobes and sensitive regions on his neck. Behind the ears and back of his neck are very sensitive. Whisper something deliciously sensual, loving or erotic.

FMF134

Describe in detail a new erotic adventure involving the three of you. Include elements of the love play you'll enjoy together.

FMF135

Browse an erotic book or magazine with Your Partner (his choice). Discuss pictures or images that appeal to each of you.

FMF136

Massage Your Partner's toes one at a time. Your Assistant does the same, starting with the other foot.

FMF141

Tenderly kiss Your Partner with affection. Hold and caress his face with both hands. Then kiss Your Assistant with the same affection.

FMF142

Stand still and allow Your Partner and Your Assistant to both caress and stroke your body.

FMF143

Kiss and lightly lick Your Partner's hand, palm and fingers. Choose his non-dominant hand. He matches your actions on Your Assistant's hand.

FMF144

Place soft, delicate kisses all over Your Partner's face - cheek, lips, nose, forehead, temples, chin. End with a tender, sensuous kiss. Repeat for Your Assistant.

FMF145

Experiment with different types of kisses and kissing sensations - (upside down, open mouth, closed mouth, sideways, corner, firm, soft). Alternate between Your Partner and Your Assistant.

FMF146

Gently kiss and lick Your Partner's inner arm – wrist to elbow. Your Assistant does the same for his other arm.

FMF151

All three of you close your eyes. Delicately caress Your Partner's and Your Assistant's faces, each with one hand. Trace your fingertips as lightly as you can as you explore every detail.

FMF152

While Your Partner and Your Assistant kiss, do something to set the mood. Put on some soft music, light a candle, pour a glass of wine, burn some incense, spray some perfume, etc.

FMF153

Both you and Your Assistant give Your Partner a brief but relaxing massage the way he likes it.

FMF154

Browse through a book with advanced or acrobatic sex positions together. Choose one of them for Your Partner and Your Assistant to try out (simulate the sex play for now).

FMF155

Find and view some erotic art together - use books or the internet. Discuss what you each like about it.

FMF156

Both you and Your Assistant erotically tickle any of Your Partner's exposed erogenous zones. Creatively use your fingers, a feather, a soft paintbrush or your tongues.

FMF161

Find an erotic edible and feed it to Your Partner and Your Assistant sensually. Fruit, syrup, chocolate, oysters, liquor, etc. Encourage them to savor the treats at the same time.

FMF162

Standing together, both you and Your Assistant softly stroke and caress Your Partner's entire body. Lightly squeeze parts of his body that you find delightful.

FMF163

Make up a fantasy scenario or roleplaying adventure for Your Partner and Your Assistant that they might perform for your erotic pleasure.

FMF164

Both you and Your Assistant massage a different symmetrical part of Your Partner's body (legs, arms, pecs, shoulders, etc.). Experiment with a different type of technique.

FMF165

Both you and Your Assistant delicately stroke each of Your Partner's hands and fingers with your fingertips. Swirl and circle as you explore and tickle every nerve to attention.

FMF166

Remove one item of clothing erotically then remove one item of clothing from both Your Partner and Your Assistant.

Female Male Female

Level 2 - Sensual Sensations

FMF211

Slowly and sensually lick and suck Your Partner's thumb. Your Assistant does the same for his other thumb. Stimulate every nerve with your twirling tongues.

FMF212

Have Your Partner get in any position you desire, expose his butt and allow both you and Your Assistant to administer a sensual spanking.

FMF213

With Your Partner and Your Assistant positioned so their feet are barely touching, use a vibrator to stimulate their toes and soles of their feet.

FMF214

Both you and Your Assistant expose and lightly lick Your Partner's lower back and side. Lightly bite and nibble his buttocks.

FMF215

Both you and Your Assistant each lick the soft, sensitive skin behind Your Partner's knees at the same time.

FMF216

Both you and Your Assistant whisper in Your Partner's ear how horny you are and what you want to do with his penis.

FMF221

Find and use an item with an interesting texture to stimulate/sensitize an exposed region of Your Partner's body. (soft, cold, rough, squishy, etc.) Then pleasure Your Assistant in a similar way.

FMF222

Enjoy a threeway kiss with Your Partner and Your Assistant.

FMF223

While Your Partner and Your Assistant kiss, use a soft artist or make-up brush to tickle and stimulate exposed erogenous zones on their bodies.

FMF224

Put an edible topping or liquor in your navel and entice Your Partner and Your Assistant to lick it out together.

FMF225

Kiss, lick and suck each finger of Your Partner's non-dominant hand. Apply a flavored lube or syrup if you desire. He matches your actions on Your Assistant's hand.

FMF226

Whisper in Your Partner's ear how you want to pleasure him with your hot, slick tongue. Do the same for Your Assistant.

FMF231

Both you and Your Assistant stroke and massage Your Partner's chest. Circle and flick his nipples lightly.

FMF232

Both you and Your Partner expose and lightly lick Your Assistant's lower back and side. Lightly bite and nibble her buttocks.

FMF233

Perform an erotic lap dance for both Your Partner and Your Assistant while removing an item of clothing. Play appropriate music if you desire.

FMF234

Creatively use something round and smooth to stimulate Your Partner in various ways. Repeat for Your Assistant.

FMF235

Use an artist brush dipped in flavored lube to stimulate Your Partner's nipples. Apply delicate flicks and twirls. Your Assistant gets to lick them clean.

FMF236

Drag your fingernails down Your Partner's back, chest and tummy, legs or arms - your choice. Do the same for Your Assistant.

FMF241

Both you and Your Assistant caress and lightly stroke any exposed part of Your Partner's body.

FMF242

Both you and Your Assistant massage and fondle any part of Your Partner's body still covered with clothing - do not touch any skin.

FMF243

Kneeling while Your Partner stands, kiss and lick his belly, hips and thighs. Kneed and massage his buttocks. Your Assistant stands behind him and fondles his chest.

FMF244

With Your Partner and Your Assistant positioned so their feet are barely touching, massage their feet and each toe with an oil or lube. They then stroke their feet together.

FMF245

All three hug and passionately kiss each other.

FMF246

Use a piece of fur, silk or satin to smoothly caress any/all exposed parts of Your Partner's body. Your Assistant watches and repeats your actions.

FMF251

Both you and Your Assistant use a vibrator to delicately stimulate Your Partner's nipples and each others.

FMF252

Lick, suck and lightly bite Your Partner's nipples. Blow on or suck in air around them to create warm and cool sensations. Alternate with Your Assistant's nipples.

FMF253

Apply a flavored lube to Your Partner's nipples. Tweak and tantalize them with your fingertips, then let Your Assistant lick each nipple clean.

FMF254

Creatively use an ice cube to perk up sensitive regions on Your Partner's body. Your Assistant follows each cold shock with a warm kiss or lick.

FMF255

Put on a tight, silky top that shows off your nipples (remove your bra if necessary). Entice Your Partner and Your Assistant to caress your chest and circle your nipples through the fabric.

FMF256

Rub and massage Your Partner's and Your Assistant's crotch at the same time (through their clothing if they are still wearing any).

FMF261

Both you and Your Assistant sensually lick exposed regions of Your Partner's body. Search out rarely explored erogenous zones.

FMF262

Based on the recommendation from Your Partner and Your Assistant, put on any item to look, feel, smell or taste even more sexy.

FMF263

Use a flavored lube or syrup on any rarely licked erogenous zone and entice both Your Partner and Your Assistant to lick it off together.

FMF264

Instruct Your Assistant to creatively stimulate Your Partner any way you desire.

FMF265

Pleasure yourself as visual stimulation for both Your Partner and Your Assistant.

FMF266

While Your Partner and Your Assistant stand together and kiss, kneel next to them and fondle, rub and massage their buttocks.

Female Male Female

Level 3 - Intimate Intentions

FMF311

While Your Partner and Your Assistant kiss, seductively read a short erotic passage or a dirty letter. Choose one that is very explicit and detailed.

FMF312

Both you and Your Assistant each select something sexy for Your Partner to wear (now and while making love later).

FMF313

Pretend you're a porn director/star. Get Your Partner and Your Assistant into a novel, creative position to receive or perform oral sex and detail how you want the scene to play out.

FMF314

Have Your Partner lay on his stomach. Both you and Your Assistant apply massage oil to his back and provide him a

creative, erotic massage while kissing each other.

FMF315

With one hand cupping Your Assistant's pussy and the other cupping your pussy (palm pressing on clitoris), Your Partner gently inserts one finger for each of you. Once comfortable, both pulse your PC muscles as tightly and quickly as you can for one minute.

FMF316

Use a vibrator to stimulate Your Partner's neck, chest and nipples while Your Assistant nuzzles his crotch.

FMF321

Describe in detail a pleasuring accessory you have in mind for Your Partner and Your Assistant and how you would like it used in your sex play.

FMF322

Both you and Your Assistant simulate a sex act for Your Partner (his choice of activity).

FMF323

Tell a dirty, explicitly erotic story involving two sexy elements provided by Your Partner and Your Assistant. Be as graphic as possible.

FMF324

Find and creatively use a non-sexual object to pleasure both Your Partner and Your Assistant (not necessarily at the same time).

FMF325

Describe in detail a raunchy S/M or bondage scenario involving Your Partner and Your Assistant.

FMF326

While Your Partner and Your Assistant stand together kissing and grinding their crotch together, kneel next to them and fondle, rub and massage their buttocks.

FMF331

While you and Your Assistant stand together kissing and grinding against each other, Your Partner hugs either of you and grinds his crotch on your butt.

FMF332

Use an ice cube to cool, then your lips and tongue to heat an exposed erogenous zone on Your Partner's body. Your Assistant does the same.

FMF333

Watch one scene of an explicit video with Your Partner and Your Assistant. You choose the DVD or switch over to a free online porn site.

FMF334

Get in a position that allows Your Partner to grind against your butt while Your Assistant spanks his ass.

FMF335

Suck one of Your Partner's fingers while manually pleasuring his penis (do not remove any clothing). Your Assistant pleasures you in a similar way.

FMF336

Dab some ice cream or smear a popsicle on your nipples and entice Your Partner and Your Assistant to lick them clean.

FMF341

Using flavored lube on a realistic dildo held by Your Assistant, demonstrate your oral skills as a visual treat for Your Partner.

FMF342

Get into a threeway 69 position with Your Partner and Your Assistant and nuzzle each other. Hum, purr or moan for an added thrill.

FMF343

In a threeway doggie position with Your Partner in the middle, grab a handful of his hair and pull his head back as you thrust vigorously against them for 10–20 seconds.

FMF344

Remove one item of clothing from Your Partner and Your Assistant. Choose a slow song for them to dance to while holding each other close.

FMF345

Both you and Your Partner hold a piece of frozen fruit (strawberry, mango, pineapple) in your mouth while you alternate kissing Your Assistant.

FMF346

Both you and Your Assistant warm your mouth with a hot liquid (water, coffee, tea) swallow then kiss or lightly suck on one of Your Partner's exposed erogenous zones.

FMF351

Standing, mutually grope and fondle each other (under or over clothing).

FMF352

Look through an explicit pictorial magazine or book together.

FMF353

With you and Your Assistant in a missionary position and Your Partner in a rear-entry position (no penetration - his choice of top), he thrusts and grinds to pleasure both of you.

FMF354

Use a digital camera and play erotic photographer with Your Partner and Your Assistant as your models. View them together and delete afterward (unless you really like one to print).

FMF355

Both you and Your Assistant each caress one of Your Partner's bare feet with your bare feet.

FMF356

Close your eyes while each of you sucks and licks the other person's middle finger. Use your tongues to swirl and stroke them.

FMF361

Both you and Your Assistant expose and blow "raspberries" on Your Partner's butt cheeks.

FMF362

Have Your Assistant put on some "old" underwear. Let Your Partner rip them off her (pre-cut the elastic band if necessary) so you can ravish her orally.

FMF363

Remove any clothing necessary for Your Partner and Your Assistant to teasingly lick your inner thighs. Lay back and enjoy their tickling tongues.

FMF364

Remove any clothing necessary for Your Partner and Your Assistant to teasingly lick your tummy. Lay back and enjoy their tickling tongues.

FMF365

While standing, Your Partner fondles both your pussy and Your Assistant's. He alternates kissing both of you passionately.

FMF366

Stroke both Your Partner's and Your Assistant's tail bone and between their butt cheeks. Use your fingers, tongue, feather, spoon, string of beads, etc. - alternate as required to stimulate both of them equally.

Female Male Female
Level 4 - Explicit & Erotic Passion

FMF411

Lightly squeeze and tug Your Partner's scrotum. Gently play with his testicles while Your Assistant kisses and licks the tip of his penis.

FMF412

kiss and lick the tip of Your Partner's penis as Your Assistant lightly tugs small amounts of pubic hair all around his genital region.

FMF413

Both you and Your Assistant apply lube to your nipples and allow Your Partner to stroke them with the tip of his penis.

FMF414

Your Partner lubricates his penis and your butt crack then thrusts against you in a sensual, doggie style, slip'n slide position – no penetration. He then does the same for Your Assistant.

FMF415

While Your Assistant plays with his nipples, gently pull the skin of Your Partner's penis taut with one hand. Use your fingertips of your other hand to stroke and massage the head.

FMF416

Use an artist brush dipped in flavored oil or lube to stimulate the head of Your Partner's penis. Flick the frenulum and swirl around the corona. Allow Your Assistant to lick it clean now and again.

FMF421

Using broad, luscious tongue strokes, lick all around the shaft of Your Partner's penis. Put the head in your mouth and suck it briefly. Your Assistant follows your lead alternating or at the same time.

FMF422

Both you and Your Assistant each attempt to take one of Your Partner's testicles in your mouth at the same time. Lick them tenderly.

FMF423

Both you and Your Assistant alternate pleasuring the head of Your Partner's penis orally with a mint, some liquor or dab of toothpaste in your mouth. Warming flavored lube is good too.

FMF424

Both you and Your Assistant tickle Your Partner's testicles, inner thighs and perineum with your tongues. Flutter your tongues like a flickering flame.

FMF425

While Your Partner and Your Assistant stand kissing, use his cock to stimulate her pussy - apply lube if desired.

FMF426

Apply some lube to the head of Your Partner's cock. Have him get in a position of your choice with Your Assistant, use it to stroke her vaginal lips and clitoris – no penetration allowed.

FMF431

In turn starting with Your Assistant, express audible sounds of passion leading up to a fake orgasm. Each rate the most convincing.

FMF432

Direct Your Partner and Your Assistant to simulate a creative new sex act of your choice.

FMF433

Using a strap-on in missionary or doggie position, penetrate Your Assistant's vagina once as slowly and deeply as you can. Grind against her. Your Partner follows your lead with his own equipment.

FMF434

Use an ice cube and your lips and tongue to cool then heat both Your Partner's penis and testicles and Your Assistant's pussy. Alternate cooling one as you warm another.

FMF435

Have Your Partner straddle your face so you can orally pleasure his testicles. Your Assistant orally pleasures the head of his penis.

FMF436

Find and creatively use a non-sexual item to pleasure both Your Partner and Your Assistant.

FMF441

Your Partner pleasures you with 30 seconds of intercourse in a rear-entry position with you standing, facing up against a wall. He repeats for Your Assistant's pleasure.

FMF442

Lightly squeeze and tug Your Assistant's vaginal lips. Massage them delicately with moist fingertips. At the same time, Your Partner uses lubed fingers to stimulate her nipples.

FMF443

Visually tease Your Partner by sensuously demonstrating fellatio using a sex toy or edible object. Your Assistant joins in or holds the item for you.

FMF444

Both you and Your Assistant pleasure Your Partner's entire penis and testicles orally at the same time. Use creative licking and sucking techniques.

FMF445

Stimulate Your Partner and Your Assistant with a vibrator at the same time. (Visual stimulation counts)

FMF446

Stimulate Your Partner with a sex toy that Your Assistant chooses. (Visual stimulation counts)

FMF451

While Your Partner watches, stroking himself, both you and Your Assistant masturbate any way you desire. Provide him visual stimulation. Come if you can.

FMF452

Both you and Your Partner kiss and lick any of Your Assistant's exposed erogenous zone that each of you desire.

FMF453

Expose, then pinch, tweak and twiddle your nipples. Use lube if desired. Then have Your Partner and Your Assistant both suck and bite them gently.

FMF454

Use a piece of soft, juicy, sticky fruit. Rub it on Your Partner's penis then lick it clean. Repeat with Your Assistant's clitoris.

FMF455

Use a vibrator to tease Your Partner's scrotum and perineum while Your Assistant licks the tip of his penis.

FMF456

Apply lube to the head of Your Partner's penis. Your Assistant straddles him and uses his cock to massage her perineum and anus – no penetration allowed. At the same time, you squat over his face so he can lick your pussy.

FMF461

Using lube in your palms, wrap your hands around Your Partner's penis and stimulate him by twisting them in opposite directions. Your Assistant then does the same.

FMF462

In a missionary position (push up style), you on the bottom, have Your Partner insert just the head of his cock into your vagina. He allows Your Assistant to spank his ass but must resist plunging deeper into you as long as he can.

FMF463

Apply lube to Your Assistant's nipples and your own, then rub, circle and flick them together. Both of you then rub your nipples on Your Partner to stimulate any of his exposed erogenous zones.

FMF464

Both you and Your Assistant lovingly kiss Your Partner's penis together and use it to stroke your lips, cheek and neck.

FMF465

Sit on Your Partner's lap facing him, guide his cock into your vagina and wrap your legs around him. Standing over him, Your Assistant offers her pussy for him to lick and suck.

FMF466

Both you and Your Assistant stand beside Your Partner in front of a mirror and watch each other as you stroke and fondle his body intimately.

Female Male Female

Level 5 - Sizzling, Sexual Stimulation

FMF511

Manually stimulate Your Partner's cock with one hand and his perineum with the other. Your Assistant nibbles on his nipples.

FMF512

Have Your Partner hold a large dildo while you and Your Assistant demonstrate how you would give him a foot-job together. Use lube if you desire.

FMF513

As a visual tease, use a realistic dildo and some lube to demonstrate how you and Your Assistant would give Your Partner a creative hand-job together.

FMF514

While Your Partner and Your Assistant stroke each other, pleasure yourself with a glass or acrylic dildo for their visual pleasure. Be as lewd as you dare.

FMF515

Give Your Partner a foot-job. Apply lube and use your toes and the soles of your feet to stimulate his penis. Your Assistant offers her pussy to him for oral pleasuring.

FMF516

While Your Partner and Your Assistant stroke each other, lube and pleasure yourself with the thickest dildo or buttplug you own. Provide a good show for their visual pleasure.

FMF521

Both Your Partner and Your Assistant will each select a piece of fetish wear or accessory (leather, stockings, boots, heels, collar etc.) for you to put on.

FMF522

While Your Partner stands, kneel before him and orally pleasure his penis just to the brink of ejaculation – then stop. Manually pleasure Your Assistant's pussy at the same time.

FMF523

Laying down so your head is hanging over an accessible edge (bed, table, sofa, etc.), orally pleasure Your Partner's penis while Your Assistant pleasures you any way she desires.

FMF524

Get into a threeway "69" position with Your Partner and Your Assistant. Pleasure each other orally.

FMF525

Straddle Your Partner's face and allow him to lick your pussy. Your Assistant plays with his nipples or his penis as Your Partner orally pleasures you.

FMF526

While you have Your Partner's cock in your mouth, Your Assistant lubes and slowly inserts the largest available dildo into your vagina. Both watch every detail as your pussy engulfs the toy.

FMF531

Using a suction cup dildo, stimulate your self without using your hands. At the same time, alternate pleasuring both Your Partner and Your Assistant orally.

FMF532

With either you or Your Assistant using a strapless strap-on, Your Partner enjoys one minute of penetration and being penetrated in a position of his choice – No thrusting. Use your PC muscles to squeeze and pulse only.

FMF533

Enjoy a minute of intercourse doggie style with Your Partner. He then pleasures Your Assistant in the same way, alternating with both of you if desired.

FMF534

Spread Your Partner's butt cheeks wide and tickle his perineum and surrounding erogenous zones with a feather or piece of silky material. Your Assistant does the same for you.

FMF535

Using lube and one or two fingers, massage Your Partner's perineum. Then penetrate his anus with smooth, gliding strokes. Your Assistant orally pleasures him at the same time.

FMF536

Use an artist brush and lube to stimulate Your Partner's perineum and surrounding erogenous zones. Tickle it as you play with his testicles. Your Assistant orally pleasures his cock.

FMF541

Circle Your Partner's scrotum just above his testicles with your thumb and index finger. Pull down gently until taut and lick his testicles. Your Assistant orally pleasures the head of his cock at the same time.

FMF542

Using a firm, pointed tongue, lick Your Partner's perineum and base of his scrotum using circles, swirls and zigzag strokes. Your Assistant orally pleasures the head of his cock

FMF543

While you lay on your front and orally pleasure Your Assistant, Your Partner straddles you and enjoys some intense rear-entry intercourse.

FMF544

Your Partner sits, legs spread, holding a dildo on each thigh. You and Your Assistant both mount one of the toys and grind against him while kissing and fondling each other's tits.

FMF545

Use the tip of a vibrator to tickle Your Partner's perineum and surrounding erogenous zones – no penetration. Use a second vibrator or lubed finger to stimulate Your Assistant in a similar way.

FMF546

Get into a doggie position with Your Partner. He is to remain still while you wiggle and circle your pelvis against him. Orally pleasure Your Assistant at the same time.

FMF551

With Your Partner sitting, straddle him with your back to his chest. Use his penis to tap and stroke your clitoris while Your Assistant sucks your nipples.

FMF552

While Your Partner stands, kneel behind him and nibble and bite his buttocks while stroking his testicles. Your Assistant kneels in front and orally pleasures his cock.

FMF553

Apply some lube between your butt cheeks. With Your Partner standing up against a wall, rub and stroke his penis between your ass while Your Assistant manually stimulates your pussy.

FMF554

In a doggie position with a strap-on or hand held dildo, penetrate Your Assistant, grab a handful of her hair and pull her head back as you thrust vigorously for 10–20 seconds. Your Partner offers her his penis to suck at the same time.

FMF555

With Your Partner lying on his back, squat on the tip of his penis and play with his nipples. Your Assistant guides Your Partner's cock to stroke and massage your pussy.

FMF556

Remove all clothing on your upper bodies. Apply massage oil to your chests and bellies. Slither and slide against each other to one song.

FMF561

Play a favorite song and orally pleasure Your Partner while he orally pleasures Your Assistant to the rhythm. Make it last the entire length of the song then stop.

FMF562

Take Your Partner's penis in your mouth and create different vibrating sensations by humming, purring, growling, etc. Your Partner follows your lead pleasuring Your Assistant in a similar way.

FMF563

While Your Partner sits, both you and Your Assistant perform a lap dance for him to one song of your choice. Seductively rub and grind yourselves on him.

FMF564

Both you and Your Assistant suck on the shaft of Your Partner's penis. Slide your lips up and down the sides of his erection as you lick and flick with your tongues.

FMF565

Use only the soft underside of your tongue to lick the head of Your Partner's penis. Repeat or alternate for Your

Assistant's pleasure.

FMF566

Use a digital camera with a zoom lens to take very close-up and intimate shots of Your Partner and Your Assistant in various explicit poses. Select one to print and frame.

Female Male Female

Level 6 - Wild, Nasty, Kinky, Taboo

FMF611

Orally pleasure Your Partner's anus in a position of your choice. Your Assistant orally pleasures his cock at the same time.

FMF612

Orally pleasure Your Assistant's anus in a position of your choice. Your Partner offers his cock to her to be sucked at the same time.

FMF613

Your choice of Nasty, Kinky or Taboo foreplay activity for Your Partner and Your Assistant to perform for you – surprise them with your wild side.

FMF614

While you give Your Partner a sensual prostate massage, Your Assistant orally pleasures him at the same time.

FMF615

In a position of your choice, attempt double penetration with Your Partner and Your Assistant using a strap-on. Enjoy slow, sensual, simultaneous vaginal and anal intercourse for a minute or two.

FMF616

Creatively use a double-ended dildo with Your Assistant. Allow Your Partner to hold and manipulate it as desired.

FMF621

Orally pleasure Your Assistant's anus in a missionary position, legs spread wide. Your Partner licks and sucks on her toes to make her wiggle.

FMF622

Insert one lubed finger in Your Partner's anus and gently massage left, right, up, down and all around – no thrusting. Your Assistant does the same for you.

FMF623

Insert a lubed buttplug into Your Assistant's anus and stimulate her with a dildo while she orally pleasures you. Your Partner sensually spanks any available ass cheeks.

FMF624

Using one or two strapless strap-ons or double dildos or one of each, enjoy threeway doggie-style anal intercourse.

FMF625

While you and Your Assistant kiss, Your Partner applies nipple clamps (or clothes pegs) to each of your nipples. Remove when one of you breaks your kiss.

FMF626

With a lubed fake pussy (penis sleeve), masturbate Your Partner's shaft just to the brink then stop. Leave his tip for Your Assistant to orally pleasure.

FMF631

Your Partner will attempt to give both you and Your Assistant a simultaneous G-Spot orgasm using his fingers (palm on clitoris, two or three fingers inserted, quick fluttering motion, strong pressure). Try to make both women squirt.

FMF632

Both you and Your Assistant pleasure yourselves with a dildo or buttplug while Your Partner watches stroking himself.

FMF633

Use an implement of your choice to erotically spank Your Partner's bare bum until it radiates a sensual heat. Let Your Assistant caresses and strokes his bum between smacks.

FMF634

Use the tip of a vibrator to tickle Your Partner's perineum and anus – no penetration. Your Assistant offers nipples to Your Partner to be sucked at the same time.

FMF635

Stimulate Your Partner and Your Assistant, each with a different buttplug or dildo at the same time.

FMF636

With Your Assistant propped in a mostly upside-down position, orally pleasure her. Your Assistant helps hold her up while giving her a rim-job.

FMF641

While Your Partner and Your Assistant take turns pleasuring you orally, stimulate them in any way you desire.

FMF642

Using a double-ended dildo or silicone beads, both you and Your Assistant get on all fours for a little "cheek to cheek" action. Your Partner offers his cock to be sucked by both of you taking turns.

FMF643

Pleasure Your Partner orally while also stimulating him anally with a lubed finger. Your Assistant nibbles, sucks and bites on Your Partner's nipples.

FMF644

Your Partner lays on his back, you straddle his cock and Your Assistant squats over his mouth so her pussy can be licked. While you ride Your Partner, suck on Your Assistant's nipples at the same time.

FMF645

Using two suction cup dildos stuck to the floor, both you and Your Assistant squat on them while kissing and thrusting in unison. Your Partner uses a vibrator to motivate both of you.

FMF646

Experiment with cross-dressing – both you and Your Assistant select some appropriate feminine wear for Your Partner to wear.

FMF651

Get into a position so both you and Your Assistant can pleasure Your Partner orally together while he stimulates both of you anally using lubed fingers.

FMF652

Select two sex toys for Your Partner and Your Assistant to play Show and Tell. In turn, they are to demonstrate their self-pleasuring technique, eyes closed, while describing the sensations.

FMF653

Roleplaying as a strict Mistress, sternly command your Love Slaves to perform and service one of your desires.

FMF654

While lying down, have Your Partner straddle you facing your feet. As he grinds on your pussy with his cock, Your Assistant slaps on his ass cheeks.

FMF655

Get into a threeway '69' position and give each other a rim-job.

FMF656

Your choice of sex position involving all three of you engaging in oral and/or anal/vaginal intercourse at the same time using any combination of toys you desire.

FMF661

Describe in detail an extreme BDSM scenario/fantasy involving all three of you. Set the stage and let Your Partner and Your Assistant add to the story in turn.

FMF662

Use one finger (and lube) to pleasure Your Assistant anally. Use your thumb or fingers from your other hand to stimulate her vaginally. Your Partner does the same for you.

FMF663

Your Partner orally pleasures Your Assistant in a missionary position, legs spread wide. While holding her legs for balance, you squat over her face so she can lick and suck pussy at the same time.

FMF664

Ride Your Partner in a reverse cowgirl position while Your Assistant squats over his face so he can lick and suck pussy at the same time.

FMF665

Both you and Your Assistant erotically and passionately nibble and bite sensitive erogenous zones on Your Partner's body. Make him ache for you in a good way.

FMF666

STOP the Foreplay and START the Sex Play.

Female Male Male

Foreplay Activities

Female Male Male

Level 1 - Warm & Loving

FMM111

From a book of fantasies or erotic letters, read a random one out loud to Your Partner while he kisses Your Assistant.

FMM112

While sensually kissing Your Partner, allow Your Assistant to tickle both of you with a feather (face, lips, ears and neck).

FMM113

Kiss and nibble along Your Partner's neck and shoulder while Your Assistant does the same to you from behind.

FMM114

Standing, hug and caress Your Partner from behind. Your Assistant kneels in front of him and strokes his lower region.

FMM115

Lovingly embrace Your Partner and Your Assistant. Hug, caress and tenderly kiss each other.

FMM116

Massage Your Partner's head with the tips of your fingers. He follows your lead to massage Your Assistant's head in the same way.

FMM121

Find a how-to article on a sex technique or activity that you have not yet experienced and read it together.

FMM122

Sit opposite and facing each other. Place a hand on each other's chest, close your eyes and synchronize breathing slowly.

FMM123

Delicately lick around one of Your Partner's ears. Your Assistant does the same on the other one. Hot breaths in his ear will give him delightful shivers of pleasure.

FMM124

Dance embraced with Your Partner and Your Assistant to one slow song. Kiss each of them lovingly when it ends.

FMM125

Kiss and lick Your Partner's wrist, inner arm and elbow. Your Assistant does the same on his other arm.

FMM126

While Your Partner and Your Assistant kiss, apply perfume to a few areas of your body where you desire extra attention.

FMM131

Describe in detail a unique, novel or exotic place to make love. Include activities you would like to experience.

FMM132

Both you and Your Assistant spider Walk your fingers delicately over parts of Your Partner's exposed body. Arouse him with a slow, light tickling and tapping motion.

FMM133

Both you and Your Assistant lick Your Partner's ear lobes and sensitive regions on his neck. Behind the ears and back of his neck are very sensitive. Whisper something deliciously sensual, loving or erotic.

FMM134

Describe in detail a new erotic adventure involving the three of you. Include elements of the love play you'll enjoy together.

FMM135

Browse an erotic book or magazine with Your Partner (his choice). Discuss pictures or images that appeal to each of you.

FMM136

Massage Your Partner's toes one at a time. Your Assistant does the same starting with the other foot.

FMM141

Tenderly kiss Your Partner with affection. Hold and caress his face with both hands. Then kiss Your Assistant with the same affection.

FMM142

Stand still and allow Your Partner and Your Assistant to both caress and stroke your body.

FMM143

Kiss and lightly lick Your Partner's hand, palm and fingers. Choose his non-dominant hand. He matches your actions on Your Assistant's hand.

FMM144

Place soft, delicate kisses all over Your Partner's face - cheek, lips, nose, forehead, temples, chin. End with a tender, sensuous kiss. Repeat for Your Assistant.

FMM145

Experiment with different types of kisses and kissing sensations - (upside down, open mouth, closed mouth, sideways, corner, firm, soft). Alternate between Your Partner and Your Assistant.

FMM146

Gently kiss and lick Your Partner's inner arm – wrist to elbow. Your Assistant does the same for his other arm.

FMM151

All three of you close your eyes. Delicately caress Your Partner's and Your Assistant's faces, each with one hand. Trace your fingertips as lightly as you can as you explore every detail.

FMM152

While Your Partner and Your Assistant kiss, do something to set the mood. Put on some soft music, light a candle, pour a glass of wine, burn some incense, spray some perfume, etc.

FMM153

Both you and Your Assistant give Your Partner a brief but relaxing massage the way he likes it.

FMM154

Browse through a book with advanced or acrobatic sex positions together. Choose one of them for Your Partner and Your Assistant to try out (simulate the sex play for now).

FMM155

Find and view some erotic art together - use books or the internet. Discuss what you each like about it.

FMM156

Both you and Your Assistant erotically tickle any of Your Partner's exposed erogenous zones. Creatively use your fingers, a feather, a soft paintbrush or your tongues.

FMM161

Find an erotic edible and feed it to Your Partner and Your Assistant sensually. Fruit, syrup, chocolate, oysters, liquor, etc. Encourage them to savor the treats at the same time.

FMM162

Standing together, both you and Your Assistant softly stroke and caress Your Partner's entire body. Lightly squeeze parts of his body that you find delightful.

FMM163

Make up a fantasy scenario or roleplaying adventure for Your Partner and Your Assistant that they might perform for your erotic pleasure.

FMM164

Both you and Your Assistant massage a different symmetrical part of Your Partner's body (legs, arms, pecs, shoulders, etc.). Experiment with a different type of technique.

FMM165

Both you and Your Assistant delicately stroke each of Your Partner's hands and fingers with your fingertips. Swirl and circle as you explore and tickle every nerve to attention.

FMM166

Remove one item of clothing erotically then remove one item of clothing from both Your Partner and Your Assistant.

Female Male Male

Level 2 - Sensual Sensations

FMM211

Slowly and sensually lick and suck Your Partner's thumb. Your Assistant does the same for his other thumb. Stimulate every nerve with your twirling tongues.

FMM212

Have Your Partner get in any position you desire, expose his butt and allow both you and Your Assistant to administer a sensual spanking.

FMM213

With Your Partner and Your Assistant positioned so their feet are barely touching, use a vibrator to stimulate their toes and soles of their feet.

FMM214

Both you and Your Assistant expose and lightly lick Your Partner's lower back and side. Lightly bite and nibble his buttocks.

FMM215

Both you and Your Assistant each lick the soft, sensitive skin behind Your Partner's knees at the same time.

FMM216

Both you and Your Assistant whisper in Your Partner's ear how horny you are and what you want to do with his penis.

FMM221

Find and use an item with an interesting texture to stimulate/sensitize an exposed region of Your Partner's body. (soft, cold, rough, squishy, etc.) Then pleasure Your Assistant in a similar way.

FMM222

Enjoy a threeway kiss with Your Partner and Your Assistant.

FMM223

While Your Partner and Your Assistant kiss, use a soft artist or make-up brush to tickle and stimulate exposed erogenous zones on their bodies.

FMM224

Put an edible topping or liquor in your navel and entice Your Partner and Your Assistant to lick it out together.

FMM225

Kiss, lick and suck each finger of Your Partner's non-dominant hand. Apply a flavored lube or syrup if you desire. He matches your actions on Your Assistant's hand.

FMM226

Whisper in Your Partner's ear how you want to pleasure him with your hot, slick tongue. Do the same for Your Assistant.

FMM231

Both you and Your Assistant stroke and massage Your Partner's chest. Circle and flick his nipples lightly.

FMM232

Both you and Your Partner expose and lightly lick Your Assistant's lower back and side. Lightly bite and nibble his buttocks.

FMM233

Perform an erotic lap dance for both Your Partner and Your Assistant while removing an item of clothing. Play appropriate music if you desire.

FMM234

Creatively use something round and smooth to stimulate Your Partner in various ways. Repeat for Your Assistant.

FMM235

Use an artist brush dipped in flavored lube to stimulate Your Partner's nipples. Apply delicate flicks and twirls. Your Assistant gets to lick them clean.

FMM236

Drag your fingernails down Your Partner's back, chest and tummy, legs or arms - your choice. Do the same for Your Assistant.

FMM241

Both you and Your Assistant caress and lightly stroke any exposed part of Your Partner's body.

FMM242

Both you and Your Assistant massage and fondle any part of Your Partner's body still covered with clothing - do not touch any skin.

FMM243

Kneeling while Your Partner stands, kiss and lick his belly, hips and thighs. Kneed and massage his buttocks. Your Assistant stands behind him and fondles his chest.

FMM244

With Your Partner and Your Assistant positioned so their feet are barely touching, massage their feet and each toe with an oil or lube. They then stroke their feet together.

FMM245

All three hug and passionately kiss each other.

FMM246

Use a piece of fur, silk or satin to smoothly caress any/all exposed parts of Your Partner's body. Your Assistant watches and repeats your actions.

FMM251

Use a vibrator to delicately stimulate Your Partner's nipples. He repeats your technique on Your Assistant's nipples.

FMM252

Lick, suck and lightly bite Your Partner's nipples. Blow on or suck in air around them to create warm and cool sensations. Alternate with Your Assistant's nipples.

FMM253

Apply a flavored lube to Your Partner's nipples. Tweak and tantalize them with your fingertips, then let Your Assistant lick each nipple clean.

FMM254

Creatively use an ice cube to perk up sensitive regions on Your Partner's body. Your Assistant follows each cold shock with a warm kiss or lick.

FMM255

Put on a tight, silky top that shows off your nipples (remove your bra if necessary). Entice Your Partner and Your Assistant to caress your chest and circle your nipples through the fabric.

FMM256

Rub and massage Your Partner's and Your Assistant's crotch at the same time (through their clothing if they are still wearing any).

FMM261

Both you and Your Assistant sensually lick exposed regions of Your Partner's body. Search out rarely explored erogenous zones.

FMM262

Based on the recommendation from Your Partner and Your Assistant, put on any item to look, feel, smell or taste even more sexy.

FMM263

Use a flavored lube or syrup on any rarely licked erogenous zone and entice both Your Partner and Your Assistant to lick it off together.

FMM264

Instruct Your Assistant to creatively stimulate Your Partner any way you desire.

FMM265

Pleasure yourself as visual stimulation for both Your Partner and Your Assistant.

FMM266

While Your Partner and Your Assistant stand together and kiss, kneel next to them and fondle, rub and massage their buttocks.

Female Male Male

Level 3 - Intimate Intentions

FMM311

While Your Partner and Your Assistant kiss, seductively read a short erotic passage or a dirty letter. Choose one that is very explicit and detailed.

FMM312

Both you and Your Assistant each select something sexy for Your Partner to wear (now and while making love later).

FMM313

Pretend you're a porn director/star. Get Your Partner and Your Assistant into a novel, creative position to receive or perform oral sex and detail how you want the scene to play out.

FMM314

Have Your Partner lay on his stomach. Both you and Your Assistant apply massage oil to his back and provide him a

creative, erotic massage while kissing each other.

FMM315

While cupping both men's crotch in one hand each, have them pulse their PC muscles as tightly and quickly as possible for a minute.

FMM316

Use a vibrator to stimulate Your Partner's neck, chest and nipples while Your Assistant nuzzles his crotch.

FMM321

Describe in detail a pleasuring accessory you have in mind for Your Partner and Your Assistant and how you would like it used in your sex play.

FMM322

Have Your Partner and Your Assistant simulate a sex act of your choice.

FMM323

Tell a dirty, explicitly erotic story involving two sexy elements provided by Your Partner and Your Assistant. Be as graphic as possible.

FMM324

Find and creatively use a non-sexual object to pleasure both Your Partner and Your Assistant (not necessarily at the same time).

FMM325

Describe in detail a raunchy S/M or bondage scenario involving Your Partner and Your Assistant.

FMM326

While Your Partner and Your Assistant stand together kissing and grinding their crotch together, kneel next to them and fondle, rub and massage their buttocks.

FMM331

While you and Your Partner stand together kissing and grinding against each other, Your Assistant hugs either of you and grinds his crotch on your butt.

FMM332

Use an ice cube to cool, then your lips and tongue to heat an exposed erogenous zone on Your Partner's body. Your Assistant does the same.

FMM333

Watch one scene of an explicit video with Your Partner and Your Assistant. You choose the DVD or switch over to a free online porn site.

FMM334

Get in a position that allows Your Partner to grind against your butt and Your Assistant to grind against his.

FMM335

Suck one of Your Partner's fingers while manually pleasuring his penis (do not remove any clothing). Your Assistant pleasures you in a similar way.

FMM336

Dab some ice cream or smear a popsicle on your nipples and entice Your Partner and Your Assistant to lick them clean.

FMM341

Using flavored lube on a realistic dildo held by Your Assistant, demonstrate your oral skills as a visual treat for Your Partner.

FMM342

Get into a threeway 69 position with Your Partner and Your Assistant and nuzzle each other. Hum, purr or moan for an added thrill.

FMM343

In a threeway doggie position with Your Partner in the middle, grab a handful of his hair and pull his head back as you thrust vigorously against them for 10–20 seconds.

FMM344

Remove one item of clothing from Your Partner and Your Assistant. Choose a slow song for them to dance to while holding each other close.

FMM345

Both you and Your Partner hold a piece of frozen fruit (strawberry, mango, pineapple) in your mouth while you alternate kissing Your Assistant.

FMM346

Both you and Your Assistant warm your mouth with a hot liquid (water, coffee, tea) swallow then kiss or lightly suck on one of Your Partner's exposed erogenous zones.

FMM351

Standing, mutually grope and fondle each other (under or over clothing).

FMM352

Look through an explicit pictorial magazine or book together.

FMM353

With Your Assistant in a missionary position with Your Partner and you in a doggie position, make them grind together with your thrusting.

FMM354

Use a digital camera and play erotic photographer with Your Partner and Your Assistant as your models. View them together and delete afterward (unless you really like one to print).

FMM355

Both you and Your Assistant each caress one of Your Partner's bare feet with your bare feet.

FMM356

Close your eyes while each of you sucks and licks the other person's middle finger. Use your tongues to swirl and stroke them.

FMM361

Both you and Your Assistant expose and blow "raspberries" on Your Partner's butt cheeks.

FMM362

Have Your Partner put on some "old" underwear. Let Your Assistant rip them off him (pre-cut the elastic band if necessary) so you can ravish him orally.

FMM363

Remove any clothing necessary for Your Partner and Your Assistant to teasingly lick your inner thighs. Lay back and enjoy their tickling tongues.

FMM364

Remove any clothing necessary for Your Partner and Your Assistant to teasingly lick your tummy. Lay back and enjoy their tickling tongues.

FMM365

Standing, fondle both Your Partner's and Your Assistant's penis and testicles while you alternate kissing them passionately.

Stroke both Your Partner's and Your Assistant's tail bone and between their butt cheeks. Use your fingers, tongue, feather, spoon, string of beads, etc. - alternate as required to stimulate both of them equally.

Female Male Male

Level 4 - Explicit & Erotic Passion

FMM411

Lightly squeeze and tug Your Partner's scrotum. Gently play with his testicles while Your Assistant kisses and licks the tip of his penis.

FMM412

kiss and lick the tip of Your Partner's penis as Your Assistant lightly tugs small amounts of pubic hair all around his genital region.

FMM413

Apply lube to both Your Partner's and Your Assistant's penis and rub your nipples with their tips.

FMM414

Lubricate both men's penis and your butt crack. With you as the start of a sensual, doggie style, slip'n slide, have them thrust against you and each other – no penetration.

FMM415

While Your Assistant plays with his nipples, gently pull the skin of Your Partner's penis taut with one hand. Use your fingertips of your other hand to stroke and massage the head.

FMM416

Use an artist brush dipped in flavored oil or lube to stimulate the head of Your Partner's penis. Flick the frenulum and swirl around the corona. Allow Your Assistant to lick it clean now and again.

FMM421

Using broad, luscious tongue strokes, lick all around the shaft of Your Partner's penis. Put the head in your mouth and suck it briefly. Repeat with Your Assistant's cock.

FMM422

Both you and Your Assistant each attempt to take one of Your Partner's testicles in your mouth at the same time. Lick them tenderly.

FMM423

Alternate pleasuring the head of Your Partner's and Your Assistant's penis orally with a mint, some liquor or dab of toothpaste in your mouth. Warming flavored lube is good too.

FMM424

Both you and Your Assistant tickle Your Partner's testicles, inner thighs and perineum with your tongues. Flutter your tongues like a flickering flame.

FMM425

While Your Partner and Your Assistant kiss, massage their cocks with lube - one in each hand. Use creative stroking techniques.

FMM426

Your Partner and Your Assistant both stand and look into each other's eyes while each sucking one finger of the other man. Kneel beside them and manually pleasure their cocks.

FMM431

In turn, starting with Your Assistant, express audible sounds of passion leading up to a fake orgasm. Each rate the most convincing.

FMM432

Direct Your Partner and Your Assistant to simulate a creative new sex act of your choice.

FMM433

While Your Partner and Your Assistant stand kissing, kneel beside them, apply lube to their cocks and creatively rub them together.

FMM434

Use an ice cube and your lips and tongue to cool then heat both Your Partner's and Your Assistant's penis and testicles. Alternate cooling one as you warm another.

FMM435

Have Your Partner straddle your face so you can orally pleasure his testicles. Your Assistant orally pleasures the head of his penis.

FMM436

Find and creatively use a non-sexual item to pleasure both Your Partner and Your Assistant.

FMM441

Have 30 seconds of femoral coitus (non-penetrative intercourse) standing, rear-entry with you facing up against a wall. Your Assistant joins from the rear.

FMM442

Have 30 seconds of femoral coitus (non-penetrative intercourse) doggie style. Your Assistant joins from the rear.

FMM443

Visually tease Your Partner by sensuously demonstrating fellatio using a sex toy or edible object. Your Assistant joins in or holds the item for you.

FMM444

Both you and Your Assistant pleasure Your Partner's entire penis and testicles orally at the same time. Use creative licking and sucking techniques.

FMM445

Stimulate Your Partner and Your Assistant with a vibrator at the same time. (Visual stimulation counts)

FMM446

Stimulate Your Partner with a sex toy that Your Assistant chooses. (Visual stimulation counts)

FMM451

While Your Partner watches, stroking himself, both you and Your Assistant masturbate any way you desire. Provide him visual stimulation. Edge yourselves if desired.

FMM452

Both you and Your Partner kiss and lick any of Your Assistant's exposed erogenous zone that each of you desire.

FMM453

Expose, then pinch, tweak and twiddle your nipples. Use lube if desired. Then have Your Partner and Your Assistant both suck and bite them gently.

FMM454

Use a piece of soft, juicy, sticky fruit. Rub it on Your Partner's penis then lick it clean. Repeat with Your Assistant.

FMM455

Use a vibrator to tease Your Partner's scrotum and perineum while Your Assistant licks the tip of his penis.

FMM456

Apply lube to the head of Your Partner's penis. Your Assistant straddles him and uses his cock to massage his perineum and anus – no penetration allowed. At the same time, you lick the tip of his penis.

FMM461

Using lube in your palms, wrap your hands around Your Partner's penis and stimulate him by twisting them in opposite directions. Then do the same for Your Assistant.

FMM462

In a missionary position (push up style), you on the bottom, have Your Partner insert just the head of his cock into your vagina. He allows Your Assistant to spank his ass but must resist plunging deeper into you as long as he can.

FMM463

Your Assistant straddles Your Partner in a way that allows him to slide his penis over his anus slowly and sensually – Your Partner is not allowed to move. You offer your mouth for him to slide his cock into at the same time.

FMM464

Both you and Your Assistant lovingly kiss Your Partner's penis together and use it to stroke your lips, cheek and neck.

FMM465

Sit on Your Partner's lap facing him, guide his cock into your vagina and wrap your legs around him. Standing, Your Assistant offers his penis for you to both lick and suck.

FMM466

Both you and Your Assistant stand beside Your Partner in front of a mirror and watch each other as you stroke and fondle his body intimately.

Female Male Male

Level 5 - Sizzling, Sexual Stimulation

FMM511

Manually stimulate Your Partner's cock with one hand and his perineum with the other. Your Assistant nibbles on his nipples.

FMM512

Have Your Partner hold a large dildo while you and Your Assistant demonstrate how you would give him a foot-job together. Use lube if you desire.

FMM513

As a visual tease, use a realistic dildo and some lube to demonstrate how you and Your Assistant would give Your Partner a creative hand-job together.

FMM514

While Your Partner and Your Assistant stroke each other's cock, pleasure yourself with a glass or acrylic dildo for their visual pleasure. Be as lewd as you dare.

FMM515

Give Your Partner a foot-job. Apply lube and use your toes and the soles of your feet to stimulate his penis. Your Assistant offers his cock to him for oral pleasuring.

FMM516

While Your Partner and Your Assistant stroke each other's cock, lube and pleasure yourself with the thickest dildo or buttplug you own. Provide a good show for their visual pleasure.

FMM521

Both Your Partner and Your Assistant will each select a piece of fetish wear or accessory (leather, stockings, boots, heels, collar etc.) for you to put on.

FMM522

While Your Partner stands, kneel before him and orally pleasure his penis just to the brink of ejaculation – then stop. Stroke Your Assistant's cock at the same time.

FMM523

Laying down so your head is hanging over an accessible edge (bed, table, sofa, etc.), orally pleasure Your Assistant's penis while Your Partner pleasures you any way he desires.

FMM524

Get into a threeway "69" position with Your Partner and Your Assistant. Pleasure each other orally.

FMM525

Straddle Your Partner's face and allow him to lick your pussy. Your Assistant plays with his nipples or his penis as Your Partner orally pleasures you.

FMM526

While you have Your Partner's cock in your mouth, Your Assistant lubes and slowly inserts the largest available dildo into your vagina. Both men watch every detail as your pussy engulfs the toy.

FMM531

Using a suction cup dildo, stimulate your self without using your hands. At the same time, orally pleasure both Your Partner and Your Assistant.

FMM532

Your Partner enjoys one minute of penetration and being penetrated in a position of his choice – No thrusting. Use your PC muscles to squeeze and pulse only. You use a strapless strap-on if he desires.

FMM533

Enjoy a minute of intercourse doggie style with Your Partner. Your Assistant offers his cock to either of you for oral pleasuring.

FMM534

Spread Your Partner's butt cheeks wide and tickle his perineum and surrounding erogenous zones with a feather or piece of silky material. Your Assistant does the same for you.

FMM535

Using lube and one or two fingers, massage Your Partner's perineum. Then penetrate his anus with smooth, gliding strokes. Your Assistant orally pleasures him at the same time.

FMM536

Use an artist brush and lube to stimulate Your Partner's perineum and surrounding erogenous zones. Tickle it as you play with his testicles. Your Assistant offers his cock to him for oral pleasuring.

FMM541

Circle Your Partner's scrotum just above his testicles with your thumb and index finger. Pull down gently until taut and lick his testicles. Your Assistant orally pleasures the head of his cock at the same time.

FMM542

Using a firm, pointed tongue, lick Your Partner's perineum and base of his scrotum using circles, swirls and zigzag strokes. Your Assistant orally pleasures the head of his cock

FMM543

While you lay on your front and orally pleasure Your Assistant, Your Partner straddles you and enjoys some intense rear-entry intercourse.

FMM544

In a missionary position with Your Partner, spread and lift your legs high. Both men lick and suck on your toes to make you wiggle on his cock.

FMM545

Use the tip of a vibrator to tickle Your Partner's perineum and surrounding erogenous zones – no penetration. Use a second vibrator or lubed finger to stimulate Your Assistant in a similar way.

FMM546

Get into a doggie position with Your Partner. He is to remain still while you wiggle and circle your pelvis against him. Suck Your Assistant's cock at the same time.

FMM551

With Your Partner sitting, straddle him with your back to his chest. Use his penis to tap and stroke your clitoris while Your Assistant sucks your nipples.

FMM552

While Your Partner stands, kneel behind him and nibble and bite his buttocks while stroking his testicles. Your Assistant kneels in front and orally pleasures his cock.

FMM553

Apply some lube between your butt cheeks. With Your Partner standing up against a wall, rub and stroke his penis between your ass while you bend over to orally pleasures Your Assistant's cock.

FMM554

Apply some lube between Your Partner's butt cheeks. With you standing up facing against a wall, Your Partner penetrates you and Your Assistant joins in behind (with or without penetration). They thrust against you and each other in unison.

FMM555

With Your Partner lying on his back, squat on the tip of his penis and play with his nipples. Your Assistant guides Your Partner's cock to stroke and massage your pussy.

FMM556

Remove all clothing on your upper bodies. Apply massage oil to your chests and bellies. Slither and slide against each other to one song.

FMM561

Play a favorite song and orally pleasure both Your Partner and Your Assistant to the rhythm. Make it last the entire length of the song then stop.

FMM562

Take Your Partner's penis in your mouth and create different vibrating sensations by humming, purring, growling, etc. Your Partner follows your lead pleasuring Your Assistant in the same way.

FMM563

While Your Partner sits, both you and Your Assistant perform a lap dance for him to one song of your choice. Seductively rub and grind yourselves on him.

FMM564

Both you and Your Assistant suck on the shaft of Your Partner's penis. Slide your lips up and down the sides of his erection as you lick and flick with your tongues.

FMM565

Use only the soft underside of your tongue to lick the head of Your Partner's penis. Repeat or alternate for Your Assistant's pleasure.

FMM566

Use a digital camera with a zoom lens to take very close-up and intimate shots of Your Partner and Your Assistant in various explicit poses. Select one to print and frame.

Female Male Male

Level 6 - Wild, Nasty, Kinky, Taboo

FMM611

Orally pleasure Your Partner's anus in a position of your choice. Your Assistant orally pleasures his cock at the same time.

FMM612

Orally pleasure Your Partner's anus in a position of your choice. Your Assistant offers his cock to Your Partner to be sucked at the same time.

FMM613

Your choice of Nasty, Kinky or Taboo foreplay activity for Your Partner and Your Assistant to perform for you – surprise them with your wild side.

FMM614

While you give Your Partner a sensual prostate massage, he does the same for Your Assistant.

FMM615

In a position of your choice, allow the men to attempt double penetration. Enjoy slow, sensual, simultaneous vaginal and anal intercourse for a minute or two.

FMM616

Creatively use a double-ended dildo with Your Partner. Allow Your Assistant to hold and manipulate it as desired.

FMM621

Orally pleasure Your Partner's anus in a missionary position, legs spread wide. Your Assistant licks and sucks on his toes to make him wiggle.

FMM622

Insert one lubed finger in Your Partner's anus and gently massage left, right, up, down and all around – no thrusting. Your Assistant does the same for you.

FMM623

Attempt to take both Your Partner's and Your Assistant's cocks in your mouth at the same time.

FMM624

Drip hot wax on both Your Partner and Your Assistant (chest or buttocks) while they lay next to each other.

FMM625

While Your Partner and Your Assistant kiss, apply nipple clamps (or clothes pegs) to their nipples. Remove when one of them breaks their kiss.

FMM626

With a lubed fake pussy (penis sleeve), masturbate Your Partner's shaft just to the brink then stop. Leave his tip for Your Assistant to orally pleasure.

FMM631

Use your fingers and lube to pleasure Your Partner anyway you desire. Stimulate Your Assistant using your other hand in the same way at the same time.

FMM632

Both you and Your Partner pleasure yourselves with a dildo or buttplug while Your Assistant watches.

FMM633

Use an implement of your choice to erotically spank Your Partner's bare bum until it radiates a sensual heat. Let Your Assistant caresses and strokes his bum between smacks.

FMM634

Use the tip of a vibrator to tickle Your Partner's perineum and anus – no penetration. Your Assistant offers his cock to Your Partner to be sucked at the same time.

FMM635

Stimulate Your Partner and Your Assistant each with a different buttplug or dildo at the same time.

FMM636

With Your Partner propped in a mostly upside-down position, orally pleasure him. Your Assistant helps hold him up while giving him a rim-job.

FMM641

While Your Partner and Your Assistant take turns pleasuring you orally, stimulate them in any way you desire.

FMM642

Using a double-ended dildo or silicone beads, both you and Your Partner get on all fours for a little "cheek to cheek" action. Your Assistant offers his cock to be sucked by both of you taking turns.

FMM643

Pleasure Your Partner orally while also stimulating him anally with a lubed finger. Your Assistant nibbles, sucks and bites on Your Partner's nipples.

FMM644

Your Assistant lays on his back, you straddle his cock and Your Partner squats over his mouth so his testicles can be licked. While you ride Your Partner, orally pleasures Your Assistant's cock at the same time.

FMM645

Creatively explore a pleasurable combination of a dildo and two cocks at the same time.

FMM646

Experiment with cross-dressing – both you and Your Assistant select some appropriate feminine wear for Your Partner to wear.

FMM651

Get into a position so both you and Your Assistant can pleasure Your Partner orally together while he stimulates both of you anally using lubed fingers.

FMM652

Select two sex toys for Your Partner and Your Assistant to play Show and Tell. In turn, they are to demonstrate their self-pleasuring technique, eyes closed, while describing the sensations.

FMM653

Roleplaying as a strict Mistress, sternly command your Love Slaves to perform and service one of your desires.

FMM654

While lying down, have Your Partner straddle you facing your feet. As he grinds on your pussy with his cock, Your Assistant slaps on his ass cheeks.

FMM655

Get into a threeway '69' position and give each other a rim-job.

FMM656

Your choice of sex position involving all three of you engaging in oral and/or anal/vaginal intercourse at the same time.

FMM661

Describe in detail an extreme BDSM scenario/fantasy involving all three of you. Set the stage and let Your Partner and Your Assistant add to the story in turn.

FMM662

Grab Your Partner and Your Assistant and run to an unusual location in your home to have a quickie in a position of your choice – stop just before either of them have an orgasm.

FMM663

Attempt to take both Your Partner's and Your Assistant's cocks in your mouth at the same time.

FMM664

Ride Your Partner in a reverse cowgirl position while sucking Your Assistant's cock at the same time.

FMM665

Both you and Your Assistant erotically and passionately nibble and bite sensitive erogenous zones on Your Partner's body. Make him ache for you in a good way.

FMM666

STOP the Foreplay and START the Sex Play.

Male Female Female

Foreplay Activities

Male Female Female

Level 1 - Warm & Loving

MFF111

Both you and Your Assistant give feather-light kisses along Your Partner's neck and jawline. Breathe softly next to her ear to make her shiver with delight.

MFF112

Massage Your Partner's head with the tips of your fingers. Stroke her hair. She follows your lead to massage Your Assistant's head in the same way.

MFF113

Sit opposite and facing each other. Place a hand on each other's chest, close your eyes and synchronize breathing slowly.

MFF114

Kiss and lick Your Partner's wrist, inner arm and elbow. Your Assistant does the same on her other arm.

MFF115

Both you and Your Assistant spider Walk your fingers delicately over parts of Your Partner's exposed body. Arouse her with a slow, light tickling and tapping motion.

MFF116

From a book of fantasies or erotic letters, read a random one out loud to Your Partner while she kisses Your Assistant.

MFF121

Describe in detail a new erotic adventure involving the three of you. Include elements of the love play you'll enjoy together.

MFF122

Standing, hug and caress Your Partner from behind. Your Assistant kneels in front and caresses her lower region.

MFF123

Kiss and nibble along Your Partner's neck and shoulder while Your Assistant does the same to you from behind.

MFF124

Kiss and lightly lick Your Partner's hand, palm and fingers. Choose her non-dominant hand. She matches your actions on Your Assistant's hand.

MFF125

Find a how-to article on a sex technique or activity that you have not yet experienced and read it together.

MFF126

While sensually kissing Your Partner, allow Your Assistant to tickle both of you with a feather (face, lips, ears and neck).

MFF131

Both you and Your Assistant delicately stroke each of Your Partner's hands and fingers with your fingertips. Swirl and circle as you explore and tickle every nerve to attention.

MFF132

While Your Partner and Your Assistant kiss, apply cologne to a few areas of your body where you desire extra attention.

MFF133

Lovingly embrace Your Partner and Your Assistant. Hug, caress and tenderly kiss each other.

MFF134

Place soft, delicate kisses all over Your Partner's face - cheek, lips, nose, forehead, temples, chin. End with a tender,

sensuous kiss. Repeat for Your Assistant.

MFF135

Both you and Your Assistant lick Your Partner's ear lobes and sensitive regions on her neck. Behind the ears and back of her neck are very sensitive. Whisper something deliciously sensual, loving or erotic.

MFF136

Describe in detail a unique, novel or exotic place to make love. Include activities you would like to experience.

MFF141

Gently kiss and lick Your Partner's inner arm – wrist to elbow. Your Assistant does the same for her other arm.

MFF142

Delicately lick around one of Your Partner's ears. Your Assistant does the same on the other one. Hot breaths in her ear will give her delightful shivers of pleasure.

MFF143

While Your Partner and Your Assistant kiss, do something to set the mood. Play soft music, light a candle, pour a glass of wine, burn some incense, apply cologne, etc.

MFF144

Dance embraced with Your Partner and Your Assistant to one slow song. Kiss each of them lovingly when it ends.

MFF145

Stand still and allow Your Partner and Your Assistant to both caress and stroke your body.

MFF146

Find and view some erotic art together - use books or the internet. Discuss what you each like about it.

MFF151

Both you and Your Assistant erotically tickle any of Your Partner's exposed erogenous zones. Creatively use your fingers, a feather, a soft paintbrush or your tongues.

MFF152

Find an erotic edible and feed it to Your Partner and Your Assistant sensually. Fruit, syrup, chocolate, oysters, liquor, etc. Encourage them to savor the treats at the same time.

MFF153

Standing together, both you and Your Assistant softly stroke and caress Your Partner's entire body. Lightly squeeze parts of her body that you find delightful.

MFF154

Make up a fantasy scenario or roleplaying adventure for Your Partner and Your Assistant that they might perform for your erotic pleasure.

MFF155

All three of you close your eyes. Delicately caress Your Partner's and Your Assistant's faces, each with one hand. Trace your fingertips as lightly as you can as you explore every detail.

MFF156

Remove one item of clothing erotically then remove one item of clothing from both Your Partner and Your Assistant.

MFF161

Massage Your Partner's toes one at a time. Your Assistant does the same, starting with the other foot.

MFF162

Experiment with different types of kisses and kissing sensations - (upside down, open mouth, closed mouth, sideways, corner, firm, soft). Alternate between Your Partner and Your Assistant.

MFF163

Tenderly kiss Your Partner with affection. Hold and caress her face with both hands. Then kiss Your Assistant with the same affection.

MFF164

Browse through a book with advanced or acrobatic sex positions together. Choose one of them for Your Partner and Your Assistant to try out (simulate the sex play for now).

MFF165

All browse an erotic book or magazine with Your Partner (her choice). Discuss pictures or images that appeal to each of you.

MFF166

Both you and Your Assistant give Your Partner a brief but relaxing massage the way she likes it.

Male Female Female

Level 2 - Sensual Sensations

MFF211

Both you and Your Assistant massage and fondle any part of Your Partner's body still clothed - do not touch any skin.

MFF212

With Your Partner and Your Assistant positioned so their feet are barely touching, massage their feet and each toe with an oil or lube. They then stroke their feet together.

MFF213

Both you and Your Assistant each use a piece of fur, silk or satin to smoothly caress any/all exposed parts of Your Partner's body.

MFF214

Lick, suck and lightly bite Your Partner's nipples. Blow on or suck in air around them to create warm and cool sensations. Alternate with Your Assistant's nipples.

MFF215

Creatively use an ice cube to perk up sensitive regions on Your Partner's body. Your Assistant follows each cold shock with a warm kiss or lick.

MFF216

Both you and Your Assistant each gently suck one of Your Partner's nipples into your mouth at the same time. Add a vibrating sensation by humming or use a vibrator on your cheek.

MFF221

Both you and Your Partner stroke and caress Your Assistant's legs and inner thighs.

MFF222

Both you and Your Assistant sensually lick exposed regions of Your Partner's body. Search out rarely explored erogenous zones.

MFF223

Use a flavored lube or syrup on any rarely licked erogenous zone and entice both Your Partner and Your Assistant to lick it off together.

MFF224

Instruct Your Assistant to creatively stimulate Your Partner any way you desire.

MFF225

Slowly and sensually lick and suck Your Partner's thumb. Your Assistant does the same for her other thumb. Stimulate every nerve with your twirling tongues.

MFF226

Fondle, rub and massage both Your Partner's pussy and Your Assistant's pussy at the same time (through their clothing if they are still wearing any).

MFF231

While Your Partner and Your Assistant stand together and kiss, kneel next to them and fondle, rub and massage their buttocks.

MFF232

Enjoy a threeway kiss with Your Partner and Your Assistant.

MFF233

Use a vibrator to delicately stimulate Your Partner's nipples. She repeats your technique on Your Assistant's nipples.

MFF234

Kneeling while Your Partner stands, kiss and lick her belly, hips and thighs. Kneed her buttocks gently. Your Assistant stands behind her and fondles her breasts.

MFF235

Using massage oil, both you and Your Assistant gently each massage one of Your Partner's breasts. Circle but do not touch her nipples.

MFF236

Apply a flavored lube to Your Partner's nipples. Tweak and tantalize them with your fingertips then let Your Assistant lick each nipple clean.

MFF241

Both you and Your Assistant each lick the soft, sensitive skin behind Your Partner's knees at the same time.

MFF242

Put an edible topping or liquor in your navel and entice Your Partner and Your Assistant to lick it out together.

MFF243

Whisper in Your Partner's ear how you want to pleasure her with your hot tongue. Do the same for Your Assistant.

MFF244

Kiss, lick and suck each finger of Your Partner's non-dominant hand. Apply a flavored lube or syrup if you desire. She matches your actions on Your Assistant's hand.

MFF245

Both you and Your Assistant stroke and caress Your Partner's breasts. Lightly circle her nipples.

MFF246

Have Your Partner remove her bra and put on a silky top. Then, both you and Your Assistant caress her breasts and circle her nipples through the fabric.

MFF251

Both you and Your Assistant expose and lightly lick Your Partner's lower back and side. Lightly bite and nibble her buttocks.

MFF252

Creatively use a string of pearls or round beads to stimulate Your Partner in various ways. Repeat for Your Assistant.

MFF253

Both you and Your Assistant perform an erotic dance together while removing an item of clothing each. Play appropriate music if desired.

MFF254

Use an artist brush dipped in flavored lube to stimulate Your Partner's nipples. Apply delicate flicks and twirls. Your Assistant gets to lick them clean.

MFF255

Both you and Your Assistant caress and lightly stroke any/all exposed parts of Your Partner's body.

MFF256

Have Your Partner get in any position you desire, expose her butt and allow both you and Your Assistant to administer a sensual spanking.

MFF261

Lightly drag your fingernails down Your Partner's back, chest and tummy, legs or arms – your choice. Do the same for Your Assistant.

MFF262

Both you and Your Assistant whisper in Your Partner's ear how horny you are and how badly you want your fingers and tongue deep inside her. Let her feel your package and imagine what else you have planned for her.

MFF263

With Your Partner and Your Assistant positioned so their feet are barely touching, use a vibrator to stimulate their toes and soles of their feet.

MFF264

While sitting still, allow both Your Partner and Your Assistant to caress your body and each other with only their breasts. Have them brush sensitive regions with just their nipples.

MFF265

While Your Partner and Your Assistant kiss, use a soft artist or make-up brush to tickle and stimulate exposed erogenous zones on their bodies.

MFF266

Find and use an item with an interesting texture to stimulate/sensitize an exposed region of Your Partner's body. (soft, cold, rough, squishy, etc.) Then pleasure Your Assistant in a similar way.

Male Female Female

Level 3 - Intimate Intentions

MFF311

Watch one scene of an explicit video with Your Partner and Your Assistant. You choose the DVD or switch over to a free online porn site.

MFF312

Suck one of Your Partner's fingers while manually pleasuring her pussy (do not remove any clothing). Your Assistant pleasures you in a similar way.

MFF313

Dab some ice cream or smear a popsicle on your nipples and entice Your Partner and Your Assistant to lick them clean.

MFF314

Both you and Your Assistant massage a different symmetrical part of Your Partner's body (legs, arms, breasts, shoulders, etc.). Experiment with a different type of technique.

MFF315

Have Your Partner lay on her stomach. Both you and Your Assistant apply massage oil to her back and provide her a creative, erotic massage while kissing each other.

MFF316

Both you and Your Assistant each kiss and lick one of Your Partner's breasts at the same time – all over except her nipples.

MFF321

Look through an explicit pictorial magazine or book together. Discuss what you each consider erotic and arousing.

MFF322

Close your eyes while each of you sucks and licks the other person's middle finger. Use your tongues to swirl and stroke them.

MFF323

Remove any clothing necessary for Your Partner and Your Assistant to teasingly lick your inner thighs. Lay back and enjoy their tickling tongues.

MFF324

Describe in detail how you would like to include a strap-on in a new sex position or activity involving Your Partner and Your Assistant.

MFF325

Stroke both Your Partner's and Your Assistant's tail bone and between their butt cheeks. Use your fingers, tongue, feather, spoon, string of beads, etc. - alternate as required to stimulate both of them equally.

MFF326

Get in a position for Your Partner and Your Assistant to lick and suck your cock at the same time.

MFF331

Standing, fondle both Your Partner's and Your Assistant's pussy while you alternate kissing them passionately.

MFF332

Both you and Your Assistant expose and blow "raspberries" on Your Partner's butt cheeks.

MFF333

Remove one item of clothing from Your Partner and Your Assistant. Choose a slow song for them to dance to while holding each other close.

MFF334

Both you and Your Assistant each caress one of Your Partner's bare feet with your bare feet.

MFF335

While Your Partner and Your Assistant kiss, seductively read a short erotic passage or a dirty letter. Choose one that is very explicit and detailed.

MFF336

Use a digital camera and play erotic photographer with Your Partner and Your Assistant as your models. View them together and delete afterward (unless you really like one to print).

MFF341

Have Your Partner and Your Assistant simulate a sex act of your choice. Encourage them to thrust and grind against each other as vigorously as you want. Have them use a dildo or two as a prop if desired.

MFF342

Describe in detail a pleasuring accessory you have in mind for Your Partner and Your Assistant and how you would like it used in your sex play.

MFF343

Find and creatively use a non-sexual object to pleasure both Your Partner and Your Assistant (not necessarily at the same time).

MFF344

With one hand cupping Your Partner's pussy and the other cupping Your Assistant's pussy (palm pressing on clitoris), gently insert one finger. Once comfortable, have them both pulse their PC muscles as tightly and quickly as possible for one minute.

MFF345

Dip a finger into Your Partner's vagina and let Your Assistant savor her taste. Then, dip a finger into Your Assistant's vagina and let Your Partner savor her flavor. Next, they both let you taste them in a similar way.

MFF346

Use an ice cube to cool, then your lips and tongue to heat an exposed erogenous zone on Your Partner's body. Your Assistant does the same.

MFF351

Using a flavored lube, massage each of Your Partner's toes on one foot then lick and suck them clean. Your Assistant does the same for the other foot at the same time.

MFF352

In turn, starting with Your Assistant, express audible sounds of passion leading up to a fake orgasm. Each rate the most convincing.

MFF353

Both you and Your Assistant warm your mouth with a hot liquid (water, coffee, tea) swallow then kiss or lightly suck on one of Your Partner's exposed erogenous zones.

MFF354

Use a vibrator to stimulate Your Partner's neck, chest and nipples while Your Assistant nuzzles her pussy.

MFF355

Get into a threeway 69 position with Your Partner and Your Assistant and nuzzle each other. Hum, purr or moan for an added thrill.

MFF356

Pretend you're a porn director/star. Get Your Partner and Your Assistant into a novel, creative position to perform/ simulate a sex act. Detail how you want the scene to play out. Provide props if desired.

MFF361

Tell a dirty, explicitly erotic story involving two sexy elements provided by Your Partner and Your Assistant. Be as graphic as possible.

MFF362

Sit, legs spread, so Your Partner and Your Assistant can both grind their pussy on one of your thighs at the same time while facing you. Fondle both their breasts and alternate kissing each of them passionately.

MFF363

While Your Partner and Your Assistant stand together kissing and grinding their pussy on each other's thigh, kneel next to them and fondle, rub and massage their buttocks.

MFF364

Standing, mutually grope and fondle each other (under or over clothing).

MFF365

Remove any clothing necessary for Your Partner and Your Assistant to teasingly lick your belly and above your crotch. Lay back and enjoy their tickling tongues.

MFF366

Both you and Your Partner hold a piece of frozen fruit (strawberry, mango, pineapple) in your mouth while you alternate kissing Your Assistant.

Male Female Female

Level 4 - Explicit & Erotic Passion

MFF411

Sensuously demonstrate cunnilingus using an edible object (mango, peach, chocolate on Your Partner's fingers, etc.) – think juicy and messy. At the same time, Your Assistant sensuously demonstrates fellatio using a sex toy or edible object.

MFF412

Pleasure Your Partner's entire pussy orally. Your Assistant orally pleasures her nipple. Both use creative licking and sucking techniques.

MFF413

Stimulate Your Partner with a sex toy that Your Assistant chooses. (Visual stimulation counts)

MFF414

Hold a large dildo while Your Partner and Your Assistant demonstrate how they would perform a foot-job together. Use lube if desired.

MFF415

Expose then pinch, tweak and twiddle your nipples. Use a flavored lube if desired. Then have Your Partner and Your Assistant each suck and bite them as hard as you like.

MFF416

Use a piece of soft, juicy, sticky fruit to tickle Your Partner's clitoris then have Your Assistant lick it clean. Repeat as often as you want.

MFF421

Get into a position that enables you to simultaneously use two vibrators to tease both Your Partner's and Your Assistant's pussy. Stroke their lips and vaginal entrance. Lightly circle each clitoris without directly touching it.

MFF422

Creatively stimulate Your Partner and Your Assistant, each with a different vibrator at the same time.

MFF423

Apply some lube to the head of your cock. In a position of your choice, use it to stroke Your Partner's vaginal lips and clitoris – no penetration allowed. Repeat for Your Assistant.

MFF424

In a missionary or doggie position, penetrate Your Partner's vagina once as slowly and deeply as you can. Grind against her. Repeat for Your Assistant.

MFF425

Lightly squeeze and tug Your Partner's vaginal lips. Massage them delicately with moist fingertips. At the same time, Your Assistant uses lubed fingers to stimulate her nipples.

MFF426

Both you and Your Assistant kiss and lick any exposed erogenous zone you desire on Your Partner's body.

MFF431

Using lube and two fingers, massage Your Partner's pussy. Then penetrate her vagina with smooth, gliding strokes. Use your other hand to mirror your actions for Your Assistant's pleasure.

MFF432

Insert a dildo of Your Partner's choice into her vagina while Your Assistant licks her clitoris. Move the dildo in slow, smooth strokes.

MFF433

While Your Assistant tickles her tummy with her tongue, lightly tug small amounts of pubic hair all around Your Partner's pussy. If she is shaved, stroke her mound softly.

MFF434

Sit, legs spread, so Your Partner and Your Assistant can both rub their pussy on one of your thighs at the same time while facing you. Encourage them to grind hard as you lick, suck and nibble on their breasts.

MFF435

Both you and Your Assistant stand beside Your Partner in front of a mirror and watch each other as you stroke and fondle her body intimately.

MFF436

In a missionary position, insert just the head of your cock into Your Partner's vagina. Allow Your Assistant to use her hand to wiggle it back and forth and around.

MFF441

Use broad tongue strokes to lick slowly up and down Your Partner's pussy. Use the underside of your tongue on her clitoris. Repeat for Your Assistant.

MFF442

Pleasure Your Partner orally while Your Assistant kisses her passionately and plays with her tits.

MFF443

With Your Partner laying on her back, legs spread wide, both you and Your Assistant delicately flutter your tongues up, down and around her pussy and inner thigh like a flickering flame always moving.

MFF444

Your Partner and Your Assistant both kneel doggie style and look into each other's eyes while each sucking one finger of the other woman. Kneel behind them and manually pleasure their pussies.

MFF445

Apply hot (slow) and cool (faster) breaths on Your Partner's clitoris. Moisten with your tongue and suck in air for more cooling sensations. Your Assistant does the same on both her nipples.

MFF446

Insert one or two fingers in Your Partner's vagina (moisten if necessary) and gently massage left, right, up, down and all around – no thrusting. Your Assistant fondles and strokes your penis at the same time.

MFF451

In a missionary position (you on top push up style), insert just the head of your cock into Your Partner's vagina. Allow Your Assistant to sensually spank your ass. Resist plunging deeper as long as you can.

MFF452

Apply lube to Your Partner's and Your Assistant's nipples and have then rub, circle and flick them together. They then both rub their nipples across exposed regions of your body or face.

MFF453

Use an artist brush dipped in lube to delicately stimulate Your Partner's clitoris. Flick up, down and across - swirl in circles and zigzags. Your Assistant uses another brush to stimulate her nipples in a similar way at the same time.

MFF454

Using a suction cup dildo (or one you hold) and your hard cock, both Your Partner and Your Assistant thrust and grind together while kissing each other.

MFF455

Find and creatively use a non-sexual object to pleasure both Your Partner and Your Assistant (not necessarily at the same time).

MFF456

With Your Partner in a missionary position, legs spread wide, slide your penis over her pussy slowly and gently at first, then with more pressure and speed. Your Assistant strokes you both from behind.

MFF461

Both Your Partner and Your Assistant apply massage oil or lube to each other's breasts. They then use them to stimulate any of your exposed erogenous zones and each other.

MFF462

Nibble and suck on Your Partner's vaginal lips. Twirl your tongue inside her vagina – wiggle it in as deep as you can. Repeat for Your Assistant.

MFF463

Describe in detail a raunchy S/M or bondage scenario involving Your Partner and Your Assistant.

MFF464

Use an ice cube to cool followed by Your Assistant's lips and tongue to heat Your Partner's nipples and clitoris. Stimulate various erogenous zones with hot and cold sensations.

MFF465

Delicately massage Your Partner's clitoris and vaginal lips with a flavored lube. Your Assistant follows with sensual licking and sucking.

MFF466

Both Your Partner and Your Assistant lovingly kiss your penis together and use it to stroke their lips, cheek and neck.

Male Female Female

Level 5 - Sizzling, Sexual Stimulation

MFF511

Insert one lubed finger in Your Partner's anus and gently massage left, right, up, down and all around – no thrusting. Your Assistant does the same for you.

MFF512

Sit and have Your Partner straddle you (her back to your chest). Play with her nipples while Your Assistant orally pleasures both of you.

MFF513

Use a dildo or buttplug and orally pleasure Your Partner at the same time while she also stimulates Your Assistant's pussy with a vibrator or dildo.

MFF514

While Your Partner orally pleasures Your Assistant, nibble and bite her buttocks while playing with her pussy.

MFF515

All three remove all clothing on your upper bodies. Apply massage oil to your chests and bellies. Slither and slide against each other to one song.

MFF516

Use an artist brush and lube to stimulate Your Partner's anus. Tickle it as Your Assistant plays with her clitoris or nipples.

MFF521

With Your Partner standing, facing a wall, press hard against her, kissing her neck and fingering her pussy. Your Assistant joins from the rear stimulating you in a similar way.

MFF522

Gently suck Your Partner's clitoris in your mouth and create different vibrating sensations by humming, moaning, growling, etc. Your Partner follows your lead pleasuring Your Assistant in the same way.

MFF523

Use the tip of a vibrator to tickle Your Partner's perineum and anus – no penetration. At the same time, Your Assistant offers her pussy or nipples for Your Partner to lick and suck.

MFF524

With Your Partner laying on her back, straddle her face so she can orally pleasure you. Your Assistant uses a vibrator, dildo or buttplug to pleasure her at the same time.

MFF525

Experiment with a new, creative "scissoring" position for Your Partner and Your Assistant that allows you to stimulate both of them with a vibrator as they grind and thrust together.

MFF526

While Your Partner sits, both you and Your Assistant perform an erotic lap dance for her to one song of your choice. Seductively rub and grind yourselves on her. Seductively entice her to caress and fondle your assets.

MFF531

Gently suck and nibble on Your Partner's vaginal lips (labia) – one side then the other. Massage them with your lips and tongue. Your Assistant offers her nipples for Your Partner to lick and suck.

MFF532

With Your Partner laying on her back, legs raised and spread wide, watch closely as you ever so slowly insert a dildo. Your Assistant holds a mirror so she can see how her pussy engulfs the fake cock. Repeat with your real cock.

MFF533

Use a digital camera with a zoom lens to take very close-up and intimate shots of Your Partner and Your Assistant in various explicit poses. Select one to print and frame.

MFF534

While Your Partner uses her fingers to expose her clitoris for you, use only the soft underside of your tongue to delicately caress and stroke it. Repeat for Your Assistant.

MFF535

While Your Partner stands, kneel behind her. Nibble and bite her buttocks while stroking her thighs. Your Assistant kneels in front and orally pleasures her.

MFF536

Select two sex toys for Your Partner and Your Assistant to play Show and Tell. In turn, they are to demonstrate their self-pleasuring technique, eyes closed, while describing the sensations.

MFF541

Using lube, insert your two middle fingers in Your Partner's vagina with palm on her clitoris. Flutter your fingers up and down quickly. Trigger a G-Spot orgasm or come close. Using your other hand, do the same for Your Assistant.

MFF542

With Your Partner using a realistic dildo or strap-on as a fake cock, watch as Your Assistant demonstrates her best blowjob technique in a position of your choice.

MFF543

Have Your Partner put on some "old" underwear. Let Your Assistant rip them off her (pre-cut the elastic band if necessary) so you can ravish her orally.

MFF544

In a doggie position, penetrate Your Partner, grab a handful of her hair and pull her head back as you thrust vigorously for 10–20 seconds. Repeat for Your Assistant.

MFF545

Sitting, legs spread, hold a dildo on each thigh. Your Partner and Your Assistant both mount one of the toys and grind against you while kissing and each other and stroking you at the same time.

MFF546

Get into a threeway 69 position and pleasure each other orally. Your Partner gets to choose orientation.

MFF551

Lube and pleasure Your Partner with a dildo or vibrator of her choice. Allow her to guide your hand or verbally coach you on technique. Repeat for Your Assistant.

MFF552

Pleasure Your Partner with the thinnest dildo or smallest vibrator available. Your Assistant sucks on her nipples at the same time.

MFF553

Pleasure Your Partner with a dildo while you lick her clitoris and Your Assistant plays with her nipples.

MFF554

While lying down, have Your Partner straddle you facing your feet. As she grinds on your penis (with or without penetration), Your Assistant sensually slaps her ass cheeks.

MFF555

Research and Discuss the possibility of fisting (vaginal and anal). Plan how/when you might do it and identify each of your roles in the activity.

MFF556

Laying down so your head is hanging over an accessible edge (bed, table, sofa, etc.), orally pleasure Your Partner's pussy. At the same time, Your Assistant orally pleasures you.

MFF561

While Your Partner and Your Assistant stroke each other's clitoris, pleasure yourself with a glass/acrylic/metal dildo or buttplug for their visual pleasure. Be as lewd as you dare.

MFF562

With Your Partner standing, kneel before her and orally pleasure her pussy. Your Assistant joins doggie style using her hands to caress you any way she desires.

MFF563

Spread Your Partner's butt cheeks wide and tickle her perineum and anus with a feather or piece of silky material. Your Assistant stimulates you in a similar way.

MFF564

Use your fingers and lube to pleasure Your Partner anyway you desire. Stimulate Your Assistant using your other hand in the same way at the same time.

MFF565

Using a firm, pointed tongue, lick Your Partner's perineum using circles, swirls and zigzag strokes. Your Assistant sucks on her nipples at the same time.

MFF566

Get into a threeway '69' position and give each other a rim-job.

Male Female Female

Level 6 - Wild, Nasty, Kinky, Taboo

MFF611

Using your fingers or any other sex toys of your choice, stimulate Your Partner anally and Your Assistant vaginally at the same time.

MFF612

In a missionary position, lift Your Partner's legs high and penetrate her deeply. Both you and Your Assistant licks and sucks on her toes to make her wiggle on your cock.

MFF613

While lying down, have Your Partner straddle you facing your feet. As she grinds her pussy on you (with or without penetration), anally stimulate her with a lubed finger/thumb. Your Assistant sensually spanks her for added sensation.

MFF614

Orally pleasure Your Partner's anus in a position of your choice. Your Assistant orally pleasures her clitoris at the same time.

MFF615

While Your Partner lies between Your Assistant's legs missionary style, both kissing passionately, pleasure her with a minute of vigorous rear-entry intercourse. Pull her hair while Your Assistant holds her tight.

MFF616

Describe in detail a BDSM activity for Your Partner and Your Assistant to perform for your erotic amusement.

MFF621

Roleplaying as a strict Master, sternly command your Love Slaves to perform and service one of your desires.

MFF622

Laying down so your head is hanging over an accessible edge (bed, table, sofa, etc.), orally pleasure Your Partner's pussy. At the same time, Your Assistant uses a strap-on for missionary anal intercourse.

MFF623

Insert a lubed buttplug into Your Partner's anus and stimulate her with a dildo while she orally pleasures you. Your Assistant sensually spanks any available ass cheeks.

MFF624

Attempt to give both Your Partner and Your Assistant a simultaneous G-Spot orgasm using your fingers (palm on clitoris, two/three fingers inserted, quick fluttering motion, strong pressure). Try to make both of them squirt.

MFF625

Using two suction cup dildos stuck to the floor, both Your Partner and Your Assistant squat on them, facing each other so they can lick and suck on your cock together while thrusting in unison.

MFF626

Using a strapless strap-on or double dildo, enjoy threeway doggie-style anal intercourse. Your Partner's choice of orientation.

MFF631

Both you and Your Assistant erotically and passionately nibble and bite sensitive erogenous zones on Your Partner's body. Make her ache for you in a good way.

MFF632

Describe in detail an extreme BDSM scenario/fantasy involving all three of you. Set the stage and let Your Partner and Your Assistant add to the story in turn.

MFF633

Insert a lubed buttplug into Your Partner's anus and stimulate her with a dildo while you orally pleasure her clitoris. Your Assistant sucks on her tits at the same time.

MFF634

Using a double-ended dildo, Your Partner and Your Assistant enjoy mutual intercourse in a position of your choice. Choose one of them to perform fellatio on you or receive anal intercourse from you at the same time.

MFF635

Pleasure Your Partner orally while also stimulating her anally with a lubed finger. Your Assistant offers her tits for licking and sucking.

MFF636

Using a double-ended anal dildo or silicone beads, both you and Your Partner get on all fours for a little "cheek to cheek" action. At the same time, Your Assistant uses a vibrator to stimulate either or both of you.

MFF641

Your choice of Nasty, Kinky or Taboo foreplay activity for Your Partner and Your Assistant to perform for you – surprise them with your wild side.

MFF642

Have Your Partner lay on her back, legs raised. Use a dildo to pleasure her vaginally while Your Assistant squats over her mouth for oral pleasuring. At the same time, both kiss, lick and suck on Your Partner's toes.

MFF643

Creatively use one or more double-ended dildos involving all three of you in some way.

MFF644

Perform anal intercourse in a position of Your Partner's choice. At the same time, Your Assistant uses a vibrator to stimulate either or both of you.

MFF645

Drip hot wax on both Your Partner and Your Assistant (breasts, thighs or buttocks) while they lay next to each other.

MFF646

While Your Partner and Your Assistant kiss, apply nipple clamps (or clothes pegs) to their nipples. Remove when one of them breaks their kiss.

MFF651

Your Assistant allows Your Partner to masturbate her with the largest, most realistic dildo available in a position of her choice. Position yourself to receive oral pleasuring at the same time.

MFF652

Both you and Your Partner pleasure yourself with an anal dildo or butt plug while Your Assistant watches, stroking herself.

MFF653

Use an implement of your choice to erotically spank Your Partner's bare ass until it radiates a sensual heat. Let Your Assistant caress and stroke it between smacks.

MFF654

With Your Partner wearing a strap-on, position Your Assistant to experience double penetration.

MFF655

Stimulate Your Partner and Your Assistant, each with a different buttplug or dildo at the same time.

MFF656

Both you and Your Assistant bend over and allow Your Partner to insert lubricated buttplugs (one for each including herself) – remove only when you are both finished playing or other activities require.

MFF661

With Your Partner propped in a mostly upside-down position, orally pleasure her pussy. Your Assistant helps hold her up while giving her a rim-job

MFF662

Using one or more strapless strap-ons or suction cup dildos, your choice of sex position involving all three of you engaging in oral and/or anal/vaginal intercourse at the same time.

MFF663

While you lay on your back, have Your Partner or Your Assistant squat on cock while the other squats over your mouth. Both of them hold still kissing each other while you lick and thrust to pleasure them.

MFF664

Orally pleasure Your Partner's anus in a missionary position, legs spread wide. While holding her legs for balance, Your Assistant squats over her face so she can lick and suck pussy at the same time.

MFF665

Use one finger (and lube) to pleasure Your Partner anally. Use your thumb or fingers from your other hand to stimulate her vaginally. She pleasures Your Assistant in a similar way.

MFF666

STOP the Foreplay and START the Sex Play.

Male Female Male

Foreplay Activities

Male Female Male

Level 1 - Warm & Loving

MFM111

Both you and Your Assistant give feather-light kisses along Your Partner's neck and jawline. Breathe softly next to her ear to make her shiver with delight.

MFM112

Massage Your Partner's head with the tips of your fingers. Stroke her hair. She follows your lead to massage Your Assistant's head in the same way.

MFM113

Sit opposite and facing each other. Place a hand on each other's chest, close your eyes and synchronize breathing slowly.

MFM114

Kiss and lick Your Partner's wrist, inner arm and elbow. Your Assistant does the same on her other arm.

MFM115

Both you and Your Assistant spider Walk your fingers delicately over parts of Your Partner's exposed body. Arouse her with a slow, light tickling and tapping motion.

MFM116

From a book of fantasies or erotic letters, read a random one out loud to Your Partner while she kisses Your Assistant.

MFM121

Describe in detail a new erotic adventure involving the three of you. Include elements of the love play you'll enjoy together.

MFM122

Standing, hug and caress Your Partner from behind. Your Assistant kneels in front and caresses her lower region.

MFM123

Kiss and nibble along Your Partner's neck and shoulder while Your Assistant does the same from behind.

MFM124

Kiss and lightly lick Your Partner's hand, palm and fingers. Choose her non-dominant hand. She matches your actions on Your Assistant's hand.

MFM125

Find a how-to article on a sex technique or activity that you have not yet experienced and read it together.

MFM126

While sensually kissing Your Partner, allow Your Assistant to tickle both of you with a feather (face, lips, ears and neck).

MFM131

Both you and Your Assistant delicately stroke each of Your Partner's hands and fingers with your fingertips. Swirl and circle as you explore and tickle every nerve to attention.

MFM132

While Your Partner and Your Assistant kiss, apply cologne to a few areas of your body where you desire extra attention.

MFM133

Lovingly embrace Your Partner and Your Assistant. Hug, caress and tenderly kiss each other.

MFM134

Place soft, delicate kisses all over Your Partner's face - cheek, lips, nose, forehead, temples, chin. End with a tender,

sensuous kiss. Your Assistant then does the same.

MFM135

Both you and Your Assistant lick Your Partner's ear lobes and sensitive regions on her neck. Behind the ears and back of her neck are very sensitive. Whisper something deliciously sensual, loving or erotic.

MFM136

Describe in detail a unique, novel or exotic place to make love. Include activities you would like to experience.

MFM141

Gently kiss and lick Your Partner's inner arm – wrist to elbow. Your Assistant does the same for her other arm.

MFM142

Delicately lick around one of Your Partner's ears. Your Assistant does the same on the other one. Hot breaths in her ear will give her delightful shivers of pleasure.

MFM143

While Your Partner and Your Assistant kiss, do something to set the mood. Play soft music, light a candle, pour a glass of wine, burn some incense, apply cologne, etc.

MFM144

Dance embraced with Your Partner and Your Assistant to one slow song. Kiss each of them lovingly when it ends.

MFM145

Stand still and allow Your Partner and Your Assistant to both caress and stroke your body.

MFM146

All browse a sex store website of your choice. Discuss the various products and how you would like to use any in your love play.

MFM151

Both you and Your Assistant erotically tickle any of Your Partner's exposed erogenous zones. Creatively use your fingers, a feather, a soft paintbrush or your tongues.

MFM152

Find an erotic edible and feed it to Your Partner and Your Assistant sensually. Fruit, syrup, chocolate, oysters, liquor, etc. Encourage them to savor the treats at the same time.

MFM153

Standing together, both you and Your Assistant softly stroke and caress Your Partner's entire body. Lightly squeeze parts of her body that you find delightful.

MFM154

Make up a fantasy scenario or roleplaying adventure for Your Partner and Your Assistant that they might perform for your erotic pleasure.

MFM155

All three of you close your eyes. Delicately caress Your Partner's and Your Assistant's faces each with one hand. Trace your fingertips as lightly as you can as you explore every detail.

MFM156

Remove one item of clothing erotically then remove one item of clothing from both Your Partner and Your Assistant.

MFM161

Massage Your Partner's toes one at a time. Your Assistant does the same starting with the other foot.

MFM162

Both you and Your Assistant alternate experimenting with different types of kisses and kissing sensations with Your Partner - (upside down, open mouth, closed mouth, sideways, corner, firm, soft).

MFM163

Tenderly kiss Your Partner with affection. Hold and caress her face with both hands. Your Assistant follows, kissing her with the same affection.

MFM164

Browse through a book with advanced or acrobatic sex positions together. Choose one of them for Your Partner and Your Assistant to try out (simulate the sex play for now).

MFM165

All browse an erotic book, magazine or website with Your Partner (her choice). Discuss pictures or images that appeal to each of you.

MFM166

Both you and Your Assistant give Your Partner a brief but relaxing massage the way she likes it.

Male Female Male

Level 2 - Sensual Sensations

MFM211

Both you and Your Assistant massage and fondle any part of Your Partner's body still clothed - do not touch any skin.

MFM212

With Your Partner and Your Assistant positioned so their feet are barely touching, massage their feet and each toe with an oil or lube. They then stroke their feet together.

MFM213

Both you and Your Assistant each use a piece of fur, silk or satin to smoothly caress any/all exposed parts of Your Partner's body.

MFM214

Both you and Your Assistant each lick, suck and lightly bite one of Your Partner's nipples at the same time. Blow on or suck in air around them to create warm and cool sensations.

MFM215

Creatively use an ice cube to perk up sensitive regions on Your Partner's body. Your Assistant follows each cold shock with a warm kiss or lick.

MFM216

Both you and Your Assistant each gently suck one of Your Partner's nipples into your mouth at the same time. Add a vibrating sensation by humming or use a vibrator on your cheek.

MFM221

Both you and Your Assistant stroke and caress Your Partner's legs and inner thighs.

MFM222

Both you and Your Assistant sensually lick exposed regions of Your Partner's body. Search out rarely explored erogenous zones.

MFM223

Use a flavored lube or syrup on any rarely licked erogenous zone and entice both Your Partner and Your Assistant to lick it off together.

MFM224

Instruct Your Assistant to creatively stimulate Your Partner any way you desire.

MFM225

Slowly and sensually lick and suck Your Partner's thumb. Your Assistant does the same for her other thumb. Stimulate every nerve with your twirling tongues.

MFM226

Fondle, rub and massage both Your Partner's pussy and Your Assistant's cock at the same time (through their clothing if they are still wearing any).

MFM231

While Your Partner and Your Assistant stand together and kiss, kneel next to them and fondle, rub and massage their buttocks.

MFM232

Enjoy a threeway kiss with Your Partner and Your Assistant.

MFM233

Use a vibrator to delicately stimulate Your Partner's nipples. She repeats your technique on Your Assistant's nipples.

MFM234

Kneeling while Your Partner stands, kiss and lick her belly, hips and thighs. Kneed her buttocks gently. Your Assistant stands behind her and fondles her breasts.

MFM235

Using massage oil, both you and Your Assistant gently each massage one of Your Partner's breasts. Circle but do not touch her nipples.

MFM236

Apply a flavored lube to Your Partner's nipples. Tweak and tantalize them with your fingertips, then let Your Assistant lick each nipple clean.

MFM241

Both you and Your Assistant each lick the soft, sensitive skin behind Your Partner's knees at the same time.

MFM242

Put an edible topping or liquor in Your Partner's navel, then both you and Your Assistant lick it out together.

MFM243

Whisper in Your Partner's ear how you want to pleasure her with your hot tongue. Your Assistant does the same.

MFM244

Kiss, lick and suck each finger of Your Partner's non-dominant hand. Apply a flavored lube or syrup if you desire. She matches your actions on Your Assistant's hand.

MFM245

Both you and Your Assistant stroke and caress Your Partner's breasts. Lightly circle her nipples.

MFM246

Have Your Partner remove her bra and put on a silky top. Then, both you and Your Assistant caress her breasts and circle her nipples through the fabric.

MFM251

Both you and Your Assistant expose and lightly lick Your Partner's lower back and side. Lightly bite and nibble her buttocks.

MFM252

Creatively use a string of pearls or round beads to stimulate Your Partner in various ways. Repeat for Your Assistant.

MFM253

Both you and Your Assistant perform an erotic dance together while each removing an item of clothing. Play appropriate music if desired.

MFM254

Use an artist brush dipped in flavored lube to stimulate Your Partner's nipples. Apply delicate flicks and twirls. Your Assistant gets to lick them clean.

MFM255

Both you and Your Assistant caress and lightly stroke any/all exposed parts of Your Partner's body.

MFM256

Have Your Partner get in any position you desire, expose her butt to allow both you and Your Assistant to administer a sensual spanking.

MFM261

Lightly drag your fingernails down Your Partner's back, chest and tummy, legs or arms – your choice. Do the same for Your Assistant.

MFM262

Both you and Your Assistant whisper in Your Partner's ear how horny you are and how badly you want your fingers and tongue deep inside her. Let her feel your packages and imagine what else you have planned for her.

MFM263

With Your Partner and Your Assistant positioned so their feet are barely touching, use a vibrator to stimulate their toes and soles of their feet.

MFM264

While you and Your Assistant both sit still, allow Your Partner to caress your bodies with only her breasts. Encourage her to brush sensitive regions with just her nipples.

MFM265

While Your Partner and Your Assistant kiss, use a soft artist or make-up brush to tickle and stimulate exposed erogenous zones on their bodies.

MFM266

Both you and Your Assistant each find and use two different items each with an exciting texture to stimulate/sensitize an exposed region of Your Partner's body (soft, cold, rough, squishy, etc.).

Male Female Male

Level 3 - Intimate Intentions

MFM311

Watch one scene of an explicit video with Your Partner and Your Assistant. You choose the DVD or switch over to a free online porn site.

MFM312

Suck one of Your Partner's fingers while manually pleasuring her pussy (do not remove any clothing). Your Assistant pleasures you in a similar way.

MFM313

Dab some ice cream or smear a popsicle on your nipples and entice both Your Partner and Your Assistant to lick them clean.

MFM314

Both you and Your Assistant massage a different symmetrical part of Your Partner's body (legs, arms, breasts, shoulders, etc.). Experiment with a different type of technique.

MFM315

Have Your Partner lay on her stomach. Both you and Your Assistant apply massage oil to her back and provide her a creative, erotic massage while kissing each other.

MFM316

Both you and Your Assistant each kiss and lick one of Your Partner's breasts at the same time – all over except her nipples.

MFM321

Look through an explicit pictorial magazine or book together. Discuss what you each consider erotic and arousing.

MFM322

Close your eyes while each of you sucks and licks the other person's middle finger. Use your tongues to swirl and stroke them.

MFM323

Remove any clothing necessary for Your Partner and Your Assistant to teasingly lick your inner thighs. Lay back and enjoy their tickling tongues.

MFM324

Describe in detail how you would like to include a pleasuring accessory of your choice in a new sex position or activity involving Your Partner and Your Assistant.

MFM325

Stroke both Your Partner's and Your Assistant's tail bone and between their butt cheeks. Use your fingers, tongue, feather, spoon, string of beads, etc. - alternate as required to stimulate both of them equally.

MFM326

Get in a position for Your Partner and Your Assistant to lick and suck your cock at the same time.

MFM331

Standing, fondle both Your Partner's pussy and Your Assistant's cock while you alternate kissing them passionately.

MFM332

Both you and Your Assistant expose and blow "raspberries" on Your Partner's butt cheeks.

MFM333

Remove one item of clothing from Your Partner and Your Assistant. Choose a slow song for them to dance to while holding each other close.

MFM334

Both you and Your Assistant each caress one of Your Partner's bare feet with your bare feet.

MFM335

While Your Partner and Your Assistant kiss, seductively read a short erotic passage or a dirty letter. Choose one that is very explicit and detailed.

MFM336

Use a digital camera and play erotic photographer with Your Partner and Your Assistant as your models. View them together and delete afterward (unless you really like one to print).

MFM341

Have Your Partner and Your Assistant simulate a sex act of your choice. Encourage them to thrust and grind against each other as vigorously as you want. Include a sex toy as a prop if desired.

MFM342

Describe in detail a pleasuring accessory you have in mind for Your Partner and Your Assistant and how you would like it used in your sex play.

MFM343

Find and creatively use a non-sexual object to pleasure both Your Partner and Your Assistant (not necessarily at the same time).

MFM344

With one hand cupping Your Partner's pussy (palm pressing on clitoris) and the other cupping Your Assistant's ass, gently insert one lubed finger each. Once comfortable, have them both pulse their PC muscles as tightly and quickly as possible for one minute.

MFM345

Dip a finger into Your Partner's vagina and let Your Assistant savor her taste. He then does the same for you.

MFM346

Use an ice cube to cool, then your lips and tongue to heat an exposed erogenous zone on Your Partner's body. Your Assistant does the same.

MFM351

Using a flavored lube, massage each of Your Partner's toes on one foot, then lick and suck them clean. Your Assistant does the same for the other foot at the same time.

MFM352

In turn, starting with Your Assistant, express audible sounds of passion leading up to a fake orgasm. Each rate the most convincing.

MFM353

Both you and Your Assistant warm your mouth with a hot liquid (water, coffee, tea) swallow then kiss or lightly suck on one of Your Partner's exposed erogenous zones.

MFM354

Use a vibrator to stimulate Your Partner's neck, chest and nipples while Your Assistant nuzzles her pussy.

MFM355

Get into a threeway 69 position with Your Partner and Your Assistant and nuzzle each other. Hum, purr or moan for an added thrill.

MFM356

Pretend you're a porn director/star. Get Your Partner and Your Assistant into a novel, creative position to perform/simulate a sex act. Detail how you want the scene to play out. Provide props if desired.

MFM361

Tell a dirty, explicitly erotic story involving two sexy elements provided by Your Partner and Your Assistant. Be as graphic as possible.

MFM362

Sit, legs spread, so Your Partner can grind her pussy on one of your thighs while facing away from you. Fondle her breasts as she orally pleasures Your Assistant.

MFM363

While Your Partner and Your Assistant stand together kissing and grinding on each other's thigh, kneel next to them and fondle, rub and massage their buttocks.

MFM364

Standing, mutually grope and fondle each other (under or over clothing).

MFM365

Remove any clothing necessary for Your Partner and Your Assistant to teasingly lick your belly and above your crotch. Lay back and enjoy their tickling tongues.

MFM366

Both you and Your Assistant hold a piece of frozen fruit (strawberry, mango, pineapple) in your mouth while you alternate kissing Your Partner.

Male Female Male

Level 4 - Explicit & Erotic Passion

MFM411

Sensuously demonstrate cunnilingus using an edible object (mango, peach, chocolate on Your Partner's fingers, etc.) – think juicy and messy. At the same time, Your Assistant sensuously demonstrates fellatio using a sex toy or edible object.

MFM412

Pleasure Your Partner's entire pussy orally. Your Assistant orally pleasures her nipple. Both use creative licking and sucking techniques.

MFM413

Stimulate Your Partner with a sex toy that Your Assistant chooses. (Visual stimulation counts)

MFM414

Hold a large dildo while Your Partner and Your Assistant demonstrate how they would perform a foot-job together. Use lube if desired.

MFM415

Expose, then pinch, tweak and twiddle your nipples. Use a flavored lube if desired. Then have Your Partner and Your Assistant each suck and bite them as hard as you like.

MFM416

Use a piece of soft, juicy, sticky fruit to tickle Your Partner's clitoris then have Your Assistant lick it clean. Repeat as often as you want.

MFM421

Get into a position that enables you to simultaneously use two vibrators to tease both Your Partner's pussy and Your Assistant's genitals.

MFM422

Creatively stimulate Your Partner and Your Assistant, each with a different vibrator at the same time.

MFM423

Apply some lube to the head of your cock. In a position of your choice, use it to stroke Your Partner's vaginal lips and clitoris – no penetration allowed. Repeat for Your Assistant.

MFM424

In a missionary or doggie position, penetrate Your Partner's vagina once as slowly and deeply as you can. Grind against her. Your Assistant then does the same.

MFM425

Lightly squeeze and tug Your Partner's vaginal lips. Massage them delicately with moist fingertips. At the same time, Your Assistant uses lubed fingers to stimulate her nipples.

MFM426

Both you and Your Assistant kiss and lick any exposed erogenous zone you desire on Your Partner's body.

MFM431

Using lube and two fingers, massage Your Partner's pussy. Then penetrate her vagina with smooth, gliding strokes. Use your other hand to mirror your actions for Your Assistant's anal pleasure.

MFM432

Insert a dildo of Your Partner's choice into her vagina while Your Assistant licks her clitoris. Move the dildo in slow, smooth strokes.

MFM433

While Your Assistant tickles her tummy with his tongue, lightly tug small amounts of pubic hair all around Your Partner's pussy. If she is shaved, stroke her mound and lips softly.

MFM434

Both you and Your Assistant erotically and passionately nibble and bite sensitive erogenous zones on Your Partner's body. Make her ache for you in a good way.

MFM435

Both you and Your Assistant stand beside Your Partner in front of a mirror and watch each other as you stroke and fondle her body intimately.

MFM436

In a missionary position, insert just the head of your cock into Your Partner's vagina. Allow Your Assistant to use his hand to wiggle it back and forth and around.

MFM441

Use broad tongue strokes to lick slowly up and down Your Partner's pussy. Use the underside of your tongue on her clitoris. Your Assistant follows and does the same.

MFM442

Pleasure Your Partner orally while Your Assistant kisses her passionately and plays with her tits.

MFM443

With Your Partner laying on her back, legs spread wide, both you and Your Assistant delicately flutter your tongues up, down and around her pussy and inner thigh like a flickering flame always moving.

MFM444

Your Partner and Your Assistant both kneel doggie style, side by side, and look into each other's eyes while each sucking one finger of the other. Kneel behind them and manually pleasure them at the same time.

MFM445

Apply hot (slow) and cool (faster) breaths on Your Partner's clitoris. Moisten with your tongue and suck in air for more cooling sensations. Your Assistant does the same on both her nipples.

MFM446

Insert one or two fingers in Your Partner's vagina (moisten if necessary) and gently massage left, right, up, down and all around – no thrusting. Your Assistant fondles and strokes your penis at the same time.

MFM451

In a missionary position (you on top push up style), insert just the head of your cock into Your Partner's vagina. Allow Your Assistant to sensually spank your ass. Resist plunging deeper as long as you can.

MFM452

Apply lube to everyone's nipples. Both you and Your Assistant position yourself so Your Partner can rub, circle and flick hers on yours. Finish with her flicking her nipples across both of your lips.

MFM453

Use an artist brush dipped in lube to delicately stimulate Your Partner's clitoris. Flick up, down and across - swirl in circles and zigzags. Your Assistant uses another brush to stimulate her nipples in a similar way at the same time.

MFM454

Using a suction cup dildo (or one you hold) and your hard cock, both Your Partner and Your Assistant thrust and grind together while kissing each other.

MFM455

Find and creatively use a non-sexual object to pleasure both Your Partner and Your Assistant (not necessarily at the same time).

MFM456

With Your Partner in a missionary position, legs spread wide, slide your penis over her pussy slowly and gently at first, then with more pressure and speed. Your Assistant strokes you both from behind.

MFM461

Apply massage oil to Your Partner's breasts. Both you and Your Assistant allow her to stimulate any of your exposed erogenous zones she desires to stimulate herself.

MFM462

Nibble and suck on Your Partner's vaginal lips. Twirl your tongue inside her vagina – wiggle it in as deep as you can. Your Assistant follows doing the same.

MFM463

Describe in detail a raunchy S/M or bondage scenario involving Your Partner and Your Assistant.

MFM464

Use an ice cube to cool followed by Your Assistant's lips and tongue to heat Your Partner's nipples and clitoris. Stimulate various erogenous zones with hot and cold sensations.

MFM465

Delicately massage Your Partner's clitoris and vaginal lips with a flavored lube. Your Assistant follows with sensual licking and sucking.

MFM466

Both Your Partner and Your Assistant lovingly kiss your penis together and use it to stroke their lips, cheek and neck.

Male Female Male

Level 5 - Sizzling, Sexual Stimulation

MFM511

Insert one lubed finger in Your Partner's anus and gently massage left, right, up, down and all around – no thrusting. Your Assistant does the same for you.

MFM512

Sit and have Your Partner straddle you (her back to your chest). Play with her nipples while Your Assistant orally pleasures both of you.

MFM513

Use a dildo or buttplug and orally pleasure Your Partner at the same time while she sucks Your Assistant's cock at the same time.

MFM514

While Your Partner orally pleasures Your Assistant, nibble and bite her buttocks while playing with her pussy.

MFM515

All three remove all clothing on your upper bodies. Apply massage oil to your chests and bellies. Slither and slide against each other to one song.

MFM516

Use an artist brush and lube to stimulate Your Partner's anus. Tickle it as Your Assistant plays with her clitoris or nipples.

MFM521

With Your Partner standing, facing a wall, press hard against her, kissing her neck and fingering her pussy. Your Assistant joins from the rear stimulating you in a similar way.

MFM522

Gently suck Your Partner's clitoris in your mouth and create different vibrating sensations by humming, moaning, growling, etc. Your Partner follows your lead pleasuring Your Assistant in a similar way.

MFM523

Use the tip of a vibrator to tickle Your Partner's perineum and anus – no penetration. At the same time, Your Assistant pleasures her pussy or nipples any way he desires.

MFM524

With Your Partner laying on her back, straddle her face so she can orally pleasure you. Your Assistant uses a vibrator, dildo, buttplug or his cock to pleasure her at the same time.

MFM525

Experiment with a new, creative "scissoring" position for Your Partner and Your Assistant that allows you to stimulate both of them with a vibrator as they grind and thrust together.

MFM526

While Your Partner sits, both you and Your Assistant perform an erotic lap dance for her to one song of your choice. Seductively rub and grind yourselves on her. Seductively entice her to caress and fondle your assets.

MFM531

Gently suck and nibble on Your Partner's vaginal lips (labia) – one side then the other. Massage them with your lips and tongue. Your Assistant offers his nipples for Your Partner to lick, suck and bite.

MFM532

With Your Partner laying on her back, legs raised and spread wide, watch closely as you ever so slowly insert a dildo. Your Assistant holds a mirror so she can see how her pussy engulfs the fake cock. Repeat with your real cock.

MFM533

Use a digital camera with a zoom lens to take very close-up and intimate shots of Your Partner and Your Assistant in various explicit poses. Select one to print and frame.

MFM534

While Your Partner uses her fingers to expose her clitoris for you, use only the soft underside of your tongue to delicately caress and stroke it. Your Assistant then does the same.

MFM535

While Your Partner stands, kneel behind her. Nibble and bite her buttocks while stroking her thighs. Your Assistant kneels in front and orally pleasures her.

MFM536

Select two sex toys for Your Partner and Your Assistant to play Show and Tell. In turn, they are to demonstrate their self-pleasuring technique, eyes closed, while describing the sensations.

MFM541

Using lube, insert your two middle fingers in Your Partner's vagina with palm on her clitoris. Flutter your fingers up and down quickly. Trigger a G-Spot orgasm or come close. Your Assistant licks, sucks and lightly bites her nipples at the same time.

MFM542

With Your Partner using a realistic dildo or strap-on as a fake cock, watch as Your Assistant demonstrates his best blowjob technique in a position of your choice.

MFM543

Have Your Partner put on some "old" underwear. Let Your Assistant rip them off her (pre-cut the elastic band if necessary) so you can ravish her orally.

MFM544

In a doggie position, penetrate Your Partner, grab a handful of her hair and pull her head back as you thrust vigorously for 10–20 seconds. She sucks on Your Assistant's cock at the same time.

MFM545

Sitting, legs spread, hold a dildo on each thigh. Your Partner and Your Assistant both mount one of the toys and grind against you while kissing and each other and stroking you at the same time.

MFM546

Get into a threeway 69 position and pleasure each other orally. Your Partner gets to choose orientation.

MFM551

Lube and pleasure Your Partner with a dildo or vibrator of her choice. Allow her to guide your hand or verbally coach you on technique. Do the same for Your Assistant.

MFM552

Pleasure Your Partner with the thinnest dildo or smallest vibrator available. Your Assistant sucks on her nipples at the same time.

MFM553

Pleasure Your Partner with a dildo while you lick her clitoris and Your Assistant plays with her nipples.

MFM554

While lying down, have Your Partner straddle you facing your feet. As she grinds on your penis (with or without penetration), Your Assistant sensually slaps her ass cheeks.

MFM555

Research and discuss the activities and accessories for a fetish of your choice.

MFM556

Laying down so your head is hanging over an accessible edge (bed, table, sofa, etc.), orally pleasure Your Partner's pussy. At the same time, Your Assistant orally pleasures you.

MFM561

While Your Partner and Your Assistant stroke each other, pleasure yourself with a glass/acrylic/metal dildo or buttplug for their visual pleasure. Be as lewd as you dare.

MFM562

With Your Partner standing, kneel before her and orally pleasure her pussy. Your Assistant joins doggie style using his hands to caress you any way he desires.

MFM563

Spread Your Partner's butt cheeks wide and tickle her perineum and anus with a feather or piece of silky material. Your Assistant stimulates you in a similar way.

MFM564

Use your fingers and lube to pleasure Your Partner anyway you desire. Stimulate Your Assistant using your other hand in a similar way at the same time.

MFM565

Using a firm, pointed tongue, lick Your Partner's perineum using circles, swirls and zigzag strokes. Your Assistant sucks on her nipples at the same time.

MFM566

Get into a threeway '69' position and give each other a rim-job.

Male Female Male

Level 6 - Wild, Nasty, Kinky, Taboo

MFM611

Using your fingers or any other sex toys of your choice, stimulate Your Assistant anally and Your Partner vaginally at the same time.

MFM612

In a missionary position, lift Your Partner's legs high and penetrate her deeply. Both you and Your Assistant lick and suck on her toes to make her wiggle on your cock.

MFM613

While lying down, have Your Partner straddle you facing your feet. As she grinds her pussy on you (with or without penetration), anally stimulate her with a lubed finger/thumb. Your Assistant sensually spanks her for added sensation.

MFM614

Orally pleasure Your Partner's anus in a position of your choice. Your Assistant orally pleasures her clitoris at the same time.

MFM615

While Your Partner lies between Your Assistant's legs missionary style, both kissing passionately, pleasure her with a minute of vigorous rear-entry intercourse. Pull her hair while Your Assistant holds her tight.

MFM616

Describe in detail a BDSM activity for Your Partner and Your Assistant to perform for your erotic amusement.

MFM621

Roleplaying as a strict Master, sternly command your Love Slaves to perform and service one of your desires.

MFM622

Laying down so your head is hanging over an accessible edge (bed, table, sofa, etc.), orally pleasure Your Partner's pussy. At the same time, Your Assistant pleasures you with anal intercourse.

MFM623

Insert a lubed buttplug into Your Partner's anus and stimulate her with a dildo while she orally pleasures you. Your Assistant sensually spanks any available ass cheeks.

MFM624

While Your Assistant lays on his back, Your Partner straddles his cock. You squat over his mouth so your testicles can be licked. While Your Partner rides him, she orally pleasures your cock at the same time.

MFM625

Using two suction cup dildos stuck to the floor, both Your Partner and Your Assistant squat on them, facing each other so they can lick and suck on your cock together while thrusting in unison.

MFM626

Enjoy threeway doggie-style anal intercourse. Your Partner's choice of orientation (use a strapless strap-on if desired).

MFM631

Insert a lubed buttplug in both Your Partner and Your Assistant. Then sit, legs spread, so they can both straddle one of your thighs at the same time while facing you. Encourage them to grind hard as you lick, suck and nibble on their nipples.

MFM632

Describe in detail an extreme BDSM scenario/fantasy involving all three of you. Set the stage and let Your Partner and Your Assistant add to the story in turn.

MFM633

Insert a lubed buttplug into Your Partner's anus and stimulate her with a dildo while you orally pleasure her clitoris. Your Assistant sucks on her tits at the same time.

MFM634

Your Partner and Your Assistant enjoy intercourse in a position of your choice. Choose one of them to perform fellatio on you or receive anal intercourse from you at the same time.

MFM635

Pleasure Your Partner orally while also stimulating her anally with a lubed finger. Your Assistant offers her his cock for licking and sucking.

MFM636

Using a double-ended anal dildo or silicone beads, both you and Your Partner get on all fours for a little "cheek to cheek" action. At the same time, Your Assistant uses a vibrator to stimulate either or both of you.

MFM641

Your choice of Nasty, Kinky or Taboo foreplay activity for Your Partner and Your Assistant to perform for you – surprise them with your wild side.

MFM642

Have Your Partner lay on her back, legs raised. Use a dildo to pleasure her vaginally while Your Assistant squats over her mouth for oral pleasuring. At the same time, both kiss, lick and suck on Your Partner's toes.

MFM643

Creatively use one or more double-ended dildos involving all three of you in some way.

MFM644

Perform anal intercourse in a position of Your Partner's choice. At the same time, Your Assistant uses a vibrator to stimulate either or both of you.

MFM645

Your Partner attempts to take both yours and Your Assistant's cocks in her mouth at the same time.

MFM646

While Your Partner and Your Assistant kiss, apply nipple clamps (or clothes pegs) to their nipples. Remove when one of them breaks their kiss.

MFM651

Your Partner allows Your Assistant to masturbate her with the largest, most realistic dildo available in a position of her choice. Position yourself to receive oral pleasuring at the same time.

MFM652

Both you and Your Assistant pleasure yourself with an anal dildo or buttplug while Your Partner watches, stroking herself.

MFM653

Use an implement of your choice to erotically spank Your Partner's bare ass until it radiates a sensual heat. Let Your Assistant caress and stroke it between smacks.

MFM654

In a position of her choice, attempt double penetration with Your Partner and Your Assistant. Allow her to enjoy slow, sensual, simultaneous vaginal and anal intercourse for a minute or two.

MFM655

Stimulate Your Partner and Your Assistant each with a different buttplug or dildo at the same time.

MFM656

Both you and Your Assistant bend over and allow Your Partner to insert lubricated buttplugs (one for each including herself) – remove only when you are both finished playing or other activities require.

MFM661

With Your Partner propped in a mostly upside-down position, orally pleasure her pussy. Your Assistant helps hold her up while giving her a rim-job.

MFM662

Your choice of sex position involving all three of you engaging in oral and/or anal/vaginal intercourse at the same time using any sex toys you desire.

MFM663

While you lay on your back, have Your Partner or Your Assistant squat on cock while the other squats over your mouth. Both of them hold still kissing each other while you lick and thrust to pleasure them.

MFM664

Orally pleasure Your Assistant's anus in a missionary position, legs spread wide. While holding his legs for balance, Your Assistant squats over his face so he can lick and suck pussy at the same time.

MFM665

Use one finger (and lube) to pleasure Your Partner anally. Use your thumb or fingers from your other hand to stimulate her vaginally. She manually pleasures Your Assistant in a similar way.

MFM666

STOP the Foreplay and START the Sex Play.

Male Male Female

Foreplay Activities

Male Male Female

Level 1 - Warm & Loving

MMF111

From a book of fantasies or erotic letters, read a random one out loud to Your Partner while he kisses Your Assistant.

MMF112

While sensually kissing Your Partner, allow Your Assistant to tickle both of you with a feather (face, lips, ears and neck).

MMF113

Kiss and nibble along Your Partner's neck and shoulder while Your Assistant does the same to you from behind.

MMF114

Standing, hug and caress Your Partner from behind. Your Assistant kneels in front of him and strokes his lower region.

MMF115

Lovingly embrace Your Partner and Your Assistant. Hug, caress and tenderly kiss each other.

MMF116

Massage Your Partner's head with the tips of your fingers. He follows your lead to massage Your Assistant's head in the same way.

MMF121

Find a how-to article on a sex technique or activity that you have not yet experienced and read it together.

MMF122

Sit opposite and facing each other. Place a hand on each other's chest, close your eyes and synchronize breathing slowly.

MMF123

Delicately lick around one of Your Partner's ears. Your Assistant does the same on the other one. Hot breaths in his ear will give him delightful shivers of pleasure.

MMF124

Dance embraced with Your Partner and Your Assistant to one slow song. Kiss each of them lovingly when it ends.

MMF125

Kiss and lick Your Partner's wrist, inner arm and elbow. Your Assistant does the same on his other arm.

MMF126

While Your Partner and Your Assistant kiss, apply cologne to a few areas of your body where you desire extra attention.

MMF131

Describe in detail a unique, novel or exotic place to make love. Include activities you would like to experience.

MMF132

Both you and Your Assistant spider Walk your fingers delicately over parts of Your Partner's exposed body. Arouse him with a slow, light tickling and tapping motion.

MMF133

Both you and Your Assistant lick Your Partner's ear lobes and sensitive regions on his neck. Behind the ears and back of his neck are very sensitive. Whisper something deliciously sensual, loving or erotic.

MMF134

Describe in detail a new erotic adventure involving the three of you. Include elements of the love play you'll enjoy together.

MMF135

Browse an erotic book or magazine with Your Partner (his choice). Discuss pictures or images that appeal to each of you.

MMF136

Massage Your Partner's toes one at a time. Your Assistant does the same starting with the other foot.

MMF141

Tenderly kiss Your Partner with affection. Hold and caress his face with both hands. Then kiss Your Assistant with the same affection.

MMF142

Stand still and allow Your Partner and Your Assistant to both caress and stroke your body.

MMF143

Kiss and lightly lick Your Partner's hand, palm and fingers. Choose his non-dominant hand. He matches your actions on Your Assistant's hand.

MMF144

Place soft, delicate kisses all over Your Partner's face - cheek, lips, nose, forehead, temples, chin. End with a tender, sensuous kiss. Repeat for Your Assistant.

MMF145

Experiment with different types of kisses and kissing sensations - (upside down, open mouth, closed mouth, sideways, corner, firm, soft). Alternate between Your Partner and Your Assistant.

MMF146

Gently kiss and lick Your Partner's inner arm – wrist to elbow. Your Assistant does the same for his other arm.

MMF151

All three of you close your eyes. Delicately caress Your Partner's and Your Assistant's faces each with one hand. Trace your fingertips as lightly as you can as you explore every detail.

MMF152

While Your Partner and Your Assistant kiss, do something to set the mood. Put on some soft music, light a candle, pour a glass of wine, burn some incense, spray some cologne, etc.

MMF153

Both you and Your Assistant give Your Partner a brief but relaxing massage the way he likes it.

MMF154

Browse through a book with advanced or acrobatic sex positions together. Choose one of them for Your Partner and Your Assistant to try out (simulate the sex play for now).

MMF155

Find and view some erotic art together - use books or the internet. Discuss what you each like about it.

MMF156

Both you and Your Assistant erotically tickle any of Your Partner's exposed erogenous zones. Creatively use your fingers, a feather, a soft paintbrush or your tongues.

MMF161

Find an erotic edible and feed it to Your Partner and Your Assistant sensually. Fruit, syrup, chocolate, oysters, liquor, etc. Encourage them to savor the treats at the same time.

MMF162

Standing together, both you and Your Assistant softly stroke and caress Your Partner's entire body. Lightly squeeze parts of his body that you find delightful.

MMF163

Make up a fantasy scenario or roleplaying adventure for Your Partner and Your Assistant that they might perform for your erotic pleasure.

MMF164

Both you and Your Assistant massage a different symmetrical part of Your Partner's body (legs, arms, pecs, shoulders, etc.). Experiment with a different type of technique.

MMF165

Both you and Your Assistant delicately stroke each of Your Partner's hands and fingers with your fingertips. Swirl and circle as you explore and tickle every nerve to attention.

MMF166

Remove one item of clothing erotically then remove one item of clothing from both Your Partner and Your Assistant.

Male Male Female

Level 2 - Sensual Sensations

MMF211

Slowly and sensually lick and suck Your Partner's thumb. Your Assistant does the same for his other thumb. Stimulate every nerve with your twirling tongues.

MMF212

Have Your Partner get in any position you desire, expose his butt and allow both you and Your Assistant to administer a sensual spanking.

MMF213

With Your Partner and Your Assistant positioned so their feet are barely touching, use a vibrator to stimulate their toes and soles of their feet.

MMF214

Both you and Your Assistant expose and lightly lick Your Partner's lower back and side. Lightly bite and nibble his buttocks.

MMF215

Both you and Your Assistant each lick the soft, sensitive skin behind Your Partner's knees at the same time.

MMF216

Both you and Your Assistant whisper in Your Partner's ear how horny you are and what you want to do with his penis.

MMF221

Find and use an item with an interesting texture to stimulate/sensitize an exposed region of Your Partner's body. (soft, cold, rough, squishy, etc.) Then pleasure Your Assistant in a similar way.

MMF222

Enjoy a threeway kiss with Your Partner and Your Assistant.

MMF223

While Your Partner and Your Assistant kiss, use a soft artist or make-up brush to tickle and stimulate exposed erogenous zones on their bodies.

MMF224

Put an edible topping or liquor in your navel and entice Your Partner and Your Assistant to lick it out together.

MMF225

Kiss, lick and suck each finger of Your Partner's non-dominant hand. Apply a flavored lube or syrup if you desire. He matches your actions on Your Assistant's hand.

MMF226

Whisper in Your Partner's ear how you want to pleasure him with your hot, slick tongue. Do the same for Your Assistant.

MMF231

Both you and Your Assistant stroke and massage Your Partner's chest. Circle and flick his nipples lightly.

MMF232

Both you and Your Partner expose and lightly lick Your Assistant's lower back and side. Lightly bite and nibble his buttocks.

MMF233

Perform an erotic dance while removing an item of clothing. Play appropriate music if you desire.

MMF234

Creatively use something round and smooth to stimulate Your Partner in various ways. Repeat for Your Assistant.

MMF235

Use an artist brush dipped in flavored lube to stimulate Your Partner's nipples. Apply delicate flicks and twirls. Your Assistant gets to lick them clean.

MMF236

Drag your fingernails down Your Partner's back, chest and tummy, legs or arms - your choice. Do the same for Your Assistant.

MMF241

Both you and Your Assistant caress and lightly stroke any exposed part of Your Partner's body.

MMF242

Both you and Your Assistant massage and fondle any part of Your Partner's body still covered with clothing - do not touch any skin.

MMF243

Kneeling while Your Partner stands, kiss and lick his belly, hips and thighs. Kneed and massage his buttocks. Your Assistant stands behind him and fondles his chest.

MMF244

With Your Partner and Your Assistant positioned so their feet are barely touching, massage their feet and each toe with an oil or lube. They then stroke their feet together.

MMF245

All three hug and passionately kiss each other.

MMF246

Use a piece of fur, silk or satin to smoothly caress any/all exposed parts of Your Partner's body. Your Assistant watches and repeats your actions.

MMF251

Use a vibrator to delicately stimulate Your Partner's nipples. He repeats your technique on Your Assistant's nipples.

MMF252

Lick, suck and lightly bite Your Partner's nipples. Blow on or suck in air around them to create warm and cool sensations. Alternate with Your Assistant's nipples.

MMF253

Apply a flavored lube to Your Partner's nipples. Tweak and tantalize them with your fingertips then let Your Assistant lick each nipple clean.

MMF254

Creatively use an ice cube to perk up sensitive regions on Your Partner's body. Your Assistant follows each cold shock with a warm kiss or lick.

MMF255

Put on a tight top that shows off your chest. Entice Your Partner and Your Assistant to caress your chest and circle your nipples through the fabric.

MMF256

Rub and massage Your Partner's and Your Assistant's crotch at the same time (through their clothing if they are still wearing any).

MMF261

Both you and Your Assistant sensually lick exposed regions of Your Partner's body. Search out rarely explored erogenous zones.

MMF262

Based on the recommendation from Your Partner and Your Assistant, put on any item to look, feel, smell or taste even more sexy.

MMF263

Use a flavored lube or syrup on any rarely licked erogenous zone and entice both Your Partner and Your Assistant to lick it off together.

MMF264

Instruct Your Assistant to creatively stimulate Your Partner any way you desire.

MMF265

Pleasure yourself as visual stimulation for both Your Partner and Your Assistant. Take suggestions from them if desired.

MMF266

While Your Partner and Your Assistant stand together and kiss, kneel next to them and fondle, rub and massage their buttocks.

Male Male Female

Level 3 - Intimate Intentions

MMF311

While Your Partner and Your Assistant kiss, seductively read a short erotic passage or a dirty letter. Choose one that is very explicit and detailed.

MMF312

Both you and Your Assistant each select something sexy for Your Partner to wear (now and while making love later).

MMF313

Pretend you're a porn director/star. Get Your Partner and Your Assistant into a novel, creative position to receive or perform oral sex and detail how you want the scene to play out.

MMF314

Have Your Partner lay on his stomach. Both you and Your Assistant apply massage oil to his back and provide him a

creative, erotic massage while kissing each other.

MMF315

While cupping each other's crotch in one hand, pulse your PC muscles as tightly and quickly as you can for a minute.

MMF316

Use a vibrator to stimulate Your Partner's neck, chest and nipples while Your Assistant nuzzles his crotch.

MMF321

Describe in detail a pleasuring accessory you have in mind for Your Partner and Your Assistant and how you would like it used in your sex play.

MMF322

Have Your Partner and Your Assistant simulate a sex act of your choice.

MMF323

Tell a dirty, explicitly erotic story involving two sexy elements provided by Your Partner and Your Assistant. Be as graphic as possible.

MMF324

Find and creatively use a non-sexual object to pleasure both Your Partner and Your Assistant (not necessarily at the same time).

MMF325

Describe in detail a raunchy S/M or bondage scenario involving Your Partner and Your Assistant.

MMF326

While Your Partner and Your Assistant stand together kissing and grinding their crotch together, kneel next to them and fondle, rub and massage their buttocks.

MMF331

While you and Your Assistant stand together kissing and grinding against each other, Your Partner hugs either of you and grinds his crotch on your butt.

MMF332

Use an ice cube to cool, then your lips and tongue to heat an exposed erogenous zone on Your Partner's body. Your Assistant does the same.

MMF333

Watch one scene of an explicit video with Your Partner and Your Assistant. You choose the DVD or switch over to a free online porn site.

MMF334

Get in a position that allows Your Partner to grind against Your Assistant's butt and you to grind against his.

MMF335

Suck one of Your Partner's fingers while manually pleasuring his penis (do not remove any clothing). Your Assistant does the same for you.

MMF336

Dab some ice cream or smear a popsicle on your nipples and entice both Your Partner and Your Assistant to lick them clean.

MMF341

Using flavored lube on a dildo held by Your Assistant, demonstrate your oral skills as a visual treat for Your Partner.

MMF342

Get into a threeway 69 position with Your Partner and Your Assistant and nuzzle each other. Hum, purr or moan for an added thrill.

MMF343

In a threeway doggie position, grab a handful of Your Partner's hair and pull his head back as you thrust vigorously against them for 10–20 seconds.

MMF344

Remove one item of clothing from Your Partner and Your Assistant. Choose a slow song for them to dance to while holding each other close.

MMF345

Both you and Your Partner hold a piece of frozen fruit (strawberry, mango, pineapple) in your mouth while you alternate kissing Your Assistant.

MMF346

Both you and Your Assistant warm your mouth with a hot liquid (water, coffee, tea) swallow then kiss or lightly suck on one of Your Partner's exposed erogenous zones.

MMF351

Standing, mutually grope and fondle each other (under or over clothing).

MMF352

Look through an explicit pictorial magazine or book together.

MMF353

With Your Assistant in a missionary position with Your Partner on top and you in a rear-entry position, make them grind together with your thrusting.

MMF354

Use a digital camera and play erotic photographer with Your Partner and Your Assistant as your models. View them together and delete afterward (unless you really like one to print).

MMF355

Both you and Your Assistant each caress one of Your Partner's bare feet with your bare feet.

MMF356

Close your eyes while each of you sucks and licks the other person's middle finger. Use your tongues to swirl and stroke them.

MMF361

Both you and Your Assistant expose and blow "raspberries" on Your Partner's butt cheeks.

MMF362

Have Your Assistant put on some "old" underwear. Let Your Partner rip them off her (pre-cut the elastic band if necessary) so you can ravish her orally.

MMF363

Remove any clothing necessary for Your Partner and Your Assistant to teasingly lick your inner thighs. Lay back and enjoy their tickling tongues.

MMF364

Remove any clothing necessary for Your Partner and Your Assistant to teasingly lick your abs. Lay back and enjoy their tickling tongues.

MMF365

Standing, Your Assistant fondles both Your Partner's and your penis and testicles at the same time. You alternate kissing them passionately as she plays with two cocks.

MMF366

Stroke both Your Partner's and Your Assistant's tail bone and between their butt cheeks. Use your fingers, tongue, feather, spoon, string of beads, etc. - alternate as required to stimulate both of them equally.

Male Male Female

Level 4 - Explicit & Erotic Passion

MMF411

Lightly squeeze and tug Your Partner's scrotum. Gently play with his testicles while Your Assistant kisses and licks the tip of his penis.

MMF412

kiss and lick the tip of Your Partner's penis as Your Assistant lightly tugs small amounts of pubic hair all around his genital region.

MMF413

Your Assistant applies lube to both Your Partner's and your penis and rubs her nipples with their tips.

MMF414

Lubricate Your Partner's penis and Your Assistant's butt crack. With you in the middle of a sensual slip'n slide, stimulate them both – no penetration.

MMF415

While Your Assistant plays with his nipples, gently pull the skin of Your Partner's penis taut with one hand. Use your fingertips of your other hand to stroke and massage the head.

MMF416

Use an artist brush dipped in flavored oil or lube to stimulate the head of Your Partner's penis. Flick the frenulum and swirl around the corona. Allow Your Assistant to lick it clean now and again.

MMF421

Using broad, luscious tongue strokes, both you and Your Assistant both lick all around the shaft of Your Partner's penis at the same time. Put the head in your mouths and suck it briefly.

MMF422

Both you and Your Assistant each attempt to take one of Your Partner's testicles in your mouth at the same time. Lick them tenderly.

MMF423

Your Assistant alternates pleasuring the head of Your Partner's and your penis orally with a mint, some liquor or dab of toothpaste in your mouth. Warming flavored lube is good too.

MMF424

Both you and Your Assistant tickle Your Partner's testicles, inner thighs and perineum with your tongues. Flutter your tongues like a flickering flame.

MMF425

While you and Your Partner kiss, Your Assistant massages your cocks with lube - one in each hand using creative stroking techniques.

MMF426

You and Your Partner both stand and look into each other's eyes while each sucking one finger of the other man. Your Assistant kneels beside you and orally pleasures your cocks.

MMF431

In turn, starting with Your Assistant, express audible sounds of passion leading up to a fake orgasm. Each rate the most convincing.

MMF432

Direct Your Partner and Your Assistant to simulate a creative new sex act of your choice.

MMF433

While you and Your Partner stand kissing, Your Assistant kneels beside you, applies lube to your cocks and creatively rubs them together.

MMF434

Your Assistant uses an ice cube and her lips and tongue to cool then heat both Your Partner's and your penis and testicles. She is to alternate cooling one of you as she warms the other.

MMF435

Have Your Partner straddle your face so you can orally pleasure his testicles. Your Assistant orally pleasures the head of his penis.

MMF436

Find and creatively use a non-sexual item to pleasure both Your Partner and Your Assistant.

MMF441

Have 30 seconds of femoral coitus (non-penetrative intercourse) standing, rear-entry with Your Assistant facing up against a wall. Your Partner joins from the rear.

MMF442

Have 30 seconds of femoral coitus (non-penetrative intercourse) doggie style with Your Assistant. Your Partner joins from the rear.

MMF443

Visually tease Your Partner by sensuously demonstrating fellatio using a sex toy or edible object. Your Assistant joins in or holds the item for you.

MMF444

Both you and Your Assistant pleasure Your Partner's entire penis and testicles orally at the same time. Use creative licking and sucking techniques.

MMF445

Stimulate Your Partner and Your Assistant with a vibrator at the same time. (Visual stimulation counts)

MMF446

Stimulate Your Partner with a sex toy that Your Assistant chooses. (Visual stimulation counts)

MMF451

While Your Partner watches, both you and Your Assistant masturbate any way you desire. Provide him visual stimulation. Edge yourselves if desired.

MMF452

Both you and Your Partner kiss and lick any of Your Assistant's exposed erogenous zone that each of you desires.

MMF453

Expose then pinch, tweak and twiddle your nipples. Use lube if desired. Then have Your Partner and Your Assistant both suck and bite them gently.

MMF454

Use a piece of soft, juicy, sticky fruit. Rub it on Your Partner's penis then lick it clean. Repeat with Your Assistant's clitoris.

MMF455

Use a vibrator to tease Your Partner's scrotum and perineum while Your Assistant licks the tip of his penis.

MMF456

Apply lube to the head of Your Partner's penis. Straddle him and use his cock to massage your perineum while Your Assistant licks the tip of your penis – no penetration allowed.

MMF461

Using lube in your palms, wrap your hands around Your Partner's penis and stimulate him by twisting them in opposite directions. Your Assistant does the same for you.

MMF462

In a missionary position, you on the bottom, have Your Partner press the head of his penis against your anus. Wiggle and twist your pelvis while Your Assistant slaps his ass – no penetration allowed.

MMF463

Straddle Your Partner in a way that allows you to slide his penis over your anus as slowly and sensually as you can – he is not allowed to move. Your Assistant offers her mouth for you to slide your cock into at the same time.

MMF464

Both you and Your Assistant lovingly kiss Your Partner's penis together and use it to stroke your lips, cheek and neck.

MMF465

Sit on Your Partner's lap facing him, guide his cock between your butt cheeks and wrap your legs around him. Standing, Your Assistant offers her tits for you to both lick and suck.

MMF466

Both you and Your Assistant stand beside Your Partner in front of a mirror and watch each other as you stroke and fondle his body intimately.

Male Male Female

Level 5 - Sizzling, Sexual Stimulation

MMF511

Manually stimulate Your Partner's cock with one hand and his perineum with the other. Your Assistant nibbles on his nipples.

MMF512

Have Your Partner hold a large dildo while you and Your Assistant demonstrate how you would give him a foot-job together. Use lube if you desire.

MMF513

As a visual tease, use a large, realistic dildo and some lube to demonstrate how you and Your Assistant would give Your Partner a creative hand-job together.

MMF514

While you and Your Partner stroke each other's cock, Your Assistant pleasures herself with a glass or acrylic dildo for your visual pleasure. Encourage her to be as lewd as she dares.

MMF515

Give Your Partner a foot-job. Apply lube and use your toes and the soles of your feet to stimulate his penis. Your Assistant offers her pussy to him for oral pleasuring.

MMF516

While Your Partner and Your Assistant stroke each other, lube and pleasure yourself with the thickest dildo or buttplug you own. Provide a good show for their visual pleasure.

MMF521

Both Your Partner and Your Assistant will each select a piece of fetish wear or accessory (leather, stockings, boots, heels, collar etc.) for you to put on.

MMF522

While Your Partner stands, kneel before him and orally pleasure his penis just to the brink of ejaculation – then stop. At the same time, Your Assistant kneels behind, nibbling his butt and stroking his testicles.

MMF523

Laying down so your head is hanging over an accessible edge (bed, table, sofa, etc.), orally pleasure Your Partner's penis while Your Assistant pleasures yours.

MMF524

Get into a threeway "69" position with Your Partner and Your Assistant. Pleasure each other orally.

MMF525

Straddle Your Partner's face and allow him to lick your scrotum and perineum. Your Assistant plays with his nipples or his penis as Your Partner orally pleasures you.

MMF526

Lube and pleasure yourself with the largest dildo available while Your Assistant kisses you passionately. Insert it slowly so that Your Partner can see every detail.

MMF531

Using a suction cup dildo (or one held in place by Your Partner), stimulate your self without using your hands. Orally pleasure Your Assistant at the same time.

MMF532

Your Partner enjoys one minute of penetration and being penetrated in a position of his choice – No thrusting. Use your PC muscles to squeeze and pulse only. If desired, have Your Assistant use a strap-on.

MMF533

Enjoy a minute of femoral coitus (non-penetrative intercourse) doggie style with Your Partner. Your Assistant offers her pussy to him for oral pleasuring.

MMF534

Spread Your Partner's butt cheeks wide and tickle his perineum and surrounding erogenous zones with a feather or piece of silky material. Your Assistant does the same for you.

MMF535

Using lube and one or two fingers, massage Your Partner's perineum. Then penetrate his anus with smooth, gliding strokes. Your Assistant orally pleasures him at the same time.

MMF536

Use an artist brush and lube to stimulate Your Partner's perineum and surrounding erogenous zones. Tickle it as you play with his testicles. Your Assistant offers her pussy to him for oral pleasuring.

MMF541

Circle Your Partner's scrotum just above his testicles with your thumb and index finger. Pull down gently until taut and lick his testicles. Your Assistant orally pleasures the head of his cock at the same time.

MMF542

Using a firm, pointed tongue, lick Your Partner's perineum and base of his scrotum using circles, swirls and zigzag strokes. Your Assistant orally pleasures the head of his cock

MMF543

While Your Partner lays on his front and orally pleasures Your Assistant, straddle him and enjoy some intense rear-entry femoral coitus (non-penetrative intercourse) using lube if desired.

MMF544

In a missionary position, lift Your Partner's legs high, pressing your penis on his. Both you and Your Assistant lick and suck on his toes to make him wiggle on your cock.

MMF545

Use the tip of a vibrator to tickle Your Partner's perineum and surrounding erogenous zones – no penetration. Use a second vibrator or lubed finger to stimulate Your Assistant in a similar way.

MMF546

Get into a doggie position with Your Partner. He is to remain still while you wiggle and circle your pelvis against him. Kiss and manually stimulate Your Assistant at the same time.

MMF551

With Your Partner sitting, straddle him with your back to his chest. Use his penis to tap and stroke your cock while Your Assistant plays with both of your testicles.

MMF552

While Your Partner stands, kneel behind him and nibble and bite his buttocks while stroking his testicles. Your Assistant kneels in front and orally pleasures his cock.

MMF553

Apply some lube between your butt cheeks. With Your Partner standing up against a wall, rub and stroke his penis between your ass. Your Assistant joins in front of you.

MMF554

Apply some lube between Your Partner's butt cheeks. With him standing up facing against a wall, rub and stroke your penis between his ass. Your Assistant fondles both of your testicles and Your Partner's cock at the same time.

MMF555

With Your Partner laying on his back, straddle him (no penetration). Rub his penis with your ass while sucking Your Assistant's tits.

MMF556

Remove all clothing on your upper bodies. Apply massage oil to your chests and bellies. Slither and slide against each other to one song.

MMF561

Play a favorite song. Your Assistant orally pleasures both you and Your Partner to the rhythm. Make it last the entire length of the song then stop.

MMF562

Take Your Partner's penis in your mouth and create different vibrating sensations by humming, purring, growling, etc. Your Partner follows your lead, pleasuring Your Assistant in a similar way.

MMF563

While Your Partner sits, both you and Your Assistant perform a lap dance for him to one song of your choice. Seductively rub and grind yourselves on him.

MMF564

Both you and Your Assistant suck on the shaft of Your Partner's penis. Slide your lips up and down the sides of his erection as you lick and flick with your tongues.

MMF565

Use only the soft underside of your tongue to lick the head of Your Partner's penis. Then, orally pleasure Your Assistant's clitoris in a similar way.

MMF566

Use a digital camera with a zoom lens to take very close-up and intimate shots of Your Partner and Your Assistant in various explicit poses. Select one to print and frame.

Male Male Female

Level 6 - Wild, Nasty, Kinky, Taboo

MMF611

Orally pleasure Your Partner's anus in a position of your choice. Your Assistant orally pleasures his cock at the same time.

MMF612

Orally pleasure Your Partner's anus in a position of your choice. Your Assistant offers her nipples to Your Partner to be sucked at the same time.

MMF613

Your choice of Nasty, Kinky or Taboo foreplay activity for Your Partner and Your Assistant to perform for you – surprise them with your wild side.

MMF614

While you give Your Partner a sensual prostate massage, Your Assistant does the same for you.

MMF615

Kiss and lick Your Partner's feet then suck on his toes while Your Assistant sucks on your cock.

MMF616

Creatively use a double-ended dildo with Your Partner. Allow Your Assistant to hold and manipulate it as desired.

MMF621

Orally pleasure Your Partner's anus in a missionary position, legs spread wide. Your Assistant licks and sucks on his toes to make him wiggle.

MMF622

Insert one lubed finger in Your Partner's anus and gently massage left, right, up, down and all around – no thrusting. Your Assistant does the same for you.

MMF623

Encourage Your Assistant to attempt taking both yours and Your Partner's cocks in her mouth at the same time.

MMF624

Drip hot wax on both Your Partner and Your Assistant (chest or buttocks) while they lay next to each other.

MMF625

While you and Your Partner kiss, Your Assistant will apply nipple clamps (or clothes pegs) to your nipples. Remove when one of you breaks your kiss.

MMF626

With a lubed fake pussy (penis sleeve), masturbate Your Partner's shaft just to the brink then stop. Leave his tip for Your Assistant to orally pleasure.

MMF631

Use your fingers and lube to pleasure Your Partner anyway you desire. At the same time, stimulate Your Assistant using your other hand.

MMF632

Both you and Your Partner pleasure yourselves with a dildo or buttplug while Your Assistant watches.

MMF633

Use an implement of your choice to erotically spank Your Partner's bare bum until it radiates a sensual heat. Let Your Assistant caresses and strokes his bum between smacks.

MMF634

Use the tip of a vibrator to tickle Your Partner's perineum and anus – no penetration. At the same time, he stimulates Your Assistant in the same way.

MMF635

Stimulate Your Partner and Your Assistant each with a different buttplug or dildo at the same time.

MMF636

With Your Partner propped in a mostly upside-down position, orally pleasure him. Your Assistant helps hold him up while giving him a rim-job.

MMF641

While Your Partner and Your Assistant take turns pleasuring you orally, anally stimulate them at the same time with separate vibrators, dildos or buttplugs.

MMF642

Using a double-ended dildo or silicone beads, both you and Your Partner get on all fours for a little "cheek to cheek" action. Your Assistant offers her pussy to be sucked by both of you taking turns.

MMF643

Pleasure Your Partner orally while also stimulating him anally with a lubed finger. Your Assistant nibbles, sucks and bites on Your Partner's nipples.

MMF644

Use a buttplug or dildo to stimulate yourself while Your Partner orally pleasures your cock and Your Assistant orally pleasures his cock.

MMF645

Creatively explore a pleasurable combination of two cocks, one pussy, three hot bodies and one or more sex toys all at the same time.

MMF646

Experiment with cross-dressing – both you and Your Assistant select some appropriate feminine wear for Your Partner to wear.

MMF651

Both you and Your Assistant kneel and pleasure Your Partner orally together while he stimulates both of you anally using lubed fingers.

MMF652

Select two sex toys for Your Partner and Your Assistant to play Show and Tell. In turn, they are to demonstrate their self-pleasuring technique, eyes closed, while describing the sensations.

MMF653

Roleplaying as a strict Master, sternly command your Love Slaves to perform and service one of your desires.

MMF654

While lying down, have Your Partner straddle you facing your feet. As he grinds on your cock with his, Your Assistant slaps on his ass cheeks.

MMF655

Get into a threeway '69' position and give each other a rim-job.

MMF656

Your choice of sex position involving all three of you engaging in oral and/or anal intercourse at the same time. Have Your Assistant use a strap-on if desired.

MMF661

Describe in detail an extreme BDSM scenario/fantasy involving all three of you. Set the stage and let Your Partner and Your Assistant add to the story in turn.

MMF662

While Your Assistant sucks Your Partner's cock, attempt to give her a G-Spot orgasm using your fingers (palm on her clitoris, two or three fingers inserted, flutter upward quickly and rhythmically with fairly intense pressure).

MMF663

Describe in detail the most extreme, weird or bizarre sexual activity you can think of involving all three of you (not that you want to do it, of course).

MMF664

Orally pleasure Your Partner's anus in a missionary position, legs spread wide. Your Assistant straddles his chest so he can suck her pussy at the same time.

MMF665

Both you and Your Assistant erotically and passionately nibble and bite sensitive erogenous zones on Your Partner's body. Make him ache for you in a good way.

MMF666

STOP the Foreplay and START the Sex Play.

Male Male Male

Foreplay Activities

Male Male Male

Level 1 - Warm & Loving

MMM111

From a book of fantasies or erotic letters, read a random one out loud to Your Partner while he kisses Your Assistant.

MMM112

While sensually kissing Your Partner, allow Your Assistant to tickle both of you with a feather (face, lips, ears and neck).

MMM113

Kiss and nibble along Your Partner's neck and shoulder while Your Assistant does the same to you from behind.

MMM114

Standing, hug and caress Your Partner from behind. Your Assistant kneels in front of him and strokes his lower region.

MMM115

Lovingly embrace Your Partner and Your Assistant. Hug, caress and tenderly kiss each other.

MMM116

Massage Your Partner's head with the tips of your fingers. He follows your lead to massage Your Assistant's head in the same way.

MMM121

Find a how-to article on a sex technique or activity that you have not yet experienced and read it together.

MMM122

Sit opposite and facing each other. Place a hand on each other's chest, close your eyes and synchronize breathing slowly.

MMM123

Delicately lick around one of Your Partner's ears. Your Assistant does the same on the other one. Hot breaths in his ear will give him delightful shivers of pleasure.

MMM124

Dance embraced with Your Partner and Your Assistant to one slow song. Kiss each of them lovingly when it ends.

MMM125

Kiss and lick Your Partner's wrist, inner arm and elbow. Your Assistant does the same on his other arm.

MMM126

While Your Partner and Your Assistant kiss, apply cologne to a few areas of your body where you desire extra attention.

MMM131

Describe in detail a unique, novel or exotic place to make love. Include activities you would like to experience.

MMM132

Both you and Your Assistant spider Walk your fingers delicately over parts of Your Partner's exposed body. Arouse him with a slow, light tickling and tapping motion.

MMM133

Both you and Your Assistant lick Your Partner's ear lobes and sensitive regions on his neck. Behind the ears and back of his neck are very sensitive. Whisper something deliciously sensual, loving or erotic.

MMM134

Describe in detail a new erotic adventure involving the three of you. Include elements of the love play you'll enjoy together.

MMM135

Browse an erotic book or magazine with Your Partner (his choice). Discuss pictures or images that appeal to each of you.

MMM136

Massage Your Partner's toes one at a time. Your Assistant does the same starting with the other foot.

MMM141

Tenderly kiss Your Partner with affection. Hold and caress his face with both hands. Then kiss Your Assistant with the same affection.

MMM142

Stand still and allow Your Partner and Your Assistant to both caress and stroke your body.

MMM143

Kiss and lightly lick Your Partner's hand, palm and fingers. Choose his non-dominant hand. He matches your actions on Your Assistant's hand.

MMM144

Place soft, delicate kisses all over Your Partner's face - cheek, lips, nose, forehead, temples, chin. End with a tender, sensuous kiss. Repeat for Your Assistant.

MMM145

Experiment with different types of kisses and kissing sensations - (upside down, open mouth, closed mouth, sideways, corner, firm, soft). Alternate between Your Partner and Your Assistant.

MMM146

Gently kiss and lick Your Partner's inner arm – wrist to elbow. Your Assistant does the same for his other arm.

MMM151

All three of you close your eyes. Delicately caress Your Partner's and Your Assistant's faces each with one hand. Trace your fingertips as lightly as you can as you explore every detail.

MMM152

While Your Partner and Your Assistant kiss, do something to set the mood. Put on some soft music, light a candle, pour a glass of wine, burn some incense, spray some cologne, etc.

MMM153

Both you and Your Assistant give Your Partner a brief but relaxing massage the way he likes it.

MMM154

Browse through a book with advanced or acrobatic sex positions together. Choose one of them for Your Partner and Your Assistant to try out (simulate the sex play for now).

MMM155

Find and view some erotic art together - use books or the internet. Discuss what you each like about it.

MMM156

Both you and Your Assistant erotically tickle any of Your Partner's exposed erogenous zones. Creatively use your fingers, a feather, a soft paintbrush or your tongues.

MMM161

Find an erotic edible and feed it to Your Partner and Your Assistant sensually. Fruit, syrup, chocolate, oysters, liquor, etc. Encourage them to savor the treats at the same time.

MMM162

Standing together, both you and Your Assistant softly stroke and caress Your Partner's entire body. Lightly squeeze parts of his body that you find delightful.

MMM163

Make up a fantasy scenario or roleplaying adventure for Your Partner and Your Assistant that they might perform for your erotic pleasure.

MMM164

Both you and Your Assistant massage a different symmetrical part of Your Partner's body (legs, arms, pecs, shoulders, etc.). Experiment with a different type of technique.

MMM165

Both you and Your Assistant delicately stroke each of Your Partner's hands and fingers with your fingertips. Swirl and circle as you explore and tickle every nerve to attention.

MMM166

Remove one item of clothing erotically then remove one item of clothing from both Your Partner and Your Assistant.

Male Male Male

Level 2 - Sensual Sensations

MMM211

Slowly and sensually lick and suck Your Partner's thumb. Your Assistant does the same for his other thumb. Stimulate every nerve with your twirling tongues.

MMM212

Have Your Partner get in any position you desire, expose his butt and allow you and Your Assistant to both administer a sensual spanking.

MMM213

With Your Partner and Your Assistant positioned so their feet are barely touching, use a vibrator to stimulate their toes and soles of their feet.

MMM214

Both you and Your Assistant expose and lightly lick Your Partner's lower back and side. Lightly bite and nibble his buttocks.

MMM215

Both you and Your Assistant each lick the soft, sensitive skin behind Your Partner's knees at the same time.

MMM216

Both you and Your Assistant whisper in Your Partner's ear how horny you are and what you want to do with his penis or yours.

MMM221

Find and use an item with an interesting texture to stimulate/sensitize an exposed region of Your Partner's body. (soft, cold, rough, squishy, etc.) Then pleasure Your Assistant in a similar way.

MMM222

Enjoy a threeway kiss with Your Partner and Your Assistant.

MMM223

While Your Partner and Your Assistant kiss, use a soft artist or make-up brush to tickle and stimulate exposed erogenous zones on their bodies.

MMM224

Put an edible topping or liquor in your navel and entice Your Partner and Your Assistant to lick it out together.

MMM225

Kiss, lick and suck each finger of Your Partner's non-dominant hand. Apply a flavored lube or syrup if you desire. He matches your actions on Your Assistant's hand.

MMM226

Whisper in Your Partner's ear how you want to pleasure him with your hot, slick tongue. Do the same for Your Assistant.

MMM231

Both you and Your Assistant stroke and massage Your Partner's chest. Circle and flick his nipples lightly.

MMM232

Both you and Your Partner expose and lightly lick Your Assistant's lower back and side. Lightly bite and nibble his buttocks.

MMM233

Perform an erotic dance while removing an item of clothing. Play appropriate music if you desire.

MMM234

Creatively use something round and smooth to stimulate Your Partner in various ways. Repeat for Your Assistant.

MMM235

Use an artist brush dipped in flavored lube to stimulate Your Partner's nipples. Apply delicate flicks and twirls. Your Assistant gets to lick them clean.

MMM236

Drag your fingernails down Your Partner's back, chest and tummy, legs or arms - your choice. Do the same for Your Assistant.

MMM241

Both you and Your Assistant caress and lightly stroke any exposed part of Your Partner's body.

MMM242

Both you and Your Assistant massage and fondle any part of Your Partner's body still covered with clothing - do not touch any skin.

MMM243

Kneeling while Your Partner stands, kiss and lick his belly, hips and thighs. Kneed and massage his buttocks. Your Assistant stands behind him and fondles his chest.

MMM244

With Your Partner and Your Assistant positioned so their feet are barely touching, massage their feet and each toe with an oil or lube. They then stroke their feet together.

MMM245

All three hug and passionately kiss each other.

MMM246

Use a piece of fur, silk or satin to smoothly caress any/all exposed parts of Your Partner's body. Your Assistant watches and repeats your actions.

MMM251

Use a vibrator to delicately stimulate Your Partner's nipples. He repeats your technique on Your Assistant's nipples.

MMM252

Lick, suck and lightly bite Your Partner's nipples. Blow on or suck in air around them to create warm and cool sensations. Alternate with Your Assistant's nipples.

MMM253

Apply a flavored lube to Your Partner's nipples. Tweak and tantalize them with your fingertips then let Your Assistant lick each nipple clean.

MMM254

Creatively use an ice cube to perk up sensitive regions on Your Partner's body. Your Assistant follows each cold shock with a warm kiss or lick.

MMM255

Put on a tight top that shows off your chest. Entice Your Partner and Your Assistant to caress your chest and circle your nipples through the fabric.

MMM256

Rub and massage Your Partner's and Your Assistant's crotch at the same time (through their clothing if they are still wearing any).

MMM261

Both you and Your Assistant sensually lick exposed regions of Your Partner's body. Search out rarely explored erogenous zones.

MMM262

Based on the recommendation from Your Partner and Your Assistant, put on any item to look, feel, smell or taste even more sexy.

MMM263

Use a flavored lube or syrup on any rarely licked erogenous zone and entice both Your Partner and Your Assistant to lick it off together.

MMM264

Instruct Your Assistant to creatively stimulate Your Partner any way you desire.

MMM265

Pleasure yourself as visual stimulation for both Your Partner and Your Assistant.

MMM266

While Your Partner and Your Assistant stand together and kiss, kneel next to them and fondle, rub and massage their buttocks.

Male Male Male

Level 3 - Intimate Intentions

MMM311

While Your Partner and Your Assistant kiss, seductively read a short erotic passage or a dirty letter. Choose one that is very explicit and detailed.

MMM312

Both you and Your Assistant each select something sexy for Your Partner to wear (now and while making love later).

MMM313

Pretend you're a porn director/star. Get Your Partner and Your Assistant into a novel, creative position to receive or perform oral sex and detail how you want the scene to play out.

MMM314

Have Your Partner lay on his stomach. Both you and Your Assistant apply massage oil to his back and provide him a

creative, erotic massage while kissing each other.

MMM315

While cupping each other's crotch in one hand, pulse your PC muscles as tightly and quickly as you can for a minute.

MMM316

Use a vibrator to stimulate Your Partner's neck, chest and nipples while Your Assistant nuzzles his crotch.

MMM321

Describe in detail a pleasuring accessory you have in mind for Your Partner and Your Assistant and how you would like it used in your sex play.

MMM322

Have Your Partner and Your Assistant simulate a sex act of your choice.

MMM323

Tell a dirty, explicitly erotic story involving two sexy elements provided by Your Partner and Your Assistant. Be as graphic as possible.

MMM324

Find and creatively use a non-sexual object to pleasure both Your Partner and Your Assistant (not necessarily at the same time).

MMM325

Describe in detail a raunchy S/M or bondage scenario involving Your Partner and Your Assistant.

MMM326

While Your Partner and Your Assistant stand together kissing and grinding their crotch together, kneel next to them and fondle, rub and massage their buttocks.

MMM331

While you and Your Partner stand together kissing and grinding against each other, Your Assistant hugs either of you and grinds his crotch on your butt.

MMM332

Use an ice cube to cool, then your lips and tongue to heat an exposed erogenous zone on Your Partner's body. Your Assistant does the same.

MMM333

Watch one scene of an explicit video with Your Partner and Your Assistant. You choose the DVD or switch over to a free online porn site.

MMM334

Get in a position that allows Your Partner to grind against your butt and Your Assistant to grind against his.

MMM335

Suck one of Your Partner's fingers while manually pleasuring his penis (do not remove any clothing). Your Assistant does the same for you.

MMM336

Dab some ice cream or smear a popsicle on your nipples and entice both Your Partner and Your Assistant to lick them clean.

MMM341

Using flavored lube on a dildo held by Your Assistant, demonstrate your oral skills as a visual treat for Your Partner.

MMM342

Get into a threeway 69 position with Your Partner and Your Assistant and nuzzle each other. Hum, purr or moan for an added thrill.

MMM343

In a threeway doggie position, grab a handful of Your Partner's hair and pull his head back as you thrust vigorously against them for 10–20 seconds.

MMM344

Remove one item of clothing from Your Partner and Your Assistant. Choose a slow song for them to dance to while holding each other close.

MMM345

Both you and Your Partner hold a piece of frozen fruit (strawberry, mango, pineapple) in your mouth while you alternate kissing Your Assistant.

MMM346

Both you and Your Assistant warm your mouth with a hot liquid (water, coffee, tea) swallow then kiss or lightly suck on one of Your Partner's exposed erogenous zones.

MMM351

Standing, mutually grope and fondle each other (under or over clothing).

MMM352

Look through an explicit pictorial magazine or book together.

MMM353

With Your Assistant in a missionary position with Your Partner and you in a doggie position, make them grind together with your thrusting.

MMM354

Use a digital camera and play erotic photographer with Your Partner and Your Assistant as your models. View them together and delete afterward (unless you really like one to print).

MMM355

Both you and Your Assistant each caress one of Your Partner's bare feet with your bare feet.

MMM356

Close your eyes while each of you sucks and licks the other person's middle finger. Use your tongues to swirl and stroke them.

MMM361

Both you and Your Assistant expose and blow "raspberries" on Your Partner's butt cheeks.

MMM362

Have Your Partner put on some "old" underwear. Let Your Assistant rip them off him (pre-cut the elastic band if necessary) so you can ravish him orally.

MMM363

Remove any clothing necessary for Your Partner and Your Assistant to teasingly lick your inner thighs. Lay back and enjoy their tickling tongues.

MMM364

Remove any clothing necessary for Your Partner and Your Assistant to teasingly lick your abs. Lay back and enjoy their tickling tongues.

MMM365

Standing, fondle both Your Partner's and Your Assistant's penis and testicles while you alternate kissing them passionately.

MMM366

Stroke both Your Partner's and Your Assistant's tail bone and between their butt cheeks. Use your fingers, tongue, feather, spoon, string of beads, etc. - alternate as required to stimulate both of them equally.

Male Male Male

Level 4 - Explicit & Erotic Passion

MMM411

Lightly squeeze and tug Your Partner's scrotum. Gently play with his testicles while Your Assistant kisses and licks the tip of his penis.

MMM412

kiss and lick the tip of Your Partner's penis as Your Assistant lightly tugs small amounts of pubic hair all around his genital region.

MMM413

Apply lube to both Your Partner's and Your Assistant's penis and rub your nipples with their tips.

MMM414

Lubricate Your Partner's penis and Your Assistant's butt crack. With you in the middle of a sensual slip'n slide, stimulate them both – no penetration.

MMM415

While Your Assistant plays with his nipples, gently pull the skin of Your Partner's penis taut with one hand. Use your fingertips of your other hand to stroke and massage the head.

MMM416

Use an artist brush dipped in flavored oil or lube to stimulate the head of Your Partner's penis. Flick the frenulum and swirl around the corona. Allow Your Assistant to lick it clean now and again.

MMM421

Using broad, luscious tongue strokes, lick all around the shaft of Your Partner's penis. Put the head in your mouth and suck it briefly. Repeat with Your Assistant's cock.

MMM422

Both you and Your Assistant each attempt to take one of Your Partner's testicles in your mouth at the same time. Lick them tenderly.

MMM423

Alternate pleasuring the head of both Your Partner's and Your Assistant's penis orally with a mint, some liquor or dab of toothpaste in your mouth. Warming flavored lube is good too.

MMM424

Both you and Your Assistant tickle Your Partner's testicles, inner thighs and perineum with your tongues. Flutter your tongues like a flickering flame.

MMM425

While Your Partner and Your Assistant kiss, massage their cocks with lube - one in each hand. Use creative stroking techniques.

MMM426

Your Partner and Your Assistant both stand and look into each other's eyes while each sucking one finger of the other man. Kneel beside them and manually pleasure their cocks.

MMM431

In turn, starting with Your Assistant, express audible sounds of passion leading up to a fake orgasm. Each rate the most convincing.

MMM432

Direct Your Partner and Your Assistant to simulate a creative new sex act of your choice.

MMM433

While Your Partner and Your Assistant stand kissing, kneel beside them, apply lube to their cocks and creatively rub them together.

MMM434

Use an ice cube and your lips and tongue to cool then heat both Your Partner's and Your Assistant's penis and testicles. Alternate cooling one as you warm another.

MMM435

Have Your Partner straddle your face so you can orally pleasure his testicles. Your Assistant orally pleasures the head of his penis.

MMM436

Find and creatively use a non-sexual item to pleasure both Your Partner and Your Assistant.

MMM441

Have 30 seconds of femoral coitus (non-penetrative intercourse) standing, rear-entry with you facing up against a wall. Your Assistant joins from the rear.

MMM442

Have 30 seconds of femoral coitus (non-penetrative intercourse) doggie style. Your Assistant joins from the rear.

MMM443

Visually tease Your Partner by sensuously demonstrating fellatio using a sex toy or edible object. Your Assistant joins in or holds the item for you.

MMM444

Both you and Your Assistant pleasure Your Partner's entire penis and testicles orally at the same time. Use creative licking and sucking techniques.

MMM445

Stimulate Your Partner and Your Assistant with a vibrator at the same time. (Visual stimulation counts)

MMM446

Stimulate Your Partner with a sex toy that Your Assistant chooses. (Visual stimulation counts)

MMM451

While Your Partner watches, both you and Your Assistant masturbate any way you desire. Provide him visual stimulation. Edge yourselves if desired.

MMM452

Both you and Your Partner kiss and lick any of Your Assistant's exposed erogenous zone that each of you desires.

MMM453

Expose then pinch, tweak and twiddle your nipples. Use lube if desired. Then have Your Partner and Your Assistant both suck and bite them gently.

MMM454

Use a piece of soft, juicy, sticky fruit. Rub it on Your Partner's penis then lick it clean. Repeat with Your Assistant.

MMM455

Use a vibrator to tease Your Partner's scrotum and perineum while Your Assistant licks the tip of his penis.

MMM456

Apply lube to the head of Your Partner's penis. Straddle him and use his cock to massage your perineum while Your Assistant licks the tip of your penis – no penetration allowed.

MMM461

Using lube in your palms, wrap your hands around Your Partner's penis and stimulate him by twisting them in opposite directions. Your Assistant does the same for you.

MMM462

In a missionary position, you on the bottom, have Your Partner press the head of his penis against your anus. Wiggle and twist your pelvis while Your Assistant slaps his ass – no penetration allowed.

MMM463

Straddle Your Partner in a way that allows you to slide his penis over your anus as slowly and sensually as you can – he is not allowed to move. Your Assistant offers his mouth for you to slide your cock into at the same time.

MMM464

Both you and Your Assistant lovingly kiss Your Partner's penis together and use it to stroke your lips, cheek and neck.

MMM465

Sit on Your Partner's lap facing him, guide his cock between your butt cheeks and wrap your legs around him. Standing, Your Assistant offers his penis for you to both lick and suck.

MMM466

Both you and Your Assistant stand beside Your Partner in front of a mirror and watch each other as you stroke and fondle his body intimately.

Male Male Male

Level 5 - Sizzling, Sexual Stimulation

MMM511

Manually stimulate Your Partner's cock with one hand and his perineum with the other. Your Assistant nibbles on his nipples.

MMM512

Have Your Partner hold a large dildo while you and Your Assistant demonstrate how you would give him a foot-job together. Use lube if you desire.

MMM513

As a visual tease, use a realistic dildo and some lube to demonstrate how you and Your Assistant would give Your Partner a creative hand-job together.

MMM514

While Your Partner and Your Assistant stroke each other's cock, pleasure yourself with a glass or acrylic dildo for their visual pleasure. Be as lewd as you dare.

MMM515

Give Your Partner a foot-job. Apply lube and use your toes and the soles of your feet to stimulate his penis. Your Assistant offers his cock to him for oral pleasuring.

MMM516

While Your Partner and Your Assistant stroke each other's cock, lube and pleasure yourself with the thickest dildo or buttplug you own. Provide a good show for their visual pleasure.

MMM521

Both Your Partner and Your Assistant will each select a piece of fetish wear or accessory (leather, stockings, boots, heels, collar etc.) for you to put on.

MMM522

While Your Partner stands, kneel before him and orally pleasure his penis just to the brink of ejaculation – then stop. Stroke Your Assistant's cock at the same time.

MMM523

Laying down so your head is hanging over an accessible edge (bed, table, sofa, etc.), orally pleasure Your Partner's penis while Your Assistant pleasures yours.

MMM524

Get into a threeway "69" position with Your Partner and Your Assistant. Pleasure each other orally.

MMM525

Straddle Your Partner's face and allow him to lick your scrotum and perineum. Your Assistant plays with his nipples or his penis as Your Partner orally pleasures you.

MMM526

Lube and pleasure yourself with the largest dildo available while Your Assistant kisses you passionately. Insert it slowly so that Your Partner can see every detail.

MMM531

Using a suction cup dildo (or one held in place by Your Partner), stimulate your self without using your hands. Orally pleasure Your Assistant at the same time.

MMM532

Your Partner enjoys one minute of penetration and being penetrated in a position of his choice – No thrusting. Use your PC muscles to squeeze and pulse only.

MMM533

Enjoy a minute of femoral coitus (non-penetrative intercourse) doggie style with Your Partner. Your Assistant offers his cock to him for oral pleasuring.

MMM534

Spread Your Partner's butt cheeks wide and tickle his perineum and surrounding erogenous zones with a feather or piece of silky material. Your Assistant does the same for you.

MMM535

Using lube and one or two fingers, massage Your Partner's perineum. Then penetrate his anus with smooth, gliding strokes. Your Assistant orally pleasures him at the same time.

MMM536

Use an artist brush and lube to stimulate Your Partner's perineum and surrounding erogenous zones. Tickle it as you play with his testicles. Your Assistant offers his cock to him for oral pleasuring.

MMM541

Circle Your Partner's scrotum just above his testicles with your thumb and index finger. Pull down gently until taut and lick his testicles. Your Assistant orally pleasures the head of his cock at the same time.

MMM542

Using a firm, pointed tongue, lick Your Partner's perineum and base of his scrotum using circles, swirls and zigzag strokes. Your Assistant orally pleasures the head of his cock

MMM543

While Your Partner lays on his front and orally pleasures Your Assistant, straddle him and enjoy some intense rear-entry femoral coitus (non-penetrative intercourse) using lube if desired.

MMM544

In a missionary position, lift Your Partner's legs high, pressing your penis on his. Both you and Your Assistant lick and suck on his toes to make him wiggle on your cock.

MMM545

Use the tip of a vibrator to tickle Your Partner's perineum and surrounding erogenous zones – no penetration. Use a second vibrator or lubed finger to stimulate Your Assistant in a similar way.

MMM546

Get into a doggie position with Your Partner. He is to remain still while you wiggle and circle your pelvis against him. Suck Your Assistant's cock at the same time.

MMM551

With Your Partner sitting, straddle him with your back to his chest. Use his penis to tap and stroke your cock while Your Assistant plays with both of your testicles.

MMM552

While Your Partner stands, kneel behind him and nibble and bite his buttocks while stroking his testicles. Your Assistant kneels in front and orally pleasures his cock.

MMM553

Apply some lube between your butt cheeks. With Your Partner standing up against a wall, rub and stroke his penis between your ass. Your Assistant joins in front of you.

MMM554

Apply some lube between Your Partner's butt cheeks. With him standing up facing against a wall, rub and stroke your penis between his ass. Your Assistant joins in behind.

MMM555

With Your Partner laying on his back, straddle him (no penetration). Rub his penis with your ass while sucking Your Assistant's cock.

MMM556

Remove all clothing on your upper bodies. Apply massage oil to your chests and bellies. Slither and slide against each other to one song.

MMM561

Play a favorite song and orally pleasure both Your Partner and Your Assistant to the rhythm. Make it last the entire length of the song then stop.

MMM562

Take Your Partner's penis in your mouth and create different vibrating sensations by humming, purring, growling, etc. Your Partner follows your lead pleasuring Your Assistant in the same way.

MMM563

While Your Partner sits, both you and Your Assistant perform a lap dance for him to one song of your choice. Seductively rub and grind yourselves on him.

MMM564

Both you and Your Assistant suck on the shaft of Your Partner's penis. Slide your lips up and down the sides of his erection as you lick and flick with your tongues.

MMM565

Use only the soft underside of your tongue to lick the head of Your Partner's penis. Repeat or alternate for Your Assistant's pleasure.

MMM566

Use a digital camera with a zoom lens to take very close-up and intimate shots of Your Partner and Your Assistant in various explicit poses. Select one to print and frame.

Male Male Male

Level 6 - Wild, Nasty, Kinky, Taboo

MMM611

Orally pleasure Your Partner's anus in a position of your choice. Your Assistant orally pleasures his cock at the same time.

MMM612

Orally pleasure Your Partner's anus in a position of your choice. Your Assistant offers his cock to Your Partner to be sucked at the same time.

MMM613

Your choice of Nasty, Kinky or Taboo foreplay activity for Your Partner and Your Assistant to perform for you – surprise them with your wild side.

MMM614

While you give Your Partner a sensual prostate massage, Your Assistant does the same for you.

MMM615

Kiss and lick Your Partner's feet then suck on his toes while Your Assistant sucks on your cock.

MMM616

Creatively use a double-ended dildo with Your Partner. Allow Your Assistant to hold and manipulate it as desired.

MMM621

Orally pleasure Your Partner's anus in a missionary position, legs spread wide. Your Assistant licks and sucks on his toes to make him wiggle.

MMM622

Insert one lubed finger in Your Partner's anus and gently massage left, right, up, down and all around – no thrusting. Your Assistant does the same for you.

MMM623

Attempt to take both Your Partner's and Your Assistant's cocks in your mouth at the same time.

MMM624

Drip hot wax on both Your Partner and Your Assistant (chest or buttocks) while they lay next to each other.

MMM625

While Your Partner and Your Assistant kiss, apply nipple clamps (or clothes pegs) to their nipples. Remove when one of them breaks their kiss.

MMM626

With a lubed fake pussy (penis sleeve), masturbate Your Partner's shaft just to the brink then stop. Leave his tip for Your Assistant to orally pleasure.

MMM631

Use your fingers and lube to pleasure Your Partner anyway you desire. Stimulate Your Assistant using your other hand in the same way at the same time.

MMM632

Both you and Your Partner pleasure yourselves with a dildo or buttplug while Your Assistant watches.

MMM633

Use an implement of your choice to erotically spank Your Partner's bare bum until it radiates a sensual heat. Let Your Assistant caresses and strokes his bum between smacks.

MMM634

Use the tip of a vibrator to tickle Your Partner's perineum and anus – no penetration. Your Assistant offers his cock to Your Partner to be sucked at the same time.

MMM635

Stimulate Your Partner and Your Assistant each with a different buttplug or dildo at the same time.

MMM636

With Your Partner propped in a mostly upside-down position, orally pleasure him. Your Assistant helps hold him up while giving him a rim-job.

MMM641

While Your Partner and Your Assistant take turns pleasuring you orally, anally stimulate them at the same time with separate vibrators, dildos or buttplugs.

MMM642

Using a double-ended dildo or silicone beads, both you and Your Partner get on all fours for a little "cheek to cheek" action. Your Assistant offers his cock to be sucked by both of you taking turns.

MMM643

Pleasure Your Partner orally while also stimulating him anally with a lubed finger. Your Assistant nibbles, sucks and bites on Your Partner's nipples.

MMM644

Use a buttplug or dildo to stimulate yourself while Your Partner orally pleasures your cock and Your Assistant orally pleasures his cock.

MMM645

Creatively explore a pleasurable combination of a dildo and three cocks at the same time.

MMM646

Experiment with cross-dressing – both you and Your Assistant select some appropriate feminine wear for Your Partner to wear.

MMM651

Both you and Your Assistant kneel and pleasure Your Partner orally together while he stimulates both of you anally using lubed fingers.

MMM652

Select two sex toys for Your Partner and Your Assistant to play Show and Tell. In turn, they are to demonstrate their self-pleasuring technique, eyes closed, while describing the sensations.

MMM653

Roleplaying as a strict master, sternly command your Love Slaves to perform and service one of your desires.

MMM654

While lying down, have Your Partner straddle you facing your feet. As he grinds on your cock with his, Your Assistant slaps on his ass cheeks.

MMM655

Get into a threeway '69' position and give each other a rim-job.

MMM656

Your choice of sex position involving all three of you engaging in oral and/or anal intercourse at the same time.

MMM661

Describe in detail an extreme BDSM scenario/fantasy involving all three of you. Set the stage and let Your Partner and Your Assistant add to the story in turn.

MMM662

Grab Your Partner and Your Assistant and run to an unusual location in your home to have a quickie in a position of your choice – stop just before either of you have an orgasm.

MMM663

Describe in detail the most extreme, weird or bizarre sexual activity you can think of involving all three of you (not that you want to do it, of course).

MMM664

Orally pleasure Your Partner's anus in a missionary position, legs spread wide. Your Assistant straddles his chest so he can suck his cock at the same time.

MMM665

Both you and Your Assistant erotically and passionately nibble and bite sensitive erogenous zones on Your Partner's body. Make him ache for you in a good way.

MMM666

STOP the Foreplay and START the Sex Play.

More Frisky Ideas & Games

We hope you're always on the look out for more ways to enhance your relationship and spice up your love life. We believe a vibrant sex life is essential to maintaining a healthy and happy relationship. It's also a vital aspect of your personal well being. The shared intimacy and pleasures of lovemaking is something we all need. But we also crave passion and excitement to keep us feeling more alive. Satisfy your desires by continuing to learn about and experiment with creative ways to make sex thrilling together. Challenge each other to step out of your sexual comfort zone and explore your full erotic potential.

Come visit our blog at **www.friskyforeplay.com/ideas** to discover more sexy ideas and fun games for couples. We also run a number of other blogs and websites that you may find interesting:

- www.couplesgames.net
- www.sexquestionsforcouples.com
- www.frisky-sexual-fantasies.com
- www.sexysuggestions.com

Also check out our other books available on Amazon:

- 469 Fun Sex Questions for Couples - Ignite your desire with hot talk
- 123 Frisky Sexual Fantasies & Erotic Roleplay Ideas - Sexy scenarios for couples who dare to play naughty
- Sex Games & Foreplay Ideas for Couples - Be naughty and play dirty together

If you have an iPhone or iPad, check out our creative sex apps currently available in the App Store. Just do a search for:

- iLoveRandomSex
- Succulent Expressions
- Sex Questions 42
- Frisky Foreplay
- Spicy Dares & Desires

Printed in Great Britain
by Amazon

81309681R00120